ALBANIAN MAFIA WARS

ALBANIAN MAFIA WARS

THE RISE OF EUROPE'S DEADLIEST NARCOS

JOHN LUCAS

ABERFELDY

Contents

PROLOGUE: INNOCENTS 1

    PART ONE: MAFIA SHQIPTARE 9

BLOOD AND HONOUR 10

A HOLE IN THE GROUND.. 21

RISE OF THE PROFESSOR... 28

SPOILS OF WAR 37

BROWN GOLD 53

HUNTING THE PROFESSOR 60

BESA BEHAVIOUR 66

BALKANS BARONS 74

BLOODY STATES... 83

SOUTH OF THE BORDER.. 94

    PART TWO: MAFIA UK 102

MURDER CITY.. 103

TONY MONTANAS.. 112

TURF WARS, PART ONE... 124

TURF WARS, PART TWO... 132

HELLBANIANZ.. 144

ADDICTED TO ACTION... 148

CRACKDOWN... 154

    PART THREE: MAFIA STATE... 161

FAMILY MISFORTUNES.. 162

THE COLOMBIAN CONNECTION... 170

DRUG WARS... 173

BODY COUNTS... 177

BALKANS ESCOBAR... 181

NARCO-STATE.. 188

FUTURE PROSPECTS 199

EPILOGUE: LOCKDOWN 205

INDEX.. 214

All I have in this world is my balls and my word and I don't break them for no one. — *Tony Montana*

You can get much further with a kind word and a gun than you can with a kind word alone. — *Al Capone*

PROLOGUE: INNOCENTS

The sun was beating down hard on the city of Durres. While hundreds of tourists were setting up camp for the day on the glorious white sand beaches, the cops hunting one of the country's most dangerous fugitives gripped their pistols, fingers perched nervously over the trigger guards.

With Dritan Dajti's reputation for cunning and his willingness to use extreme violence, the arrest team was on high alert. Terse instructions crackled over their radios. Backup cars packed with more anxious cops waited on every street corner, just in case Dajti somehow managed to evade the raiders preparing to crash through his front door.

But all the caution in the world wouldn't be enough to mitigate the dangers they faced, not when the men who were supposed to be enforcing the law couldn't even trust their own side. By the end of that sweltering summer's day, Albania would be mourning its most serious national tragedy for more than a decade.

The celebrated Durres coast lies on the edge of Mediterranean Europe just seventeen miles west of Tirana. Not only does it lure those living and working in Albania's bustling capital, it tempts holidaymakers from across the country and beyond. Once a Greek colony, before Roman generals and later marauding Italian princes made it their home, the ancient ruins and glittering bays that yawn out into the Adriatic Sea have turned it into one of the country's most auspicious attractions.

Yet this backwater paradise also has a reputation as one of the continent's key transit points for South American cocaine, rivalling Rotterdam and Antwerp for the sheer volume of pure Colombian snow passing through its docks every year. And with the drugs trade, inevitably, comes violence.

Nothing illustrates that fact as starkly as the morning of August 7, 2009. Dritan Dajti had been on the run for six years, ever since he had decided that the prospect of a long stretch behind bars was simply too much to face. Dajti had been charged with gunning down a construction company owner who refused to pay protection money. But his first appearance in a Tirana courtroom went disastrously wrong. In a move inspired by gangster classic *The Godfather*, a crony secreted a pistol in the men's bathroom. After a short recess, Dajti emerged and dramatically whipped out the gun in the dock, threatening the guards and fleeing with the help of another gang member waiting outside on a motorbike.

Yes, it was a daring escape, but Dajti was no celebrated Robin Hood figure. In the view of most ordinary Albanians the shaven-headed thug had cheated justice. For the authorities, shame was heaped on top of their humiliation when six police officers were later arrested for corruption in connection with the plot. Dajti was condemned in his absence to twenty years in jail. But even though a reward of one million leks, or $8,700, was offered for information leading to his arrest, Dajti was able to evade capture for years, probably with the help of more corrupt cops. The fugitive didn't exactly spend his time on the run lying low. He entrenched himself as the head of a criminal organisation involved in extortion, drug trafficking, robbery and murder.

By the time of his final showdown with the law, Dajti was living in a luxury apartment in Durres, where his mob controlled the port. Recently, he had also been extorting another local businessman. It was, after all, his stock-in-trade. Dajti's problem was that his latest victim was no pushover and he simply wouldn't bend to the gangster's will. It took just one anonymous phone to bring dozens of officers flocking to the beach-front home where Dajti was believed to be sleeping. The police smashed down the door in a morning raid, hoping to catch the mobster still in bed. But he wasn't there. Instead, in the early hours of the afternoon, his Volkswagen Tuareg was spotted nearby. Then, what initially appeared to be a stroke of good luck became a bloody disaster.

A unit was diverted from the main squad and swooped on the car, but Dajti wound down the windows and sprayed them with bullets. The ensuing gun battle sent bystanders diving for cover as hot metal tore through flesh again and again. By the end of the carnage, four police officers — Fatos Xhanin, Altin Dizdar, Kastriot Freskaj and Sajmir Duchollar — lay dead. One of Dajti's henchmen was also killed, while Dajti's driver was arrested. Several others suffered gunshot wounds. Dajti himself was critically injured, but he was rushed to hospital and, against all the odds, survived.

Inside his car, police discovered two handguns and two police radios. Detectives later found they had been betrayed by a corrupt officer who had texted one of Dajti's gang just twenty minutes before the raid, tipping him off. A further probe found that at least five police officers were suspected of being in Dajti's pocket, after their names and numbers were found on his personal phone. Records showed frequent contacts between Dajti and the bent cops.

The shootout was the worst killing of police officers since an economic catastrophe had tipped the country into civil war back in 1997. The firefight was quickly dubbed the "Durres Massacre," with Prime Minister Sali Berisha calling it an "ugly crime" that deserved swift punishment.

"They died during an operation against one of the most dangerous criminals of Albania," he said of the fallen cops. "Dritan Dajti was a big threat. As the head of the criminal gang in the country and beyond, he constituted a permanent threat for the public order and security."

The Council of Ministers declared the following Saturday a national day of mourning, and the four police officers "Martyrs of Nation," giving them the right to be buried in a special cemetery in Tirana. But the honour was of little comfort to their devastated families.

Despite Sali Berisha's insistence that Dajti would see swift justice for the outrage, it took nearly five years to bring him to trial. There was nothing wrong with the prosecution case, rather it was the fact that so many lawyers declined to represent the quadruple cop killer, believing their own safety to be at risk from rival gangsters, as well as from police colleagues lusting for revenge. Eventually, the Serious Crimes Court had to enforce disciplinary measures against twenty-five barristers who flatly refused to take the case.

Dajti was not demurred by the justice process. During his almost year-long trial in 2013, he grinned, mocked the court and frequently erupted in violent rages, even snarling at a judge when told the legal proceedings were not personal.

"I have it personal with you now," he shouted to the court. "I know the laws. Don't forget that you are talking with Dritan Dajti."

Finally, the unrepentant gangster was jailed for life. Except, as is so often the case with the baffling Albanian justice system, that wasn't quite the end of the matter.

In February 2019, Dajti appealed the sentence. In proceedings held away from the glare of the public and media, judges found in his favour. His life sentence was commuted to twenty-five years, meaning that because Dajti had been in custody since 2009, he would serve just fifteen more years, at most, for taking the lives of four police officers. Three of the judges who made the decision were later investigated for corruption. The prosecutor's office appealed the appeal outcome, but for now, at least, the decision stands.

***

Just a few weeks after the ruling in the Dritan Dajti case, the seemingly distant issue of the ruthless Albanian mafia devastated the lives of a family in a rural Hertfordshire commuter town.

On March 22, 2019, Ravik Gurra, a fifty-year-old barrister who lived with his wife and two teenage daughters in a £400,000 semi-detached home in Harpenden, about twenty miles from London, was sipping coffee outside a café in Elbasan, Albania. At the time, his nation of birth was taking on the Turkish national team in the FIFA European Championship qualifiers. As the commentary from the television washed over him, Gurra may well have been in a contemplative mood.

While his professional life in Britain, where he had primarily lived since moving to London to study law in 1998, was unremarkable and consisted mostly of translating for the police, courts and the Home Office, his work in Albania was much more exhilarating. In addition to defending members of the Communist terror group Revenge for Justice, Gurra had also fought cases on behalf of the drug trafficker, murderer and extortionist Emiljano Shullazi and members of the Capja crime family of Elbasan, some of whom had been implicated in drug trafficking and a number of mafia-style assassinations.

The trouble was, Gurra kept losing the cases. Perhaps he had received some threats from disgruntled clients. Perhaps not. It is entirely possible that Gurra's courtroom defeats were not even playing on his mind and instead he was thinking only of getting back to the family home to spend time with his loved ones.

In any case, as Gurra listened to the football and the excited chatter of his companions, a stranger approached the table. Without hesitation, the assassin raised the silenced pistol in his right hand and pumped three bullets into the lawyer's head. The attack was so swift and well-executed that when Gurra initially slumped in his seat, his friends suspected a heart attack. But as the tyres of the getaway car screeched into action, the reality of the situation became clear.

Gurra's murder sent shockwaves through Albania's legal world. The country's professional association for criminal lawyers suspended all work for several days in protest and called on the government to pour all available resources into finding his killers. In the event, the only thing the police managed to achieve was to find the remains of the burnt-out getaway car.

The line given to the media was that perhaps Gurra had lost one case too many. That was certainly the impression given to me when a contact within Albania's legal establishment, who I met while researching another story, told me about the case.

"This has made all criminal barristers in Albania take notice," he said, "because it shows none of us are safe from the mafia. And the story from your point of view is that the same thing could happen in your country, because these people do not respect borders and they have no fear of the police. They have too much power."

Back in Harpenden, the murder generated only small surface ripples outside of the family home. At Gurra's local Anglican church, which he attended regularly with his wife, a service was held and a simple notice placed in the parish magazine, reading: "RIP, Ravik Gurra." His wife and children remained in the home they had shared but revealed little of their heartache to neighbours. The only external sign of their anguish came in the form of a new alarm system fitted to the outside of the house. They were too afraid to speak to the press.

But one resident revealed how Gurra would often chat to him about the football, Liverpool FC in particular, and was open about his work, although not about the nature of his clientele. On one occasion, while installing railings on a shared driveway, he had joked, "Don't worry, they're not prison bars. I see enough of them at work." The picture painted was one of a gregarious, intelligent, considerate and humourous family man; a victim of a heinous tragedy.

***

At the time of Ravik Gurra's murder, I already knew that Albanian criminals were having an increasingly significant impact on Britain's underworld, the cocaine trade in particular. The name of an East London street gang, the Hellbanianz, had grown synonymous with Albanian drug dealers in Britain and across Europe.

But Ravik Gurra's murder shone a light on an even murkier dimension of this phenomenon, suggesting that these criminal groups were much more dangerous than many people realised, thanks to their roots in a corrupt, politically unstable environment back home. I wanted to understand more about where killers like Dritan Dajti came from and how murders like that of Ravik Gurra can take place, seemingly with little chance of justice being served. I also wanted to write this book because within the endless debate about drug policy, we always know the names of the experts, the policy-makers, the government ministers and leaders, but rarely do we bother to learn about the individuals on the other side, the CEOs of the drugs world, the people who make all the money. I think it's important that we know their names.

What you are about to read is a concise history of the global Albanian mafia, as far as it can be written. When I began my research a couple of issues quickly became apparent. Predictably, while first hand sources are always hard to come by in the underworld, they are even more elusive in the tightly-knit world inhabited by Albanian gangsters. Secondly, the story of Albanian organised crime has some considerable sprawl. The mafia has tentacles in practically every European country, as well as in North America, Canada, South America and Australia. Therefore, for practical reasons, I've had to focus on what I consider to be the most significant cases and the most important players. This isn't a biography of any particular individual. I wanted to break down the evolution of a criminal movement that's taken more than two decades to flourish into a readable and logical narrative — not easy to do when so much is shrouded by lies, criminal codes, corruption and questionable legal procedures.

A note on sources:

Some people with invaluable expertise chose to speak with me, while others refused. As a result, I am immeasurably grateful to those who did speak, both in Britain and Albania. Most asked not to be identified, for obvious reasons, and where they have been directly quoted I have usually given them a pseudonym. I am also thankful for the efficiency with which the Metropolitan Police, the British courts service, the US Department of Justice and EULEX responded to my enquiries.

It would have been impractical to reference every single newspaper or website article that I've read during my research, given that this is a narrative, not an academic account. But I am grateful for the excellent work done by the Organized Crime and Corruption Reporting Project (OCCRP), which has helpfully documented many of Eastern Europe's most notorious gangsters in a handy online database. If you want to explore the continent's underworld outside of the Albanian mafia, head there. I have also made use of reporting by Balkan Insight, Exit, Panorama (Albania),

Shqiptarja.com, Balkanweb.com, Albaniandailynews.com, and News24.com, among others. If not for those outlets creating a public record of Albania's criminal travails, it would have been impossible to get this project off the ground.

I have also made use of various books, most of which are referenced in the text, but *The Albanians, A Modern History*, by Miranda Vickers, *The Balkans 1804-2012*, by Misha Glenny, *Kosovo, War and Revenge*, by Tim Judah, and *New State, Modern Statesman (Hashim Thaci- A Biography)*, by Roger Boyes and Suzy Jagger are not mentioned by name, so I will do so here in lieu of a full bibliography.

Because this is a global story, I've used the US dollar as a standard currency, even though it is written from a British perspective. In addition, I have anglicized most names by removing accents and other diacritical marks to make the book easier for English language readers.

PART ONE: MAFIA SHQIPTARE

BLOOD AND HONOUR

It was October 1963, and a heavyset, middle-aged man with a greying buzzcut settled uncomfortably into his seat before some of America's most venerated politicians. He coughed, fidgeted and wiped a little sweat from his upper lip. But he wasn't nervous about speaking to Washington's so-called big shots. Joseph Valachi was more concerned about the hundreds of murderous gangsters he was about to make extremely angry.

What he went on to reveal would stun politicians, law enforcement officers and the nation in general, forever altering many people's perception of Italian-Americans. Valachi was a gangland assassin, hoping to earn leniency by describing the inner structures of a hitherto secret criminal society, known as La Cosa Nostra, or simply the Mafia. But for this soldier in New York's Genovese crime family, giving evidence to the US Senate committee on organised crime was far worse than committing murder. He was breaking *omerta*, the code of silence, becoming the first mobster to do so publicly.

Today, La Cosa Nostra is largely in decline and the world faces an even greater threat from multiple mafias which compete, and also cooperate, in a globalized world within a vast array of illegal industries. Whereas the original Mafia was largely concerned in gambling, protection, unions and racketeering, transnational crime syndicates now thrive on the demand for illegal weapons, class A drugs and modern-day slaves. And while many of Joseph Valachi's contemporaries could trace their heritage back to the island of Sicily, some of today's most dangerous criminals originate from an almost equally tiny territory, the Republic of Albania.

Nestled in south-eastern Europe, on the Adriatic coast of the Balkan Peninsula, Albania is neighbour to Montenegro in the north-west, Kosovo in the north-east, Macedonia to the east and Greece to the south-east. Across the Adriatic Sea to the west, is Italy. But as a people, the Albanian nation is rather more complicated, with a global diaspora propelled by conflicts dating back centuries.

Albania's modern history began in November 1912, when it declared independence from the Ottoman Empire. Before then, most of the country had either been at war with invading forces or under the Turkish yoke for the best part of five hundred years, a period that saw not just the first mass exodus of ethnic Albanians into Italy and the surrounding Balkan territories, but the conversion of many of the country's Christians to Islam.

In parallel with the declaration of independence came the bloodshed of the First Balkan War. Serbia had its eye on the port of Durres, prompting Italy, Austria and Hungary to back an independent Albania as a bulwark against Serbia's imperial ambitions, which were openly supported by Russia. In a bid to stave off a wider conflict, the Treaty of Bucharest was signed in August 1913, giving Albania recognition by the Great Powers. This left the country with its first official national borders, containing 28,000 square kilometers of land and a population of some one million people. Tens of thousands of ethnic Albanians remained stranded in areas outside the new territory.

When World War One broke out in 1914, the fledgling Albanian state collapsed along religious and tribal lines. The country's newly installed figurehead, the German Prince William, fled and signed up to fight on the Eastern front for his homeland. As the latest European conflict snowballed, Albania was occupied by Italy and Greece in the south, Austria-Hungary in the north, and France in the east. By the time the guns fell silent, Italy held most of Albania, with Serbia having encroached in the north and Greek and French forces holding large swathes of the country. A rebellion followed, and some degree of statehood was restored by the intervention of the United States.

By 1924, after more internecine warfare, Albania became a republic under the bloodthirsty rule of Ahmed Bey Zogu, who in 1928 transformed the country into a kingdom, styling himself King Zog I. He lasted until 1939, when the Italian fascist dictator Benito Mussolini invaded at the outbreak of World War Two, making Albania one of the first countries to be occupied by the Axis Powers. Zog fled to Greece, then London. When the Italians surrendered in September 1943, the country was quickly occupied by the Germans before Albanian guerillas could seize the capital.

By the time the war was over, Albania had spent decades in a state of permanent flux, with many of its citizens fleeing to Western Europe and America, as well as surrounding territories. It was crying out for some form of stability — and received it in the form of another brutal dictatorship.

In January 1946, Enver Hoxha, who had been a partisan fighter and rising star in the Communist Party during occupation, became president of what was now the People's Republic of Albania. In a famous speech, Hoxha outlined the heavy toll the war had taken on Albania:

> "The sacrifices of our people were very great. Out of a population of one million, 28,000 were killed, 12,600 wounded, 10,000 were made political prisoners in Italy and Germany, and 35,000 made to do forced labour, of ground; all the communications, all the ports, mines and electric power installations were destroyed, our agriculture and livestock were plundered, and our entire national economy was wrecked."

For Hoxha and the Communist Party, it was time to rebuild. This meant initiating a land grab; the rounding up of clan chiefs, dissidents and intellectuals; and the implementation of hardline Stalinism and work camps. Some estimates put the number of political murders under the Communist regime as high as 25,000.

The southern Tosk ethnic group, with their traditional disregard for authority, were now out of favour, while the Ghegs, from the north, made up most of the ruling party.

Still, there were certain positives. The University of Tirana was established, diseases such as malaria were almost eradicated and the ancient law of the Albanian blood feud was outlawed. Hoxha died in 1985 but the Communist regime stumbled on until 1991, when the country held its first free elections.

Today, Albania has a population of just under three million people, but there are an estimated eight million ethnic Albanians in the world. Many of them reside within the borders of Albania's immediate neighbours, but millions more live in Western countries, facilitating the growth of a global mafia like no other.

***

The Albanian mafia has no *capo de tutti capi*, or boss of bosses, no Commision, and no *omerta*. Instead, it has its own codes, its own values, and a unique structure, or lack of one, that in some ways makes it difficult to define. Albanian organised crime does, however, share some qualities with most other mafias: inherent secrecy, a shared language, and family ties between members— all factors that make infiltration and the cultivation of informants incredibly challenging.

The important thing to remember is that unlike La Cosa Nostra, the term "Albanian mafia" does not describe a hierarchical, strictly mono-ethnic criminal fraternity. Rather, it serves as useful shorthand for Albanian serious organised crime groups in general— whether or not they are based around traditional clans, or have hundreds or just a few members. Because the Albanian mafia is so hard to define it's often the subject of much debate among academics, law enforcement experts and journalists.

The traditional definition of the Albanian mafia, favoured by the FBI, goes something like this: There are thought to be around twenty Albanian criminal clans—known as *fares* or a *fis*. According to tradition, each clan is bonded by blood and marriage, and uses the Albanian customary idea of *besa*, or trust, to enforce a code of honour. On a practical level, each clan could have thousands of

13

members around the world, but a small leadership council known as a *Bajrak*. Sub-groups are led by a *Krye*, or Boss, and under them a *Kryetar*, or Underboss. Serving under the *Kryetar* is a *Mik*, or Friend, who acts as a go-between for the leadership and the footsoldiers. In some larger organisations there could be even more levels and the entire structure is kept together by enforcing strict discipline. Even close relatives could face harsh punishment for deviating from the rules.

Recruits to these criminal clans are said to take an oath, called a *bese*, upon initiation, similar to the rituals conducted by La Cosa Nostra. Inductees are given the status of blood brother, making intermarriage between their families strictly forbidden, forever. If tradition is strictly followed, then the brotherhood ritual involves two men tying their little fingers together and pricking the ends, until drops of blood fall into glasses filled with water and raki. Then the men link arms, hold the glasses to each other's lips, and drink.

In reality, it is highly unlikely that modern Albanian mafia groups do any such thing. But the above concepts originate in the *Kanun of Lek Dukagjini*, a set of laws created by a medieval prince who once ruled the north of the country and codified hundreds of rules for Albanians to live by. It was suppressed under Communism but made a comeback during the 1990s, particularly in the North, where it is followed more closely by the Gheg ethnic subgroup than by those in the mainly Tosk South[1].

Thanks to the *Kanun*, the concepts of trust, honour, and loyalty remain strong among Albanians today, and numerous sayings denote just how seriously they are taken. There is: *"Shqiptaret vdesin dhe besen nuk e shkelin,"* or "Albanians would die rather than break honor." And another that translates as: "When the Albanian gives his world, he gives his son."

For many, the four pillars of the *Kanun*— Personal Honour, or *Nderi*; Hospitality, or *Mikpritja*; Right Conduct, or *Sjellja*; and Kin Loyalty, or *Fis*—are far more important than any national, international or religious laws, although the *Kanun* is by no means a strictly criminal code. But a reputation for loyalty and reliability is a key reason why Albanian crime groups have been so successful in

---

[1] The key difference between the groups is their dialect.

14

the international underworld. They might not speak the same language as their Italian or South American brethren, for example, but they keep their promises— for better or worse.

Law enforcement agents have spoken of the problems they encounter with tackling these family-based Albanian crews. Marko Nicovic, vice president of the International Narcotics Agency, once told Toronto's *National Post*, "Kosovo Albanians make the perfect mafia, even better than the Sicilians. They are a small ethnic group made up of clans or families that have very close to family relations. The brotherhood, or *fis*, is impenetrable by outsiders. It is difficult to find translators to work with police and impossible to get an informer or agent inside the organisations."

While the orthodox definition has some truth to it, the reality is that most active Albanian crime groups are much smaller and less hierarchical than the traditional clan structure.[2] In fact, hundreds if not thousands of autonomous Albanian gangs have been uncovered in the last two decades. One explanation for the vast number of apparently independent outfits also comes from the concept of honour outlined in the *Kanun*. Albanian gangsters often say that their sense of honour prevents them from taking orders. According to them, criminal relationships are reciprocal and when a so-called boss makes decisions, instructions are usually given with respect, to avoid dishonouring others. Therefore, the Albanian mafia operates more like a loose network of smaller, highly organised gangs that all share the same basic values.

In some respects, the Albanian mob operates in a similar way to the Russian mafia. The academic Mark Galeotti wrote in his book *The Vory*, "Each network will have authority figures who either give orders or, more often, have the social, physical, economic and

---

[2] There are many large and successful Albanian mafia groups which clearly do have a single, powerful leader. As we shall see, heroin kingpin Aldo Bare wielded absolute power over his organisation. Similarly, the transatlantic drugs trafficker Daut Kadriovoksi was said by the FBI to head up a powerful mafia family and was described as an Albanian "Godfather". The US-based Krasniqi and Thaqi organisations were based around a central leadership group of just a few family members. Meanwhile, the network run by "Mike" Dika and "Timmy" Lika, also in New York, had dozens of co-conspirators who were not strictly part of a "family".

15

coercive power to ensure that in the main people heed their views. Most, though, have relatively little hierarchy and no sense of wider strategy."

And while some of the heavyweight Albanian syndicates do work within a more traditional structure, it is not at all certain that family or clan ties are always at the heart of the organisation. Some are based around social or regional associations, while there is also plenty of evidence that criminals of other ethnicities, such as Romanians, Turks, Italians and Britons can and do play key roles in Albanian organised crime groups.

Partly because of this loose-knit style, law enforcement agencies struggle to get their people inside these outfits. The FBI's John Farley outlined the problem in 2009 when commenting on the aforementioned Lika and Dika network:

"There is no true hierarchy. It's hard to determine exactly where the leadership is, and where the organisation ends and where it begins. It's mostly a loose-knit group where whoever has the goods at the time, whoever has the connections at the time, moves up the chain and takes control of that, and then it can switch. They go to each other for whoever has an 'in' to whatever criminal activity is being pursued. It's very difficult to counter, because we can't determine the hierarchy, because it is fluid. So it's a very different way, it's an emerging problem."

The Albanian mafia does have one other particular characteristic that sets it apart from other crime groups: a reputation for using the most extreme violence. This goes far beyond the typical crimes of La Cosa Nostra, such as execution-style shootings, beatings and car bombs. Albanian gangsters have been known to behead their enemies, blow them up with dynamite or RPGs, and blatantly assassinate police and politicians. Again, the *Kanun* lies at the heart of this cultural tick.

Quite simply, while personal honour is of the utmost importance, it is also easily besmirched. To redress insults to honour of a varied and almost infinite kind, the tradition of *hakmarrje*, or blood feud, has been followed for centuries. The *Kanun* was designed to bring order to this ancient system of revenge killing, but not to stop it. For example, the *Kanun* says that a man who has been dishonoured can kill the guilty party, but that his family could then face an assassination in revenge. The pattern could continue indefinitely.

According to Article 601 of the *Kanun*, dishonour can be caused when someone is called a liar; spat at; pushed; struck; has a promise to them broken; if someone takes his weapon; insults his wife; violates his hospitality; insults his friend; breaks into his house or fails to pay a debt. It leaves a lot of leeway for minor problems to escalate, particularly when Article 600 states, "An offence to honour is not paid with property, but by the spilling of blood."[3]

The long-term effect of this eye-for-an-eye approach to justice has been to leave some Albanian men trapped within a deeply macho culture. Although many honour-based disputes can actually be mediated peacefully according to the *Kanun*, for example by pledging *besa* to create a period of peace, among the criminal fraternity violence is usually seen as the only option. Even today, blood feuds can last for many years and cross international borders.

For example, back in 2000 an Albanian man named Denis Ceka escaped to Britain after shooting his former friend Mikel Manahasa. He claimed the killing was accidental but he was jailed in absentia for twelve years. Mikel's brother Petrit and cousin Shpetim Selhaka tracked Ceka to Northampton. Ceka didn't know the cousin, who befriended him and persuaded him to move to Wood Green, North London. He later invited Ceka to a party in Hounslow. As the fugitive killer walked in, Petrit Manahasa emerged and knifed him to death. Both men were later jailed in Albania, where they had returned to a hero's welcome.

Retribution from the Albanian mob is equally swift and relentless. Other criminal organisations, such as La Cosa Nostra, have sometimes been surprised at how quickly Albanian gangsters resort

---

[3] In the tradition of the Kanun, women and children were immune from the consequences of the blood feud, and in fact a revenge killing could not even be carried out if the intended victim was in the company of a woman. But apart from costing the lives of thousands of young men, blood feuds resulted in economic hardship for families because their menfolk were either killed or sent into hiding with relatives and were therefore unable to provide an income. The Kanun states that if all the men of a family are killed, then the eldest, unmarried daughter becomes the man of the house.

to murder. But far from becoming pariahs in the criminal underworld, it has allowed them to rise to the top.[4] These days, some of the more sophisticated groups deliberately restrict their use of violence, relying on their reputations instead. It tends to attract less interest from law enforcement, but has the same effect.

***

While the world of Albanian organized crime may be confusing and often contradictory, the above summary does teach us one thing: Albanian criminals can be infinitely flexible, unpredictable and dangerous. And what has not been in doubt for the past two decades is the serious manner in which they are viewed by Western intelligence and law enforcement agencies.

As we shall see, sanctions imposed on Yugoslavia by the United Nations in the 1990s marked the beginning of the Albanian mafia's global expansion. Until just a few years previously, organised crime had been largely suppressed under Communism. Suddenly, traditional smuggling routes used for decades became goldmines, as goods such as cigarettes, chocolate and even washing machines became valuable illicit commodities. There had always been money to be made transporting heroin and cannabis along the same routes into Western Europe, but now criminals could maximise their profits by dealing in less risky products. By re-investing the cash and continuing to exploit the chaos and porous borders, Albanian mafia gangs developed a near monopoly on heroin in some parts of the continent.

By the turn of the twenty-first century, it was thought that up to eighty-five percent of the heroin in Greece and seventy percent in Germany had been trafficked by ethnic Albanian narcos, many associated with either traditional clans or fighters from the Kosovo Liberation Army (KLA). Europol estimated that by 2001 up to forty per cent of the drug in Europe had been supplied by Albanians, a figure echoed by the Italian Ministry of Social Solidarity in 2005. Furthermore, Albanian mafia groups were also selling the drug on

---

[4] One notable case is that of Alex Rudaj, whose New York-based Corporation took on the city's traditional Five Families in an orgy of violence.

18

the streets themselves, in countries such as Germany, Belgium, Greece and Switzerland, apparently controlling both the supply and retail ends of the operation.

Even in Italy, where Albanians had to compete with La Cosa Nostra, the Camorra, and the 'Ndrangheta, it was the Albania mafia, with its fearsome reputation for violence, which began to dominate the underworld. Soon, Albanian mobsters were working in partnership with these organisations, solidifying and expanding their control over Europe's smuggling routes.

Narcotics were not the only commodities being transported across the continent in the back of lorries. Human trafficking was also big business and notorious brothels with enforced labour sprung up across Eastern Europe during the Balkan wars. It was a particularly lucrative market for Albanian criminals. For example, by 2005 nearly three quarters of those convicted of human trafficking in Macedonia were ethnic Albanian. Most of the girls and women were trafficked from places like Romania, the Ukraine and Moldova and traded throughout Kosovo, Serbia, Bosnia, Albania and Montenegro. Similar operations began to appear in countries such as Germany, Great Britain and Italy.

In 2001, a UK Home Office briefing revealed that Albanian mafia gangs had all but seized control of Britain's vice trade, most noticeably in London's West End—an area previously dominated by Maltese and English criminals. In 2006, Europol published *The Threat From Organised Crime*, which focused solely on the Albanian mob. By 2006, Interpol had more than 500 Albanians on its wanted list for drug trafficking, testimony to the mafia's expansive criminal activities. Albanians also muscled in on traditional La Cosa Nostra territory in New York, most notably in the case of the aforementioned Alex Rudaj organisation. Another report, 2011's *EU Organised Crime Assessment*, revealed how Albanian crooks were flooding Europe with home-grown cannabis.

By 2012, the Scottish Crime and Drug Enforcement Agency (SCDEA) noted that Albanian crime groups posed a significant threat north of the border in Britain.

"The Albanians are a bit of a challenge because they have a military background in their homelands, and their criminal elements have a very violent history," director Graeme Pearson said at the time. "They are very difficult groups to penetrate."

More recently, there have been stark warnings about the number of Albanian children being trafficked to the UK to work within organised crime. In 2017, the children's charity Barnados said nearly thirty per cent of the estimated 13,000 child slaves in the UK were Albanian, second only to the thousands of Vietnamese youngsters forced to work in nail bars or cannabis factories.

Then came the National Crime Agency's 2017 *National Strategic Assessment of Serious and Organised Crime.* The agency found that 0.8 per cent of the 39,414 people in Britain thought to be involved in serious organised crime were Albanian, a relatively miniscule figure which was equal to the number of Nigerians and only slightly fewer than the percentage of Polish criminals.

Nevertheless, the report singled out Albanians for special mention, stating, "Albanian crime groups involved in drug trafficking have established a high-profile influence within UK organised crime and have considerable control across the UK drug trafficking market, with particular impact and high-level influence on the cocaine market."

The report went on to explain, briefly, how and why: "Criminals from the Balkans are increasingly expanding their network of influence, forming direct relationships with cocaine suppliers in South America. The threat faced from Albanian crime groups is significant. London is their primary hub, but they are established across the UK."

In recent years, the British state has been fighting back, and as of March 2018 there were 726 Albanians in British jails, three times the number in 2013.

The Albanian mafia will never have its 'Valachi moment'. At least, there will never be a single person like Joseph Valachi who can set out how the whole thing works, because it's far too complex. But this book will attempt to provide a narrative account of the rise of the Albanian mafia, its most dangerous narcos, and what it all means for the future. And to truly understand what's happening today we must go back to where it all started— to the pyramids.

A HOLE IN THE GROUND

L eonard Prifti had lost everything, even his parents. And as chaos and lawlessness raged around him, he knew it wouldn't be long until he found himself facing either the wrong end of an AK-47, or starvation. At just fourteen years old, there was no realistic prospect of survival in these conditions. Hungry, alone, and with little consideration for what was right or wrong, only what was necessary, Leonard did what he had to do — what every other orphan in the neighbourhood had done — and pledged his allegiance to Alfred Shkurti.

The charismatic gang boss handed the young man a pistol and promised him that once he'd been trained, he could upgrade to a machine gun. Leonard would need it, he said, for all the work he would be doing for the organisation. Back then, the boy was grateful. But neither Leonard Prifti nor Alfred Shkurti could have known just how far-reaching the consequences of their meeting would be, for them both.

It could be argued that such a distasteful scene only became possible because the repressive Communist system built by Enver Hoxha was no longer in place. Just as in the Soviet Union and other Eastern European states, Albania's Reds had been remarkably effective at keeping organised crime bottled up, or at least at making sure it worked to the state's advantage. That's not to say there were no powerful criminal clans, black marketeers or corrupt officials, not to mention smugglers, but criminality impinged relatively little on civil society.

The best example of how the state tolerated organised crime dated back to the 1960s, when Hoxha's regime allowed the Border Police and the Sigurimi, the secret police, to work with Italian mafia groups smuggling cigarettes across the Adriatic Sea. It even set up a special unit, known as the 101K, to oversee the storage and transportation of tobacco from a warehouse in a village near Durres.

This apparent breach of Communist dogma was permitted partly because the domestic market could not meet the demand, but also because it raised funds for the state, with the added bonus that the deal ultimately caused harm to Albania's and Stalin's capitalist enemies by depriving Western companies of their profits. Later Belgian intelligence reports claimed the Italian mob had kicked back at least $22 million to the government in a single year, cash that helped to purchase a fleet of Alouette helicopters in the 1980s. There were also claims that the Albanian state itself was involved in the cultivation and export of poppies, in order to drag down the capitalist nations.

But ironically, while the dictator's death in April 1985 heralded a period of social and political liberalisation, culminating in the country's first free and fair elections in 1991, the weakness of the fledgling democratic system soon plunged the country into lawlessness.

There is a compelling logic behind the crisis that led to the insidious corruption of young men like Leonard Prifti. It all seems so obvious with hindsight, but at the time the economic collapse took place in slow motion, with very few observers able to grasp the enormity of what was taking place.

Firstly, the advent of democracy led to the rapid dissolution of the Sigurimi and the 101K, both legacies of the Communist era which the new democratic leaders were keen to eradicate. The unforeseen consequence was that many former officers from both groups were now free to fully immerse themselves in the world of organised crime. It was a natural progression for them. After all, many had been involved in smuggling cigarettes into Albania, and possibly drugs out, for many years. The only thing that had changed was that they were no longer picking up a regular government salary.

Using their contacts in the diaspora and within the state apparatus, they were able to operate as smugglers across the Balkans with relative impunity. For them, the timing couldn't have been better. Goods such as cigarettes and coffee were suddenly worth a small fortune thanks to the wide-ranging UN trade embargo imposed on Yugoslavia in 1992.

The journalist and Balkans expert Misha Glenny has described the embargo as "something really, really dumb," and for good reason. Writing in his classic study of global organised crime, *McMafia*, Glenny described what happened next:

"The Balkans, war-ravaged, impoverished and traumatised, were about to be turned into a smuggling and criminal machine that had few, if any, parallels in history. While the world wrung its hands and fretted over the terrible nationalist urges of the Yugoslav people and their leaderships, the Balkan mafias started putting aside their ethnic differences to engage in a breathtaking criminal collaboration."

In addition to goods passing through and out of Albania, other items started coming in. For example, the fall of Communism meant the regime's previous ban on all but essential government vehicles and public transport was lifted. Everybody now wanted a car. The problem was that nobody had the money to buy one, and in any case very few, if any, car manufacturers were prepared to set up shop in Albania. As always, professional criminals exploited the gap in the market. Cars stolen from the streets of Britain, France, Germany and elsewhere in Europe began to arrive in Durres, where they were sold on to locals at knock down prices or, if they were particularly in demand, shipped back out again to places like Dubai or China.

Still, at least the people now had the vote and the opportunity to live in a free society. Political leaders in the West were relatively happy. But if they had they looked a little closer, they would have seen the writing on the wall.

The first indication that Albania's new democratic leaders were themselves willing to play fast and loose with the rules came just months after the elections. After a period of turmoil, the Democratic Party (DP) had formed a government, under the leadership of Enver Hoxha's former cardiologist and now committed capitalist Sali Berisha. In addition to allegedly accepting donations from convicted criminals abroad, the DP also set up a company called *Shqiponija*, or The Eagle, with the purpose of illegally shipping oil to Yugoslavia. There was little effort to hide what was going on; its director was the Minister for Health, Tritan Shehu, who allegedly helped to funnel cash raised by the scheme into party coffers. Although the company was shut down in 1996, it has never been possible to trace exactly what happened to the money.

At the same time, Berisha, a Gheg from the north, filled key state positions with members of other loyal Gheg clan members, in a bid to stymie any resurgence from the Socialist Party (SP). Many of these cronies had alleged links to organised crime families. Unsurprisingly, among portions of the general population, smuggling, drug cultivation and trafficking, as well as people smuggling, were becoming acceptable occupations. But the state's apparently ambivalent attitude to criminality was soon to prove disastrous.

Albania's transition to a market economy was rapid and the new financial sector largely unregulated. There were also very few banks with the ability to lend cash to thousands of citizens who now wanted to better their lives. It was a recipe for disaster.

At first, the outlook seemed rosy. GDP increased by around ten per cent year-on-year between 1993 and 1995, and even though agriculture still accounted for around fifty per cent of the economy, it was expanding at a faster rate than anywhere else in Eastern Europe. Albania appeared to be a success story. But progress was too slow for most citizens, who wanted to elevate their living standards quickly after decades under Communism. Despite the economic growth, average monthly wages were still less than $80 and Albania remained Europe's poorest country.

Once again, criminals emerged to meet the demand. They started up private investment companies, offering extraordinarily high returns. Some of these schemes even had the support of the government, with senior officials appearing in public at company events. The first scheme was called Sejdise, after its founder Hajdin Sejdia, a Kosovar Albanian who raised millions with the aim of building a luxury hotel in the centre of Tirana. By the end of 1996, the DP had accepted huge donations from some of the companies and the prime minister and the speaker of the Albanian parliament had even been awarded medals by one firm to mark its anniversary. By the end of the year, around two thirds of the population, roughly two million people, had poured an estimated £1.2 billion dollars into the schemes. Many had even sold their homes to free up more cash. To illustrate the scale of the impending crisis, Albania's entire GDP in 1996 was just $3.3billion.

For the uninitiated, the basic premise of a pyramid scheme is this: attract investment by offering huge returns, then pay money out to early investors using income generated by newcomers. Often there is no genuine investment at all and the entire facade relies on robbing Peter to pay Paul. While many of these Albanian schemes were fraudulent from the outset, others did have real assets. But their organisers were also engaged in other criminal activities, such as smuggling, and were using profits from crime to pay investors. When the UN lifted sanctions against Yugoslavia at the end of 1995 their profits dried up, so they changed tactics and became pure frauds. That put in motion a disastrous chain of events.

Sensing the end was near, the most popular schemes boosted interest rates to as high as six per cent a month, then eight per cent as fresh elections loomed. New companies suddenly appeared, while one of the most established schemes hiked its interest rates to a staggering nineteen per cent a month. More and more people emptied their life savings into these too-good-to-be-true investment scams.

Two schemes, Xhafferi and Populli, had nearly two million depositors between them and competed recklessly for custom with another company, Sude. As 1996 drew to a close, Populli started offering more than thirty percent a month. Meanwhile, Xhafferi offered to treble depositors' money over the course of just three months. Similarly, Sude said it could double investments within just two months. Albanians sold their houses, businesses and even livestock to invest money in the schemes.

The government sat on its hands as the situation spiraled towards its inevitable conclusion. Meanwhile, warnings from the IMF and World Bank fell on deaf ears. Reluctantly, the government issued a warning about some of the schemes, but President Berisha still insisted most were genuine. The media and public rallied behind him. The IMF was trying to rain on Albania's parade, they argued.

A government committee was set up to investigate the schemes, but it never actually convened. Finance minister Ridvan Bode even had the chutzpah to put a government-friendly spin on the impending disaster.

"It could be positive," he argued, "because people will want to be more responsible and will want to work and be more careful with their money and not just invest in such fraudulent schemes that were illusions."

Sude collapsed in January 1997. Gjallica, which was originally set up in the Vlora region by three former State Security officials, followed. Rioting erupted in the city, and also in Tirana, where Sude was based. The government announced it would not compensate depositors and froze the assets of Xhafferi and Populli. The Bank of Albania began to limit daily withdrawals and by February the government had outlawed pyramid schemes entirely.

But it was far too little, far too late. Every scheme had stopped making payments and millions of Albanians had lost everything. In Lushnje, where pyramid scheme pioneer Hajdin Sejdia had been born, it was estimated that half the population had moved in with the other half because so many had sold their homes. Sejdia himself fled the country, his hotel unbuilt, leaving nothing in Tirana but an enormous hole in the ground.

RISE OF THE PROFESSOR

For a country that in 1997 had a population roughly half that of London, the impact of the economic collapse was devastating. As the crisis unfolded the nation's currency was devalued by a third and inflation rocketed by about eighteen per cent. But worse was that almost overnight, Albania erupted.

The biggest protests were in Lushnje, a south-western city in the county of Fier, where most economic activity was agricultural. The majority of its 80,000 residents lost vast sums in the pyramid schemes and thousands took to the streets. Demonstrations soon descended into violence. The chairman of the DP, Tritan Shehu, was dispatched to calm the mood. But instead, he was kidnapped by an angry mob and held hostage inside the city's football stadium. He had to be rescued by special forces.

The unrest soon spread to other towns and cities, mainly in the south, and it took just a matter of days for disorder to morph into a full-blown insurrection, with armed gangs roaming the streets, demanding the overthrow of the government[5]. The crisis was accelerated by an incident in Vlore, where protesters attacked the offices of the SHIK, the national intelligence service, resulting in the deaths of six officers and three protesters.

As the fighting intensified, arms depots were looted. In response, President Berisha opened up arms depots in the north to allow pro-government civilians to protect themselves. The entire fiasco was an unprecedented failure of government. As the protests spread nationwide, looters stole around 550,000 firearms, 840 million rounds of ammunition and 16 million grenades. Inevitably, weapons also flooded into the country from outside. At one point, it was thought that there were so many weapons that every male over the age of ten had access to a gun.

Gangs effectively took over many towns and cities, including Lushnje, Durres, Saranda, Vlore and even parts of Tirana. As government factories closed down and hundreds of smaller businesses collapsed like dominos, thousands of young Albanian men saw crime as their only option, while thousands more fled abroad to escape it, with Greece and Italy favoured destinations.

In March 1997, President Berisha was re-elected by parliament for another five-year term, but he was forced to declare a state of emergency after the vote further infuriated the public. Echoing the language of the authoritarian regime the democrats had replaced, he threatened to use the "iron hand" of the law to restore order, describing the unrest as a "communist rebellion backed by foreign intelligence agencies".

"This group has attacked the people, the institutions, broken the banks and freed prisoners. It is an armed communist rebellion," he added. "They have launched a war to take over the country."

By April, the besieged government and all ten of the country's political parties agreed to allow the exiled King Leka I to return, in

---

[5] It was not the first time armed groups had mobilised against the democratic system. Since 1996, an organisation set up by a band of committed ex-Communists calling itself Revenge for Justice had been assassinating state officials and carrying out robberies across the country (it would take another twenty years to bring the group's leaders to justice, after many found asylum in Europe. Even then, many were sentenced in absentia).

the hope that he could ease the tension. The towering six-foot eight inches monarch visited the southern city of Vlore the following month. The journalist Matthew Sweet, from the *Independent*, described the ensuing chaos as King Leka tried to address a 5,000-strong crowd:

> "The guards are sweating and nervous: there's trouble in the air. In order to address the crowd, King Leka has moved dangerously close to the edge of a raised marble concourse, and he's inches from the steep drop to the pavement. Bodies surge around him as he tries to talk to his people but the crowd is in no mood to listen. Instead, 5,000 angry protesters are urging him to join in their anti-government chants: 'Down with the parliament! Down with Berisha!' they yell, before settling on a tub-thumping chorus of 'Fuck you Sali!' Things are getting out of hand, everyone is running and shouting, rebel gunmen in the crowd spray automatic rifle fire into the air; nearby, a gang is hijacking one of the cars in the royal motorcade with a stick of dynamite. Vlora is on the brink of riot."

Amid the chaos, the government also took the desperate measure of printing money to pay pensioners and the unemployed, even though new finance minister Arben Malaj, a Socialist drafted into a government of national unity, was forced to make the startling admission that the state could not really afford to do it.

"I am sure we will be forced to print money again," he said. "This is very worrying. One of my colleagues told me we will not have the money to print money."

The IMF and World Bank were trying to help the Albanian government draft a budget, but riots and the ongoing insurrection made stability a distant prospect.

Although rioting across the country initially sprung from a spontaneous outpouring of rage, much of the subsequent civil disorder was well organised. Cities and regions established their own "salvation committees" or "rescue committees", with the intention of taking on the functions of the government, demanding the resignation of President Berisha and issuing a direct challenge to the state. Propping up many of these committees were armed gangs, which while criminal in nature also had political motivations and ties to the Socialist Party (SP).

In Vlore, where King Leka had held his first disastrous public appearance, the south's leading salvation committee had taken on the form of a shadow government, supported by an armed mob dubbed the Gang of Cole. The gang's leader, Zani Caushi, led dozens of thugs who became notorious for armed robberies, kidnapping and drug trafficking.

Caushi, a career criminal, had been locked up in a high security prison in Greece, serving 101 years for murder, when the pyramid crisis reached its crescendo. But he escaped and headed back to his home town, specifically the neighbourhood of Cole, intent on taking advantage of the chaos. Caushi established himself as an ardent supporter of the SP and his standing was such that he even acted as a bodyguard for the party's future leader Skender Gjinushi and also the Italian Prime Minister Romano Prodi during a visit in April 1997. He liked to pose in combat vests and modeled himself on a cross between Rambo and James Bond. Caushi was later photographed in a black bow tie and dinner jacket casting his vote in the June 1997 general election, which saw the DP swept from office and Sali Berisha replaced by the SP's Rexhep Medidani, while Fatos Nano became Prime Minister.

Caushi was arrested in September 1997 on suspicion of drug trafficking and the murder of at least four people, all of whom were linked to rival gangs supportive of the DP. At his 1998 trial he was found guilty only of weapons charges and released due to time served. There were murmurs that his acquittal was repayment for his support of the SP.

Caushi was arrested again in 1999, following a shootout in which three people were killed. This time, he was given a life sentence for murder, robbery and weapons charges. Other members of the Gang of Cole were also handed long sentences, for offences ranging from murder and drug trafficking to the destruction of state institutions and possession of military vehicles.

In the southern city of Berat, another SP-supporting gang led by a murderous sociopath emerged. The Gang of Altin Dardha committed at least 120 murders, sixty-three of them said to have been carried

31

out by Dardha himself. There was a story, perhaps apocryphal, that Dardha's motivation for starting the gang was to avenge the death of his father. In any case, its main purpose seemed to be to kill as many members of another mob, led by the DP-supporting Lulzim Caka, as possible. Dardha himself was later killed in a shootout.

Almost all of the emerging armed gangs had political allegiances. In Korce, the "5 Stores" and "Redeneci" gangs supported the DP and did battle with their opposition numbers, the "Shepherds". Alongside general racketeering, robbery and kidnapping, the gangs also disrupted each other's political rallies and organised election fraud. Eventually, the Korce's mayor negotiated a peace accord which was signed by the gang leaders in the town hall, showing just how far the gangs were legitimised by civil society.

Some of the deadliest gang wars took place in the central city of Elbasan, an area that eventually spawned many of Albania's most sophisticated narco gangs. Eduart Peqini, known as Mandela, led the Gang of Mandela, which was locked into a blood feud with Arjan Tosak, who led the SP-supporting Gang of Cerrik. Two leading members, also members of the SP, were later jailed for the murder of six Republican Guard officers. The city also suffered from the scourge of the Gang of Tan Kateshi, another outfit affiliated to the SP.

While the northern cities, including Tirana, suffered relatively less violence, there were still some notorious gangs operating there. One boss was Nehat Kulla, known as "the General". He had served time with Fatos Nano, the former chairman of the SP who was previously jailed for corruption. The General was later locked up for twenty years for the 1998 murder of the former interior minister Halit Shamata.

***

Of all the warlords who emerged from the chaos of the pyramid crisis, it was the aforementioned Alfred Shkurti who gained the most infamy. Like many Albanian crime bosses, his early life is shrouded in mystery. Shkurti's mother owned a general store in Lushnje and his father was a member of the State Police. A respectable family, his brother became an ambulance driver and his sister a high school

32

teacher. As an adult, Shkurti himself moved to Durres, where he also served as a police officer.

But Alfred did not hold onto his family's good name. He fled the country in 1993 after shooting a man dead during a riot. Very little is known about Shkurti's life during this period, but he settled in Italy in 1997 and it is likely he made significant criminal connections. At some point during the pyramid crisis he made the decision, like many other villains, to return home.

It is generally accepted that the Shkurti family suffered some loss of status during the pyramid crisis, with Alfred's mother losing her store and other family members their jobs. Shkurti always maintained that his reason for returning was to restore his family's honour, which may have been true to an extent. But the crisis also provided marvelous opportunities for career criminals, who used the chaos to consolidate their drug trafficking operations, extort local businesses and seek political power and influence. Alfred Shkurti began working closely with Lushnje's rescue committee in a bid to overthrow the government. But he clearly had overriding criminal interests and that put him into conflict with a rival gang leader, Artur Daja.

Daja was another fugitive murderer who had also been hiding out in Italy until the pyramid crisis erupted. Both men had known each other, or known *of* each other, for a long time. But with Daja's activities in drug dealing and prostitution clashing with Shkurti's own interests, they had fallen out. Exactly how the blood feud heated up is still a mystery, but it's thought that at least one of Shkurti's associates had been murdered in Italy. Daja was blamed.

In June 1997 Alfred Shkurti, his brother Ramadan and a group of cousins spotted some parked cars belonging to Daja and his cronies, who were having lunch nearby. They set about smashing them up with baseball bats, but a furious Daja appeared and pulled out a gun. In the shootout that followed, Daja was injured and one of his henchmen was killed. But Ramadan Shkurti and one of his cousins were also gunned down. It was Artur Daja who fired the fatal shots, execution-style. From that point on it became clear that either Alfred Shkurti or Artur Daja must die.

The grief-stricken Shkurti began to recruit more soldiers to his band. Some were family members, others were young men from his neighborhood, including several orphans, one of which was fourteen-year-old Leonard Prifti. All were expected to kill for their leader. One twenty-two-year-old recruit later described carrying out a hit on passengers in a moving car.

"A four-wheel drive came from the high school toward us," he recalled. "There were two persons inside whom I had never seen and as soon as the vehicle came by I opened fire at once and used all the bullets of the pistol. I went behind an apartment building and began rolling a cigarette of hashish. Then I waited for one of the members who gave me 20,000 Lek."

Another one of Daja's key associates, an Albanian-Macedonian called Xhevat "The Kosovar" Demiri, was shot dead in front of his wife and two children in August 1997. The following February, Lushnje gang members disguised as police officers ambushed another enemy, only managing to kill one of his bodyguards. A few days later they tried again, this time executing their target and another man in the street. On another occasion, in August 1998, one of Daja's men was dragged from his family home by Shkurti's thugs and killed.

As Alfred Shkurti systematically wiped out his opponents, his loyal followers, many of them teenagers and orphans, began to refer to him as "The Professor" or "The Great One". The gang was also apparently protected by the police — it's headquarters, known as Station No 2, sat within a heavily guarded compound right next door to the city's main police station. It was there that dozens of bombings, kidnappings and assassinations were planned, and opponents tortured.

At Shkurti's 2011 trial at the Serious Crimes Court in Tirana, one victim, Niko Qevjani, told how he was mercilessly beaten inside Station No 2 by Lushnje gang members Sajmir Alicko and his brother Arjan Alicko, supposedly for scratching their car.

"Arjan Alicko dragged me out of my car and forced me to walk to Station No 2," he said. "There he made me kneel down and asked me to pay him thirteen million leke (around $120,000) for the damage to their van. I told him that I don't have that money. Arjan Alicko and his friend Bledar Flamuri began hitting me with hard objects. They hit me even harder just because my blood spilled and stained Arjan's shirt."

Niko was eventually frogmarched to a Western Union, his face bruised and covered in blood, where he handed over about $18,000. On the way, they were stopped by police, who accepted the explanation that Niko had been in an accident.

"Alicko would go in and out of the local police station as if he was the police chief," Niko said. "No one would ever question him, even though I reported him three times."

But Shkurti's protected status did not prevent Artur Daja from striking back. As Shkurti and his henchmen travelled through Lushnje in an armoured van, the vehicle was rocked by an anti-tank missile. Incredibly, nobody was killed or injured, and that evening the Shkurti gang firebombed the home of a man suspected of involvement in the attack.

Eventually, Artur Daja's luck ran out. With the connivance of a member of his own outfit, he was kidnapped, tortured and killed in October 1998. It is said that Shkurti personally hacked off his head, which he then drove to display in all four corners of the city. Daja's torso was dragged to the town's main square, where it was publicly blown up with dynamite. The demonstrative performance was a very public restoration of Shkurti's honour. Even the man who had betrayed Daja, Bledar Haxhiu, wasn't spared — his body was later found riddled with bullets.

Despite the gratuitous violence committed by the Gang of Lushnje — officials put the death toll at twenty-five for the year — the general public saw them not just as the victors, but as heroes. Daja's gang had robbed, killed public officials and terrorised the police, and were in cahoots with the disastrous right-wing government. Shkurti's bloody campaign had restored a semblance of order. But his organisation was left in complete control of the city. Now real money could be made.

The gang cashed in through extortion, protection rackets and sometimes legitimate businesses, which were usually taken by force. Shkurti seized control of the city's football stadium, and on one notorious occasion forced ninety shareholders of a fishing company to sign over their shares to gang members in a single day. The city's lagoon was commandeered and used to store heroin and cannabis being shipped from Turkey to Italy. The gang even made, and won, "bids" for public service contracts such as road building and street cleaning. Murders were an inevitable part of the bidding process. As time went on, the Lushnje gang became more deeply involved in gun running, people trafficking, contract killing, burglary and large-scale forgery.

By 1999, a semblance of order had been restored to much of the country. Gang leaders like Alfred Shkurti were being rounded up. But that was not the end of his story. Shkurti refused to go into custody. He changed his name to Aldo Bare — the name under which he would become famous — and began a war of attrition against the police. At least one officer was assassinated. In another incident, a huge bomb was planted at the city police headquarters close to the chief's parking space. Fortunately, it was diffused. Another bomb plot failed when the would-be assassin was killed in an accidental explosion close to his target.

Aldo Bare fled to Macedonia, then onto Romania and Turkey. Although the crackdown continued, the Gang of Lushnje remained powerful in the city until at least 2005, through its network of corrupt police officers and public officials.

As one former police officer said, "It was not worth going against Bare. Every police officer knew that Bare would find a way to avoid justice, so why risk our lives in the first place?"

For the year 1997-98, Albanian police had recorded an unprecedented 1,542 murders, most linked either to gang violence or a spike in blood feuds. Much worse was that the pyramid crisis had unleashed a beast that could never be tamed. The violence, poverty, crime and corruption experienced by many young Albanians during this period would put them on an unwavering path of crime. Many swore that they would never again put their fortunes in the hands of another. Aldo Bare, and his teenage assassin Leonard Prifti, would later re-emerge in Europe, more powerful and dangerous than ever.

But in the meantime, more trouble was brewing across the border in Kosovo. It would prove to be yet another opportunity for Albanian mafia gangs to flex their muscles and expand their sphere of influence.

SPOILS OF WAR

Human kidneys can be worth more than forty times their weight in gold on the black market. In terms of cold hard cash, that can mean as much as $230,000. But in this murky trade, the rightful owner more often than not doesn't get a penny. That's because by the time a buyer is found, he's almost certainly dead. And if you believe some of the claims made after the 1998 Kosovo war, that's the way it was for Serbian prisoners being held at the remote farm building in Albania known innocuously as the Yellow House.

No wonder they were said to have begged the guards, allegedly members of the Kosovo Liberation Army (KLA), to be set free. Day after day, the soldiers were said to watch as their comrades were led out, never to return. They apparently knew the fate that awaited them — an injection or a bullet in the head, and the surgical removal of their kidneys, livers and other organs. Of course, ask former members of the KLA about the allegations and you'll hear a very different tale. These horror stories are constructs of Serbian propaganda, wicked lies, to undermine the new state of Kosovo more than two decades after the war for its freedom.

Whatever the truth of the matter, it's no surprise that the war of words is still going on today, bearing in mind the fraught and complex history between the two peoples.

The conflict stemmed from the way Yugoslavia's borders were drawn up following the end of World War Two. The federation was left with six constituent republics of Bosnia and Herzegovina; Croatia; Macedonia; Montenegro; Serbia; and Slovenia. By the end of 1992 and following the collapse of Communism, all six nations bar Serbia and Montenegro had declared independence.

War ensued in Croatia, then in Slovenia, and then most seriously in Bosnia and Herzegovina, where Bosnian Serb forces carried out heinous war crimes against the Bosnian Croat and Muslim separatists, notoriously during the siege of Sarajevo and later the Srebrenica massacre. But as the world watched on in horror, another intractable problem was bubbling away on Serbia's border with Albania.

The majority ethnic Albanian population of Kosovo was the only nationality within the Yugoslavian federation not allowed republic status and had historically been subsumed as a semi-autonomous region within Serbia. There were long-standing fears that if Kosovo was given even the faint potential to secede, it could go on to form part of a Greater Albania, merging with Macedonia and Albania.

For their part, the Serbs felt they had been forced out of Kosovo over the course of decades, to the point where they formed just ten to twenty percent of the population. The more the Kosovar Albanians pushed for greater freedoms, the more the nationalist Serbs pushed back.

Serb leader Slobodan Milosevic had ended Kosovo's autonomy in 1989 and moved to exclude Albanians from most areas of public life, including politics, the civil service, education, public companies, the health service and the police. The Albanian population responded by forming a shadow government under the Democratic League of Kosovo (LDK). But progress was slow, if non-existent.

The LDK's leader, university literature professor Ibrahim Rugova, did not favour armed struggle, and instead pursued a symbolic democracy where his 'government' was elected by the ninety percent Albanian majority, but would forever remain powerless unless Serbia acquiesced, a hopelessly unlikely prospect.

"We are not certain how strong the Serbian military presence in the province actually is," Rugova said at one point, "But we do know that it is overwhelming and that we have nothing to set against the tanks and other modern weaponry in Serbian hands....We would have no chance of successfully resisting the army. In fact, the Serbs only wait for a pretext to attack the Albanian population and wipe it out. We believe it is better to do nothing and stay alive than to be massacred."

Not everyone saw it that way. Unsurprisingly, a far more militant wing of the separatist movement emerged publicly in 1995. The Kosovo Liberation Army (KLA) began a bombing campaign against Serbian forces the following year and as tensions finally boiled over into a full-blown conflict in 1998, the political impetus rapidly shifted to the leadership of this bold new group.

The KLA's most senior official, political director Hashim Thaci, was a charismatic former history and philosophy student at the University of Pristina. The seventh of nine children, born in the tiny hamlet of Buroje in the Drenica Valley, the young Thaci had been fortunate to be admitted to the university — as part of Serbia's programme of persecution the number of ethnic Albanians allowed to attend had been cut from 40,000 to just 18,000.

Tall, handsome and with a palpable sense of purpose, Thaci was soon elected as the students' vice-rector, putting him under the microscope of the Serbian police. It was at university where he quickly learned counter-surveillance techniques, sneaking back to his home in the Drenica Valley most nights to discuss the prospect of armed resistance with other militants, including the KLA's erstwhile founder Adem Jashari.

"It was a heavy burden to be so young and to be so public," he later told his biographers, the British journalists Roger Boyes and Suzy Jagger. "I could have continued with a good life as a young man. I had siblings living in the diaspora— so it wasn't easy at the age of twenty two or twenty three to go off and start a war. It could have been different— but I never regretted it."

By 1993, Thaci was living in Switzerland among the country's Albanian diaspora. But the move had not been entirely voluntary. His family had been subject to harassment by the Serbian police, and a warrant was out for his arrest on charges of belonging to an illegal organization. Thaci dropped out of a history course at the University of Zurich and drifted further towards radical politics. Like many, he had been galvanised by the horrors of the 1995 Srebrenica massacre.

By now, Thaci had assumed leadership of the KLA's Drenica Group, which mainly consisted of radicals from his birthplace. Thaci and his fellow exiles were able to slip in and out of Albania for military training and meetings with other KLA founders. During his early militant career, Thaci picked up the nickname "The Snake". He says it owes more to his ability to "slither my way around the high mountain passes" when following smuggling routes between Kosovo and Albania, rather than as an indication of his personality. "My first nickname was the student," he said.

By the time of the Albanian pyramid crisis, Thaci was living in exile in Tirana where he was involved in obtaining weapons for the KLA[6]. Thaci later described the looting of army depots as an "extraordinary chance to expand our weapons base," mostly with stocks of pistols and AK-47s. Many of the weapons destined for KLA guerillas later made it over the border from the northern Albanian town of Kukes, built on a peninsula that gave smugglers a direct route via the White Drin River across to Prizren.

But the same period also saw Thaci removed from the country. In July 1997, Thaci's flatmate, a journalist, was stabbed to death with a screwdriver. Thaci was arrested and accused of being an arms dealer, but later released and deported to Switzerland, where he already had asylum. Thaci believes he may have been targeted for assassination by the Serbs and that his flatmate was killed in his place.[7]

---

[6] Although he has always maintained that he never fired a shot in anger, other accounts suggest Thaci took part in early fighting in Drenica.

[7] Thaci was tried on terrorism charges in Pristina the same month and sentenced to ten years, in absentia, never serving a day a prison.

When bloodthirsty Serb leader Slobodan Milosevic became President of Yugoslavia in the same year, the Albanian nationalist cause became even more pressing. There were more KLA bombings, more attacks on Serbian forces. Meanwhile, the Serbs hit back in KLA strongholds, particularly in the Drenica valley area.

There is no question that the sides were uneven. In March 1998, the International Crisis Group said the KLA had claimed responsibility for just twenty-one deaths in two years; five cops, five civilians and eleven Albanians accused of collaborating with the Serbs. Meanwhile, the Serbian army was sweeping through Kosovan villages, seizing homes and killing at will, in a blatant programme of ethnic cleansing.

One of the attacks included an assault on the compound of KLA leader Adem Jashari, who was killed alongside fifty-seven others, including women and children of the family. It was a massacre that turned the tide for the KLA, galvanising new recruits and showing those Kosovars who were still on the fence that Milosevic must be defeated. As the conflict intensified, it became clear that the United States was now tacitly backing the rebels, even though ambassador Robert Gelbard had previously labelled the KLA a terrorist organisation (a claim that was later retracted).

By September 1998 there were an estimated 250,000 displaced Kosovar Albanians, many of them hiding out in woodlands with no food, shelter or clothing. The following month, NATO carried out airstrikes against the Serbian side. Meanwhile, the Serbs committed a number of atrocities, including the January 1999 Racak massacre, in which forty-five Albanian farmers were marched up a hill and shot.

British Prime Minister Tony Blair, making the case for intervention in March 1999, described how the Albanian side was faring, noting how more than ten per cent of the population had been made homeless, with 65,000 turfed out in that month alone. Blair said "masked irregulars [were] separating out the men: we don't know what has happened to them".

With Hashim Thaci now leading renewed peace talks at Rambouillet, in France (replacing the LDK's delegation as the Kosovar Albanians' leading authority), the Albanian side, the US and Britain signed a deal to allow NATO to administer Kosovo as an autonomous region and provide a peacekeeping force. Yugoslavia and Russia refused to sign. There then followed a three-month NATO bombing campaign.

While the above summary might omit many of the complexities of the conflict and the atrocities carried out on both sides, the take home is this — if not for the intervention of NATO, the KLA would have been decimated by the much better-equipped Serbian forces. The conflict officially came to an end on June 3, 1999, when Milosevic finally allowed the NATO-led peacekeeping Kosovo Force (KFOR) into the country. But as the fog of war cleared, unsavoury allegations about the KLA emerged.

Serbian propagandists are usually happy to trumpet the links — real and overblown — between the KLA and organised crime, but they are often glossed over by Western accounts of the period. Yet there is little doubt that there was significant crossover between the militants and the Balkan underworld.

The ineffective phantom government of the LDK had raised funds chiefly through a tax on the hundreds of thousands of ethnic Albanians living abroad. This levy amounted to three percent of salaries, or ten percent of business profits. While there was no way to enforce it, many people paid up either through genuine patriotism or out of fear of being exposed as deadbeats if the government ever achieved real power. The cash was mostly spent on strengthening the LDK's parallel government, which included paying salaries for doctors and teachers (as well as providing armoured cars for its political leaders).

But when the KLA began to form its own plans for the future of Kosovo it also needed funding — and militant leaders were not too fussy about where it came from. While the West later became willing to help at a distance, the KLA's fight was supported long-term by a colourful cast of ordinary expats and businessman, as well as drug traffickers, gangsters and organised crime families.

It must be stressed that not everything was necessarily illegal or unethical. The main KLA fund, Homeland Calling, raked in about $100 million. The American branch, set up in New York by expat Florin Krasniqi, raised around $11 million. The cash went mainly on legally purchased weapons from gun stores in the US which were then shipped to Albania and then onto Kosovo, where Florin's cousin Xhevdet and nephew Adrian were both founding members of the KLA (Florin was strongly motivated by the death of Adrian in a firefight with Serb forces). Now a steel magnate, Florin was never involved in organised crime, but other fundraisers in the diaspora were. These criminal groups also set up ostensible fundraising organisations, using extortion to kick back funds directly to KLA commanders while creaming off a bit for themselves.

But while the lines sometimes appeared blurred, there were other occasions where both KLA supporters and members were involved in outright criminality of almost every colour.

As the war crimes investigator John Cencich later wrote in his book *The Devil's Garden*:

"This wasn't just a war zone; it was also the underworld. I was smack in the middle of major auto theft, heroin smuggling, and human trafficking for the purposes of prostitution. Narcotics trafficking throughout the Balkans funded many of the KLA operations. In fact, many KLA members were directly linked to syndicated crime in Albania. They were also involved in arms smuggling and had connections to the Italian mafia."

One of the most notorious gang bosses affiliated to the KLA was Princ Dobroshi, a drug trafficker who oversaw the northern section of the Balkan Route through which heroin was smuggled from Turkey into Western Europe. He was jailed in Norway for heroin trafficking in 1994 but later escaped after bribing a guard, fleeing to Croatia and then the Czech Republic, where he had plastic surgery to hide his identity.

Dobroshi was arrested again in Prague in 1999 as part of an operation that saw forty people held across Europe. He was extradited to Norway, jailed and eventually paroled in 2005. Czech security services found he had used profits from the drugs trade to buy arms for the KLA. The operation to transport him to Oslo was carried out amid the highest possible security, over fears that militants would mount a rescue attempt. Despite being suspected of several murders, Dobroshi was last known to be living as a free man in Kosovo, where he described himself as a tobacco salesman.

Then there was Agim Gashi, one of the first Albanian mafia figures to establish close ties with the Italian Calabrian mafia, known as the 'Ndrangheta. He made millions through a heroin trafficking syndicate based in Milan which stretched into Spain, Germany, France and Switzerland, via Turkey, Albania, Kosovo, Slovakia, Turkey and Egypt.

Gashi was born in Pristina, Kosovo, but moved to Milan in 1992, where he married an Italian woman. His criminal empire sprouted from a pickpocket ring, then into prostitution, and finally to drug trafficking. Gashi's heroin was shipped to Italy from Turkey, hidden inside shipments of fruits and nuts, then on to Europe.

Gashi splashed out on a luxury villa outside Milan and owned front businesses in London, Norway and Hungary, including perfume shops and beauty parlours. The Gashi network was already well-established by the time war broke out in Kosovo, at which point he began incorporating arms trafficking into his portfolio, chiefly to supply the KLA. After he was arrested while purchasing 200 automatic rifles, the *Corriere della Sera* told how Gashi had supplied Kosovan fighters with "Kalashnikov rifles, bazookas, and hand grenades". He was jailed in 1999 and his cousin, Ekrem, was gunned down in Pristina the same year while travelling through the city in his Mercedes.

Another major criminal with ties to the KLA was the Kosovan smuggler and drugs lord Naser Kelmendi. We will hear much more about him later.

By the end of the conflict, some of the Albanian crime groups that had been so keen to help their comrades break free from Serbian rule started inflicting their own form of oppression upon the civilian population. With the Serbian police gone, gangsters from Tirana, Vlore, Bajram Curri and elsewhere, took to the streets of the capital Pristina in four-by-fours, stealing from residents, journalists, aid workers and other officials who had moved in to help fleeing refugees.

Criminals then began to seize and loot the homes of fleeing Serbians, selling them on when property prices increased. It proved to be such a money spinner that they also forced ethnic Albanians out of their homes, cars and businesses, often using extreme violence to get their way.

As a British official said at the time, "[The UN] is unprepared to take over law and order. In the absence of police and legitimate rules, a vacuum has occurred. That vacuum is being filled by organised crime. Albanian gangs are inviting Kosovo Serbs to leave their apartments. Now Kosovo Albanians are being invited to leave."

The KLA's leadership was forced to deny that the organisation itself was involved in the property seizures.

"We have no such information," Hashim Thaci said. "We know there are those who have left Kosovo, but we have not forced anyone to leave, or put pressure on them to leave. That is propaganda. Anyone who has not committed crimes is free to live in Kosovo."

At one point, up to thirty people a week were being killed in connection with rising crime. There were also hundreds of revenge killings of Serbs and Roma, who were seen as collaborators or responsible for looting abandoned homes during the war. Some of the killers were KLA members. Even so, an unnamed KLA intelligence chief complained bitterly to the *Sunday Telegraph* in September 1995 of unfair treatment in the press.

"We are criticised for rising crime rates but we cannot decommission, transform and fight the mafia all at the same time," he said.

Years later, Hashim Thaci told his biographers of his own dismay over the post-war violence.

"I realised just how far deep ran the wounds in society," he said. "A crimewave was unfolding in front of me, committed by some of my own compatriots. And we were completely unprepared for it. People who had been criminals before the war returned to their old ways, uncontrolled because there were no identity cards, no order."

Yet many critics said the KLA's responsibility ran far deeper than its struggle against the mafia, and accused it of having promised a free rein to organised crime bosses in return for arms during the conflict. In fact, allegations of complicity and direct KLA involvement in organised crime went even further. For example, some critics noted the way the Thaci family made money in the post war years.

In January 1999, UN police raided the apartment of Gani Thaci, Hashim Thaci's elder brother and a former KLA soldier, in connection with an alleged firearms incident. They found a gun hidden under a mattress but also $250,000 in cash. Gani's explanation was that the cash was given to him by a Canadian construction firm working in Kosovo, Meridian Resources. The firm admitted that Gani was paid for "intermediary services" although it claimed the fee was closer to $60,000.

Meridian's Director Shaun Going said at the time, "There's no doubt the former KLA people are well-positioned in business so there is no way of doing business in this country without doing business with them or coming across them on a day-to-day basis."

In any case, Gani later became a senior figure in the Kosovo Insurance Bureau, a scheme overseen by the central bank. Later, Thaci's other brothers also seemed to be doing well. Idriz Thaci set up a business which won government tenders to help build highways and provide electricity services worth millions. A key supplier was Kosova Petrol, a firm owned by a former advisor to Hashim Thaci, Bedri Selmani. Selmani was at one point said to have evaded tax at a cost to the state of four million euros.[8] Blerim Thaci, a younger brother and also a former KLA fighter, started a firm that built 102 apartments in Pristina worth millions, but it was never clear where the funds for the project came from.[9]

Other former militants were also jostling for position in the new state. In 2000, the ex-KLA commander Ekrem Rexha was left riddled with bullets outside his home in Pristina. Rexha was a former Yugoslav army general who was known as a moderate and a close friend of Ramush Haradinaj, himself a rival of Hashim Thaci. The gunmen were never brought to justice.

In 2003, the Serbian government published its controversial *White Paper on Albanian Terrorism in Kosovo-Metohija*. It listed 156 individuals, mostly former KLA leaders and soldiers, who it said were terrorists, war criminals or mafia figures. It also identified what Serbia says is a system of criminal clans under the leadership of two main groups, the Haradinaj clan and the Drenica group, supposedly under the command of the Thaci family.[10]

Of course, given the context the report must be treated with the utmost skepticism. And in any case, it can well be argued that just because some KLA leaders accepted money from certain families to

---

[8] The control of petrol stations, of which Kosova Petrol owned twenty back in 2008, was said to have been the cause of a devastating fallout between Thaci and fellow KLA commander Ramush Haradinaj.

[9] According to Hashim Thaci's biographers, both Gani and Idriz were previously part of an "extensive network outside Kosovo" that helped to raise funds for KLA guns.

[10] According to the Serbian government, drug traffickers and gangsters such as Naser Kelmendi, and criminal members of the Musaj, Lluca, Selimi, and Lata clans, amongst others, report to Haradinaj. Meanwhile, the Drenica Group comprises members of clans such as Haliti and Ljushtaku.

help fund the war, it doesn't make them criminal godfathers. Nevertheless, the report makes for fascinating and disturbing reading.

Following the publication of the *White Paper*, sources in the West also started to throw accusations at the former KLA leadership. In 2005, the German magazine *Die Weltwoche* told how a secret intelligence report had named Hashim Thaci, by then Kosovo's prime minister; Ramush Haradinaj, the head of the Kosovan government between December 2004 and March 2005; and Xhavit Haliti, a senior parliamentarian, of running the Drenica Group like a mafia organisation.

In 2011, a Council of Europe investigation by Swiss senator and human rights investigator Dick Marty alleged that Hashim Thaci was the "boss" of a "mafia-like" crime group that emerged during the start of the Kosovo war. The two-year inquiry, sparked by claims made by former Yugoslavia war crimes prosecutor Carla del Ponte, drew on numerous intelligence sources, including the FBI, and included claims that the KLA indulged in the murder and organ-harvesting of Serbian captives. Their kidneys, it was claimed, were sold to an Albanian clinic.

Although the KLA's leadership was not directly named in relation to the organ harvesting allegations, the report also said intelligence reports from five countries claimed that Thaci and other members of the Drenica Group exerted "violent control" over the heroin trade. Pulling no punches, the report went on to say that Hashim Thaci was "commonly identified, and cited in secret intelligence reports, as the most dangerous of the KLA's 'criminal bosses'". It said that KLA units were "shaped, to a significant degree, according to the hierarchies, allegiances and codes of honour that prevail among the ethnic Albanian clans, or extended families, and which form a de facto set of laws, known as the *Kanun*, in the regions of Kosovo from which their commanders originated".

Put simply, organised crime bosses and their footsoldiers in Kosovo and Albania had formed guerrilla units for the KLA and continued their criminal activities in parallel with the fight against the Serbs.

It had echoes of the way crime lords had formed Socialist Party-supporting gangs during the Albanian pyramid crisis the previous year. In addition, the report said a "small but inestimably powerful group of KLA personalities" within the Drenica Group "apparently wrested control of most of the illicit criminal enterprises in which Kosovar Albanians were involved in the Republic of Albania".[11]

The report went on to name other senior KLA figures, including Xhavit Haliti, Kadri Veseli, Azem Syla, and Fatmir Limaj. It said all had been investigated for war crimes or criminal activity, but had "evaded effective justice". It added the chilling accusation that some had never faced prosecution because they were backed to become political leaders by the United States, giving them time to murder or intimidate witnesses against them, concluding, "This also seems to have allowed Thaci – and by extension the other members of the 'Drenica Group' to exploit their position in order to accrue personal wealth totally out of proportion with their declared activities". Even worse, Marty wrote, "first-hand sources alone have credibly implicated Haliti, Veseli, Syla and Limaj, alongside Thaci and other members of his inner circle, in having ordered – and in some cases personally overseen – assassinations, detentions, beatings and interrogations in various parts of Kosovo and, of particular interest to our work, in the context of KLA-led operations on the territory of Albania".

Thaci himself slammed the accusations as "Goebbelsian". Speaking to *The Times*, he denied any involvement in drugs or organ trafficking, and said he had never ordered any murders nor carried one out. Vowing to go after Marty in the courts, Thaci said:

"This was the most heavy offence that has been done to me personally as a citizen, a parent, a prime minister and to the whole people of Kosovo. That is a complete slander. Everyone has seen that it is a report with no facts and substance. I am completely clean with regards to the allegations and I am calm in that regard. I have been accused of these things for fifteen years now. I know that the US and the European Union

---

[11] Former Albanian president Sali Berisha had allowed significant swathes of his family's land in northern Albania to be used as a KLA staging ground (Kosovar Albanians are mainly Ghegs, like Berisha), but the report noted that Thaci also had considerable support from the incumbent Socialist government as well as "the formidable Albanian mafia". Many of the KLA's commanders based themselves in Albania, some in Tirana. The report described how this opened up new opportunities for criminals, allowing them to establish "protection rackets" and other criminal enterprises in the areas where they were operating.

countries know these are complete lies. I feel insulted as a human being because I could not have imagined before this happened that someone would go to these extreme depths to make these accusations, even less someone who calls himself a politician like Dick Marty."

On the accusations of KLA organ trafficking, he added, "That is the most despicable thing. Completely inhuman. That is why I took so much offence at these unbased accusations."

He went on, "I have been the political leader of the KLA publicly, I have never hidden my identity."

And he issued a legal threat, "Dick Marty may think this is child's play but it's not. It means he will have to face justice for what he has done. He may be a citizen of a neutral country but I do not think justice will be neutral towards him."

Marty was never pursued in the courts however, because the report, as a government document, was legally privileged.

As Thaci's biographers later noted, the organ harvesting claims appeared to have originated with three sources who told former *Daily Telegraph* journalist Michael Montgomery about an occasion on which 300 Serbs were allegedly kidnapped by KLA gunmen in 1999, taken to the Yellow House in Albania and killed for their kidneys. They had accused Ramush Haradinaj, by then Kosovo's Prime Minister, and his brother of orchestrating the atrocity. That report found its way to the desk of Carla Del Ponte, who ordered an inquiry. A subsequent report relied on eight former KLA witnesses, four of whom said they had taken scores of captured Serbs to Albania, while one said he had taken body parts to an airport near Tirana, although none said they saw an operation actually taking place.[12]

---

[12] A team of investigators from the EU's Rule of Law Mission in Kosovo, EULEX, visited the house and found a room with a black polished floor. It showed traces of blood and possibly urine, but their origins could not be determined. They also found rubbish bags outside containing medical gloves, bandages, syringes and empty boxes of muscle relaxant drugs. In addition, they found that a layer of white paint had been slathered over the building's former yellow colour. The family who lived there at the time denied all knowledge of any wrongdoing. The team was also unable to speak to the original witnesses identified by Montgomery. Later, the lead investigator Matti Raatikainen said, "The fact is that there is no evidence whatsoever in this case. No bodies, no witnesses." Carla Del Ponte later published a book, *The Hunt: Me and the War Criminals*, which repeated the organ trafficking claims. She

In recent years, Hashim Thaci has been recognised for his work in normalising relations between Kosovo and Serbia, even being nominated for a Nobel Peace Prize. He is generally viewed by Western leaders as a heroic statesman, somewhat in the mould of Nelson Mandela.

Former US Vice President Joe Biden has called him "the George Washington of Kosovo" and Madeline Albright, US Secretary of State during the Kosovo war, has praised his "vision". On a practical level, it seems highly unlikely that Thaci would have the time to head up an international crime syndicate, in between the business of running a country and representing it on the world stage at frequent international summits.

But that's not to say that the war in Kosovo didn't do much to liberate the country's criminal class. Albanian mafia groups were suddenly able to operate throughout Kosovo without the added restrictions placed on them by Serbian oppression, and whether or not the top levels of the state were complicit in their activities, crime groups certainly found allies and collaborators within the new state apparatus.

By the end of the war, the KLA was thought to have around 20,000 members, with about 10,000 going back to their old jobs and 5,000 joining the Kosovo Protection Corps, a paramilitary organization which was essentially the KLA under a new name. Another 2,500 joined the police and the K-SHIK, Kosovo's intelligence service. In other words, the KLA effectively became the state[13]. Today, Thaci is

---

also alleged that evidence taken from the Yellow House had later been destroyed. The book, in turn, sparked the Marty report. So, say Thaci's biographers, the entire narrative around the organ trafficking allegations was based on just a handful of witness statements, which had been recycled for various reports.

[13] The ethnic Albanian diaspora also fought for disputed territory in neighboring Macedonia in 2001. The National Liberation Army (NLA) wanted to seize an area in the North West of the country which borders Albanian and Kosovo in a bid to form a "Greater Albania". Again, there was an indisputable nexus between its leadership and organised crime and, like the KLA, many of its leaders entered the legitimate political sphere after the fighting was done.

still the country's elected president and Haliti is the Deputy Chairman of the Assembly of Kosovo[14].

The truth about the KLA's involvement in organised crime might forever be shrouded by the fog of war. It undoubtedly was not a 'clean' organisation, but exactly how dirty it was, and the extent to which its leaders were involved may never be known. Particularly disturbing are accusations that the West is unwilling to confront some of the most serious allegations, because of its closeness to Hashim Thaci and his allies. Bemoaning an apparent lack of willing to tackle the problem, even the KLA's former money man Florin Krasniqi,

---

[14] Hashim Thaci was dramatically indicted on war crimes charges by prosecutors at The Hague on his way to a meeting at the White House with President Trump in late June 2020. Thaci, as well as Kadri Veseli, are allegedly "criminally responsible for nearly 100 murders," according to the indictment.

Ramesh Haradinaj was indicted by the International Criminal Tribunal for the Former Yugoslavia for war crimes in 2005, but was acquitted amid allegations of witness intimidation. Another former KLA commander, Fatmir Limaj, was also acquitted. In 2008, he faced corruption and fraud charges but they were dropped when he accepted a diplomatic role abroad. A man who had been prepared to testify against him was found dead in Germany. Although it was ruled a suicide, he had also reported witness intimidation.

Haradinaj faced another trial in 2012, but was again acquitted. In 2018, Limaj, by then deputy prime minister, was further cleared of responsibility for the murders of two ethnic Albanian civilians in October 1998. He was found not guilty of charges that he did not take reasonable and necessary measures to prevent the killings. It was alleged that he had seen the bodies of the victims and was aware that the crime had been committed, but the court ruled there was "no single piece of evidence that the accused committed the criminal offence".

The Hague continues to probe alleged KLA war crimes, including organ harvesting. In January 2019, a number of former commanders were summoned to appear before the court. They were Sami Lushtaku, Rustem Mustafa, known as Remi during the war, Sokol Dobruna, Nazif Mehmeti, Remzi Shala, known during the war as "The Red Apple", and Safet Sula.

In July 2019, Shala was convicted of the 1998 kidnapping of an ethnic Albanian man who later turned up dead. He was jailed for fourteen years by the court in Prizren. At the time of writing, it was not clear what the outcome would be in the other cases. "I suppose I could be either witness or defendant, but I have no idea why I have been invited," Dobruna said at the time.

Kosovo's then-Prime Minister, Ramush Haradinaj, welcomed the hearings, adding "The KLA's war was just and sacred and this will be proven." He resigned in July 2019 to fight yet more war crimes allegations, sparking an election in October.

latterly a member of the Kosovo parliament, described Thaci in 2011 as "the head of the mafia here".

It is certainly true that the wars in the former Yugoslavia allowed vast criminal networks to strengthen, profit, expand and consolidate their power across Europe. Drugs, people and weapons began to flow more freely through the Balkan Route and the fledgling democratic governments across the region became far more tolerant of organised crime than the Communist regimes had been. As a result, drugs misery increased on the seedy backstreets of cities like Hamburg, Paris and London. In the early part of the century two men, one from Kosovo and one from Albania, moved to dominate these markets. Their names were Naser Kelmendi and Aldo Bare.

BROWN GOLD

For the Balkan mafias, the three-year time frame that unleashed the chaos of the pyramid crisis and the Kosovo war was akin to the so-called dot com boom in the United States. While tech companies in the late 1990s were cashing in on the growth of the World Wide Web and advances in connectivity, crime syndicates from Eastern Europe were thriving on increased demand for weapons and drugs, facilitated by poorly enforced borders.

Both sets of entrepreneurs also seemed to have support from the authorities in their respective countries. In America, tax cuts were helping speculators to invest in emerging markets and companies, while CEOs were making friends in high places. In the Balkans, mafia bosses had also made powerful allies among the political classes and corrupted hundreds of police and state officials.

It often isn't possible to pinpoint exactly who is in charge of an Albanian organised crime syndicate, because of the way they are made up of multiple extended criminal networks. But that isn't always the case. By the end of 2018 at least two powerful crime lords could be identified — thanks to painstaking work by a range of European law enforcement agencies, which successfully brought them to trial.

One of them was the fugitive gang leader Alfred Shkurti — now known as Aldo Bare. The other was the Kosovan gangster and KLA supporter Naser Kelmendi. As their cases show, both men rode the boom years and then crashed as their networks grew ever larger. But when times were good, their stock-in-trade was heroin.

Aldo Bare had played no part in the war in Kosovo. As a Tosk from the South, risking his life and liberty for Kosovan liberation wasn't really his bag. More prosaically, Bare's ostentatious and victorious campaign against his enemy Artur Daja and subsequent war of attrition against the police in Lushnje, had already attracted enough attention. By 2002, Bare had fled Albania all together. His part in the insurrection against the Democratic Party-led government had always been more about business than politics anyway, and Bare decided now was time to really nurture those interests — from a safe distance.

Creating his new identity had not been difficult. Bare already employed a team of master forgers, who manufactured passports and other documents for his wide-ranging criminal enterprises. Their efforts were convincing enough to get him into Turkey, where he was able to buy and rent a number of properties in Istanbul and Ankara. Even though Interpol had issued arrest warrants in 2000 and 2001, and despite the fact he had been sentenced to twenty-five years in prison in absentia for the murder of Daja, he could slip back into Albania or Macedonia quite easily. And money was no problem. Bare's drug trafficking network had been operational for some years, probably since before the pyramid crisis, and partly thanks to the ongoing regional instability it was going from strength to strength.

When it comes to success in the world of organised crime, geography is everything. Take the South American cartels. Without the climate, rich soil and expansive jungles of places like Colombia, Peru and Bolivia, the coca crop would not exist, and so the mafias there would not have grown quite so powerful. Similarly, Aldo Bare would always have been a violent, ruthless and cunning individual. But if he'd grown up on a council estate in Glasgow, he would most likely have become just another street thug. Luckily for him, thanks to its Mediterranean climate, Albania is the perfect place to grow weed. And in the decades since the upheaval of the 1990s, the country has emerged as Europe's biggest producer of outdoor grown cannabis, with most of the annual crop cultivated in the southern village of Lazarat.[15]

The drug's contribution to the economy is massive. Recent estimates suggest the industry is worth around £4.25 billion a year — equal to roughly half of GDP. Farmers offload one kilo of their crop for about £170 to buyers in Albania. The same amount on the streets of London could be worth £5,000— a mark-up of nearly 3,000 per cent. Of course, there are processing and transportation costs to consider, but that still leaves the narcos with a healthy profit. While Aldo Bare had no known involvement in Lazarat, he did cultivate the drug in his Lushnje stronghold. But that was just one dimension of his business.

The second geographic advantage for Aldo Bare — and other traffickers who emerged from the upheaval of the civil war— was Albania's key position within the centuries-old smuggling and trading path known as the Balkan Route. In the past, the route was part of the old Silk Road between the Far East and Europe, serving as the fulcrum between the continent and the Ottoman Empire. It then became the link between the NATO countries and the Soviet Union. Now, it serves as the best land bridge between the EU (and

---

[15] Lazarat has a population of just under 3,000, but roughly ninety percent are engaged in cannabis farming and at one point it was producing as much as 900 tons of cannabis as year — almost the entirety of Albania's annual crop. There have been several attempts to tame the area, resulting in shootouts with locals. Back in 2014, the Socialist government launched what was probably Europe's biggest ever drugs raid, flooding the village with around 800 troops to seize and burn cannabis fields. Even so, the following year three security personnel were killed at a checkpoint by mafia gunmen, proving that organised crime gangs in the village had not been wiped out.

by extension Britain and the United States), and Russia, the Middle East and Turkey. If goods or people are to move from one area to another by land, then the Balkans are the best way to go. And Aldo Bare was interested in moving chiefly one thing — heroin.

The route has roughly three or four branches, which all begin in Turkey, where opium from Afghanistan, Pakistan and Iran is first transported and then processed into heroin by the Turkish mafia. Traditionally, those same *babas*, or godfathers, as well as the Russian mafias, were the main traffickers of the drug into Europe and the rest of the world. One of the most successful Turkish organisations was the Baybasin clan, which was responsible for shipping hundreds of thousands of kilos of heroin into Europe, as we shall see later. But increasingly, as the 1990s became ever more chaotic, Albanian crime syndicates were purchasing tons of the drug from the Turkish barons and transporting it themselves through Bulgaria and Romania, then across the regions of the former Yugoslavia and on into Austria and Germany, or Scandinavia, or south through Albania and then across the Adriatic Sea to Italy.

The Balkan Route's central role in European drug trafficking is well known by law enforcement, particularly Interpol, which has a dedicated unit set up to tackle it. But the smugglers always find a way. They use trucks, mainly, but also cars, camper vans, and sometimes planes or trains. Where possible, such as between Istanbul and the Romanian port of Constanza, drugs move by sea. They are hidden wherever there is a space — among the load; within the load; in the fuel tank; in the roof lining; in the spare wheel, or secreted in even more creative places. Sometimes, traffickers secretly attach packages to lorries at rest stops, leaving drivers to play an unwitting part in their drugs conspiracy. Narcos then track the shipment and collect it later. Other drivers, who are in the know, have their own tricks for getting past border control. Checks can sometimes take up to eight hours, so they load their trucks with perishable goods, such as flowers, in the hope that guards feel pressured into waving them through. Bribes are a more direct way of getting past the border, while another method is to intentionally sacrifice a smaller load so that another, larger shipment, can get through.

While the route tends to follow a set path of main roads — often deserted for many miles — it is not set in stone. For example, during the break-up of Yugoslavia it became impossible to move goods through certain channels, so new ones opened up in other countries. Yet for organised crime gangs, these new tributaries were a welcome development.

During the Communist era, smuggling was commonplace, often with the tacit cooperation of officials. Yet by and large, the system kept a lid on the trafficking of illicit goods between the East and the West. When Communism collapsed and Yugoslavia's nations began fighting for independence, the West imposed sanctions. Suddenly, there was a shortage of much-desired goods. Even more profitable was the arms embargo. Within weeks, the weapons ban had predictably achieved the opposite effect and the region was flooded with arms from South America, South Africa and other former Warsaw Pact countries. The oil embargo in Serbia and Montenegro in 1992 helped criminals get rich through oil illegally imported from countries such as Albania, Macedonia and Bulgaria.

One of the reasons for this black-market boom was that most of the armed groups involved in the various struggles were poorly equipped and staffed with volunteer soldiers. As a result, they had to rely on smugglers to obtain weapons, food and other goods. There is evidence that during the 1992-95 conflict in Bosnia and Herzegovina criminals and fighters from all sides exchanged goods and even sold weapons to each other. Even the civilians who lived through the Siege of Sarajevo only did so because of a huge tunnel built underneath the city, through which an average of twenty tons of food and other commodities was delivered every day.

With the onset of the war in Kosovo and the close working relationship between the KLA and organised criminals, the gateway to Europe became increasingly porous and the criminal organisations exploiting the smuggling routes became even better established. Profits from trafficking weapons, and people (often women to work in brothels), were later spent on corrupting state officials, police and politicians, and were also re-invested into the heroin market. Just as the fall of Communism had led to the liberalisation of Eastern Europe's licit economies, prompting a new entrepreneurial class to emerge, it transformed the Balkan's criminal landscape from one in which only a few very well-connected villains could prosper into a vast, dynamic underworld with hundreds, if not thousands, of aspiring kingpins.

This situation was compounded by another Western-led geopolitical blunder. The 2001 invasion of Afghanistan— which produces more than three quarters of the world's opium— was supposed to eradicate the Taliban and bring the country under American control. At the time, the fact that the Taliban had banned poppy cultivation the previous year — leading to a ninety-one percent decrease in cultivation areas, from 82,172 hectares to just 7,606 hectares — seemed irrelevant. But in the years following the invasion, the US-backed warlords who helped to fight the Taliban, drug traffickers close to the new government, and the Taliban itself, all profited from a resurgence in the crop. By 2018, the total area under cultivation had soared to 263,000 hectares.

For Albanian and Bosnian crime groups it helped that many of their members were Muslim (albeit usually non-practicing) and could therefore establish closer ties with Al Qaeda and Taliban members in Afghanistan.

To provide some idea of the value of this market, Afghan poppy farmers can expect to be paid somewhere in the region of around $700 dollars per kilo at the farm gate. Turkish wholesalers might sell it on for a markup of around 1,800 per cent, or $12,665. By the time it hits the streets of somewhere like Britain as fully processed heroin, a kilo could cost a drug dealing gang around $31,870. It could then net them as much as $117,765 on the streets.[16]

The 2003 Serbian *White Paper* sheds further light on the profits allegedly being being made by Albanian narcos. It said that Kosovan gangsters controlled "more than eighty percent of the heroine trade, their dealers are located in at least half the European countries and they smuggle four to six tons of heroin monthly amounting to $2 billion a year".

---

[16] The global market for heroin is estimated to be worth around $68 billion, while the market for cocaine is worth $130 billion. The global market for illegal drugs in total is around $380 billion. To put that in perspective, McDonald's turns over around $27 billion a year.

While Aldo Bare wasn't Kosovan, he was also benefitting from the heroin trade. In fact, by the turn of the millennium, he had become one of the most successful criminals in Italy and the police were desperate to find this illusive kingpin known as "The Professor".

HUNTING THE PROFESSOR

The Kosovo war proved fortuitous for Aldo Bare. Not only did it open up smuggling routes across the Balkans, but other opportunities emerged in unexpected ways. For example, when the master drug trafficker Agim Gashi was caught by the Italian authorities meeting with an arms supplier on behalf of the KLA, his heroin syndicate based in Milan was broken up. But the framework for the operation was still in place. Within months of Gashi's arrest, Aldo Bare had placed a key lieutenant in charge of his own operation in Milan, with another top crony based in Turin, effectively creating twin trafficking and distribution centres in the country.

The man in charge of the Turin base was Edmond Bega, formerly the president of Lushnje's football club, seized by Bare in the wake of the pyramid crisis. His eventual arrest would spark a separate probe into the finances not just of Lushnje Football Club, but of the entire Albanian Football Association. In Milan, Bare placed his right-hand man Enver Dondollaku in control.

Aldo Bare's heroin came from Turkey, then along the Balkan Route — Bulgaria or Romania, then Macedonia and Albania and finally across the Adriatic Sea to the Italian ports of Bari and Ancona. There were numerous distribution points across the country, including in Turin, Monza, and Brescia, where three processing labs were later discovered.

At first, the shipments were delivered by speedboat, and when border controls were improved the organisation switched to bringing the drugs in by trucks or cars. The Italian authorities estimated that at least 700 kilos of heroin, 200 kilos of cocaine and untold quantities of cannabis grown in Lushnje were smuggled into Italy by the gang. At 2006 prices, the heroin alone could have netted Bare in the region of $20 million, assuming he was then selling it on wholesale. The cocaine would have made a further $10 million. And these were just the quantities the Italian cops were able to track over a period of a couple of years. Although unproven, it's likely that Bare's operation continued into Western Europe. But it was in Italy where law enforcement efforts were focused.

At first, Italian investigators struggled to deal with the scale and nature of the network. They were more used to dealing with homegrown mafia groups. In fact, as they later discovered, Bare was working directly with the 'Ndrangheta, which could ensure the smooth flow of goods through the ports and further down the chain to wholesalers and retailers. Italy's intelligence police also observed Albanian men meeting with a group of North Africans in a café in Turin, customers who probably wanted to ship the drugs back to the continent. But no matter how many traffickers were arrested, or how many seizures were made, the drugs kept flowing. Eventually, in 2004, police established that the organisation was being controlled by a man in Turkey. Underlings overheard on wiretaps called him "The Professor".

Further recorded conversations revealed that the man in question was Aldo Bare, the notorious gangster from across the Adriatic who should have been safely locked up for the murder of Artur Daja. The Italian wiretaps also led police to a seizure of 319 kilos of heroin, two kilos of cocaine and 155 kilos of chemicals used to mix the drugs. As a result, a court issued thirty-four arrest warrants, including one for Aldo Bare, who narrowly escaped arrest in Istanbul later that year. Fifteen members of his network were later sentenced to a total of 200 years imprisonment.

On one level, the operation was only a moderate success because its mastermind was still a free man. But it had also given fresh impetus to a new government in Albania as it launched a clampdown on mafia gangs. Authorities later hailed a probe into twelve of the country's largest criminal clans and claimed that more than 150 mafioso had been arrested. It was later claimed that at least 150 criminal organisations had been destroyed as a result, with at least 1,000 arrested and 191 criminals who'd been abroad extradited back to Albania.

Ironically, it was Aldo Bare's most bloodthirsty triggerman who ultimately gave him away — from beyond the grave. Leonard Prifti had been recruited to the Lushnje gang as a fresh-faced fourteen-year-old orphan and began killing for his master not long after. His favourite method of murder was to cut his enemies down in a hail of bullets fired from a Scorpion submachine gun. By 2005, Prifti, now with the nickname "The Little Chief", was firmly established as the exiled Aldo Bare's man in Lushnje, where he was in charge of all of the gang's operations. His lust for violence was such that Prifti became one of the few members of Aldo Bare's gang respected by the other members in the same way that they venerated The Professor. Yet despite his position of power, Prifti refused to delegate when it came to dishing out violence.

Prifti had been tasked by Aldo Bare with liquidating a rival gangster, Baki Taullajit. He was characteristically bold. The Little Chief simply walked up to his target in the town centre and blasted him in the head with a silenced pistol. Even though Taullajit had been without his usual bodyguards, other cronies saw the murder take place and gave chase. Minutes later, Prifti himself was cornered and shot dead in a nearby alley.

When police searched his body, they found a phone with a history showing dozens of calls to a Turkish number. Police soon traced it to Bare's new hideout in Ankara. In March 2006 armed police raided the property, where they found Bare preparing to flee with a fake Macedonian passport.

It took another three years to drag the heroin baron back to his home country, after he claimed he would be killed the moment he set foot in an Albanian prison. Aldo Bare was eventually returned to stand trial in 2011 and paraded in front of the media by masked special forces soldiers.

In court, Bare was usually flanked by half a dozen stony-faced guards. Also in the dock were nine associates; Enver Dondollaku; Arben and Enver Borici; Ilir Stergu; Afrim Hoxha; Erion Cici; Rexhep Gina; Arjan Alicko; and Jorgo Muzaka. One former gang member, Petrit Lici, gave evidence against his former boss. Arriving at court with a heavily armed escort, Lici gave testimony for around fifty minutes under the hateful gaze of his former boss. He explained how Artur Daja's head had been removed from his body and kicked around like a football in a public square.

"The day the event happened I was drinking coffee in a cafe near the city gymnasium," he said. "There I learned that Artur Daja had been killed and that some people, a good part of them I knew, had come to the city centre with his head. I became curious and left the cafeteria to go to the center of the city. Next to the monument Our Earth I saw Enver Dondollaku holding in his hand the severed head of Artur Daja. Next to him I saw Leonard Prifti, Ilir Rexhep, Enver Boric and some other people I did not know. Around the square there was a small crowd of citizens. I stayed in the square just over a minute and then I left."

Lici also revealed why the turncoat who had sold Daja out to Bare, Bledar Haxhiu, had himself been killed a month later. Lici said Haxhiu had already been in a blood feud with Lushnje gang member Edjan Xhafa, and that Aldo Bare had offered to intervene if he would give up Daja. But the only way for Haxhiu to do so was to kill the gangster himself and hand over his body in a suitcase. It wasn't what Bare had in mind, so Haxhiu, and an accomplice, were executed.

Lici's decision to cooperate with prosecutors was self-serving, but also remarkably brave. While Bare tried to come across in court as a respectable businessman, often wearing a black suit with a black turtle neck jumper underneath (actually making him appear even more villainous), his frequent violent outbursts gave him away.

At one point, enraged by the government's determination to seize the 12,000sq ft lagoon in Lushnje that Bare used as part of his drug and people smuggling operations, he screamed, "There is no motherfucker who can take the lagoon from me. I would fuck Sali Berisha's mother and anyone else who would touch that property."

When the judge ordered Bare to "calm down and don't intimidate from the courtroom," Bare continued to rant until he was removed.

"I will kill," he bellowed, "even from the position I am in, anyone who touches my property!"

As a police officer fixed his gaze on the fallen mobster, Bare sneered, "Why do you look at me like that? I can straighten you out too."

Aldo Bare was ultimately convicted of seven murders, including those of Artur Daja, a police officer and two rival gangsters. He was also found guilty of running a criminal syndicate, illegal possession of firearms, drug trafficking, desecrating graves, destroying property, and a host of other crimes. Bare was jailed for life in July 2012. Almost of all of his gang members are now dead or in prison (although some are now free once more).[17]

In March 2017, it was reported that Albania's Constitutional Court had repealed Aldo Bare's life sentence. He remains in prison for now but his exact status, and whether or not he will have a retrial, is not clear. He is still thought to have significant influence in the Albanian underworld. In any case, Lushnje's streets still run red with blood in connection with the Aldo Bare saga.

In October 2017, Aldo Bare's nephew, Xhulio Shkurti, the son of his late brother, Ramadan, survived an assassination attempt in the city. Two men, Zamir Latifi and Jurgen Hoxha, were killed. The suspected gunman was Laert Haxhiu, a relative of Bledar Haxhiu, the turncoat murdered by Bare. The following November, his associate, Saimri Tahullau, was gunned down in retaliation. Despite several attempts to arrest Haxhiu, he is still thought to be on the run.

---

[17] Some of the most significant figures, such as Arben Borici and Ilir Sterku, were jailed for life. Afrim Hoxha, got eighteen years, Erion Cici, was jailed for twenty-five, Rexhep Gina for sixteen, Arion Alico for six and Jorgo Muzaka for ten years. Enver Dondollaku got twenty-five years and Edmond Bega was jailed for thirteen years. For his cooperation, Petrit Lici had his sentence knocked down from twenty-five years to just eight.

BESA BEHAVIOUR

Ramiz "Celo" Delalic was becoming a problem. The former Bosnian military commander, whose nickname meant "Baldy", was revered by his people for his role in defending Sarajevo against the Serbs. This was despite the fact that he was widely blamed for starting the war in the first place by killing the groom's father during a Serbian wedding procession through the town's Muslim section in March 1992, a move seen as a deliberate provocation. Although never convicted of murder, Delalic had taken credit for the act, likening the shooting to the assassination of Archduke Franz Ferdinand, which sparked World War One.

"I claim the right," he bragged soon afterwards to a television crew, "to link that event with this one that happened here....and as of that moment the first barricades have started and the war in Bosnia and Herzegovina has started."

A decade-and-a-half later, Delalic still had a penchant for hogging the limelight. He had been using Naser Kelmendi's name in public, identifying him to the media as a gangster and drug trafficker. This didn't suit the Kosovo-born Kelmendi, known respectfully in the Balkan underworld as Stari or "The Old One". Unlike the flamboyant Aldo Bare, Kelmendi kept a low profile. As a result, he didn't have to live in exile and could spend his time between his home in Pristina and his business headquarters, a hotel in the Bosnian capital Sarajevo. In addition to dragging his name through the mud, Delalic was also using his contacts within the Bosnian police and security services to disrupt Kelmendi's business operations.

There was a third problem, involving Kelmendi's friend and business associate Fahrudin Radoncic. On one level, it was soap opera stuff. Delalic had been in a relationship with Radoncic's wife during the war, and Delalic loved to brag about it. But more seriously, Delalic claimed that Radoncic had collaborated with the Serbs, and he had documents to prove it.

Radoncic was not involved in crime. He was a journalist turned legitimate media magnate who had founded Bosnia's most influential newspaper. He later entered politics and became minister of security. Yet Radoncic and Kelmendi had business dealings and were good friends. To make matters worse, 'Baldy' Delalic was also a suspect in the murder of Radoncic's godfather, yet another black mark against his name.

In the weeks before his violent death, Delalic became increasingly nervous. He had a separate ongoing feud with another underworld figure, Mohamed "Ali" Gashi — a drug trafficker who was allied to Kelmendi — and as he drove past Gashi's house with his girlfriend, he murmured, "I should do something to him, because he and they are preparing something for me."[18] But in the event, Delalic decided not to act. He also received several warnings from other sources and took to wearing a bullet proof vest, checking his car for explosives every day and frequently changing apartments.

According to a 2014 indictment against Kelmendi, the aggrieved gangster met repeatedly with a number of his key lieutenants and partners on the fifteenth floor of Sarajevo's famous Twist Tower, owned by Radoncic's company Avaz. The indictment claimed that

---

[18] Gashi was eventually jailed for twenty years over a separate extortion and attempted murder plot.

the assassination of Ramiz Delalic was contracted out to a pair of professional Serbian hitmen, for a fee of around 100,000 euros. The conspirators allegedly placed their share of the fee in a small black suitcase, which Kelmendi took personally to a middleman in Serbia, who would hand over the cash to the killers once the job was done.

One of the alleged gunmen later denied being involved in the murder, but the parents of Strahinja Raseta, who was subsequently killed in a car bombing, confirmed their son had taken part. The two-man hit team arrived in Sarajevo shortly before the murder, where they moved into a flat allegedly rented by one of Kelmendi's cronies. Another henchman was busy tracking Delalic to an apartment in the city centre. Kelmendi himself left the country, heading to a seaside resort in Montenegro.

At 11.28pm on June 27, 2009, Ramiz Delalic arrived at his girlfriend's apartment in Odabasina Street Number One. Strahinja Raseta was crouched underneath the stairwell leading to the flat. His conspirator signalled with a whistle when Delalic arrived. As Delalic placed one foot on the stairwell, Raseta emerged and unloaded all twenty-seven rounds from a 9mm silenced Heckler & Koch machine gun. Delalic stumbled onto the stairs and collapsed, but incredibly he was still not dead. He gurgled something incomprehensible as blood oozed onto the pavement. Then Raseta pulled out a Magnum .357 and fired several more rounds into his head and body.

According to the indictment, it was not the first assassination arranged by Naser Kelmendi. One of several former associates who gave evidence against him claimed Kelmendi had tried to persuade him to organise the murder of a man who "should disappear" because "he screwed some people, he took 100 kilos of heroin and he did not respect the agreement". The witness said he refused to get involved, but when a man was later found dead in Sarajevo, after allegedly stealing 100 kilos of heroin from one of Kelmendi's associates, he put two and two together. Kelmendi had been his guarantor, giving his *besa* that Kalic would pay up or die. Kelmendi did not face any charges over the allegation.

Like most Albanian mafia bosses, many details of Naser Kelmendi's past will forever remain a mystery. Born in Pec, Kosovo, in 1957, the Serbian *White Paper* published in 2003 claimed that Kelmendi was part of a system of criminal clans working under the leadership of the Haradinaj family, and that Kelmendi had made a vast fortune from cigarette smuggling, generating huge sums for the KLA.

In 2012, President Obama signed a declaration under the Kingpin Act, barring Kelmendi from the United States and declaring that his assets could be frozen, as well as those of anyone doing business with him. In 2015, a US Treasury declaration confirming sanctions against Kelmendi and his three sons Besnik, Elvis and Liridon, and daughter Donata, alleged that Kelmendi "has been engaged in criminal activity for more than thirty-five years as the leader of a criminal family in the Balkans, with a network of associates across Europe".

It went on to say that Kelmendi's "criminal organization operates a drug distribution network that stretches through Afghanistan to Turkey and into Europe – primarily for the sale of heroin, but also for the trafficking of cocaine and ecstasy. Naser Kelmendi and his organization also are suspected of laundering money through front companies." John E Smith, Acting Director of the Office of Foreign Assets Control at the Treasury Department, added "Naser Kelmendi leads a powerful criminal organization that has made millions through the sale of narcotics for more than a decade."

Yet efforts to hold Kelmendi to account through the courts have only been partially successful. In 2013, Kelmendi was arrested by Kosovo police in Pristina under an international arrest warrant for charges of murder and drug trafficking. He was released the next day because there was no extradition treaty between Kosovo and Bosnia and Herzegovina, but the Special Prosecution Office of the Republic of Kosovo demanded his detention, and Kelmendi was promptly re-arrested by EULEX, the EU's Rule of Law Mission in Kosovo. Then, in July 2014, came the breathtaking indictment.

At least four turncoats gave evidence against their former boss— his high-ranking lieutenant Haris Mehanovic and three other men known only as K1, K2, and K3. Together, they were able to provide a detailed insight into Kelmendi's life story and alleged operations.

K1 had known Kelmendi since 1996 and claimed that after the war he began trafficking heroin through Kosovo, Bosnia and into Austria, Switzerland and the rest of Europe. He explained how Kelmendi had left Kosovo in 1998 and moved to Sarajevo.

Mehanovic told how he met K2 in the same city in 1999, when the latter was supplying guns to the KLA. It was through K2 that Mehanovic was introduced to Kelmendi. In his evidence, K2 said his introduction to Kelmendi included the offer of a job driving heroin to Britain, which he initially declined.

The fourth witness, K3, a "high level" drug dealer in Belgrade, said Kelmendi's criminal empire really took off after the powerful Belgrade crime syndicate led by the Zemun clan was destroyed in a government crackdown in 2003. Then, when Montenegro achieved independence from Serbia in 2006, Kelmendi found himself with a "sudden monopoly" on the drugs and cigarette market there as well. Kelmendi, of course, disputed every charge on the indictment.

What is certain is that Kelmendi was extraordinarily cautious and prone to bouts of anger. Stocky, powerfully built and with a penchant for expensive dark suits, black sunglasses, and slicked back hair, Kelmendi has an imposing presence. The members of his organisation were not allowed to call him on the phone and as K1 put it, if someone should do so, then "off with his head". When meeting in person, subordinates were ordered to remove the batteries from their phones. When Kelmendi was arrested, police found ten different phones on his person. The only people he really had faith in were his children, who were all either entrusted with direct involvement in the drugs trade or placed in charge of front companies.[19]

According to prosecutors, Kelmendi taught the rest of the gang a system of codes, such as the word "piece" to denote either one kilo of drugs or 1,000 euros. K3 told how he bought various drugs mainly from Liridon Kelmendi between 2009 and 2012, usually between one and four kilos of heroin or ecstasy a month. He also described buying speed, cocaine and cannabis.

K1 was able to shed considerable light on the nuts and bolts of the operation. He was Kelmendi's "transport manager" and was paid

---

[19] Liridon was named in the indictment as a drug trafficker, while in 2013 Elvis Kelmendi was sentenced to four years in prison for the attempted murder of Elvis Hodzic in 2010. Liridon has been convicted of carrying a gun and ammunition without permission, while Kelmendi's brother Becir has also been convicted of weapons charges.

150,000 German marks a year for his work. Kelmendi, he claimed, arranged for specially designed tables and doors to be manufactured in Turkey. The plywood items were hollow inside and could hold 150 kilos of Afghan heroin each. Drugs were also transported in trucks filled with fruit and vegetables, sometimes ten vehicles at a time, and also shipped out hidden in loads of textiles.

Kelmendi specialized in "white heroin," a purer form of the drug popular on the streets of Britain.

As K1 told the court, "The worst quality heroin was going to Switzerland and some different countries while the purest was going to England."

He described how Kelmendi's cousin Rexhep "Xheko" Kelmendi was in charge of the day-to-day operations. Xheko was later killed in a gun battle in Pec in 2013.

According to the indictment, Kelmendi was also buying huge shipments of ecstasy from Holland, sometimes 200,000 pills in a single order. They were stored in one litre plastic bottles that could hold up to 4,000 pills each and then placed in hidden compartments inside fuel tanks, or inside a specially adapted refrigerator truck. Often, the ecstasy would be transported to Turkey and swapped for heroin. Despite his cautious nature, Kelmendi did receive regular text messages from his couriers informing him of their positions throughout Europe, indicating that he took personal charge of the smuggling operations.

K2 described how he was eventually railroaded into working for Kelmendi. He said that in 2003 he was transporting fifty kilos of cocaine from Turkey to Bosnia on behalf of an associate. The drugs were hidden in a shipment of clothing. When he finally arrived in Sarajevo, he was taken by another man to a restaurant, where it transpired the real customer was Naser Kelmendi, who told him, "You will either work for me or you will be against me. I told you, if you want to be a gentleman, if you want to be a boss, you have to be by my side and not to do things on your own." The shipment had not contained cocaine, but heroin, and the charade had been carefully planned by Kelmendi to force K2 to work for him.

When K2 eventually agreed to supervise a shipment of 100,000 ecstasy pills from Holland to Turkey, Kelmendi pressured him to sign a contract mortgaging his home as a guarantee on the deal.

When the deal went sour, K2 ended up paying Kelmendi 11,000 euros a month. Now he was on the hook. In lieu of payment one month, Kelmendi told K2 to drive to Austria to pick up a truck containing tarpaulin and bring it back to Bosnia. When he arrived, Kelmendi's henchman began stripping the car and unloaded a large amount of heroin. Kelmendi told him, "Did you think that you will transport only tarpaulin for 11,000 euros?"

The Kelmendi syndicate made millions, if not billions, and owned a vast portfolio of real estate. At one point, Kelmendi gave his son Elvis five million euros to start his own business. Just for the year 2003 alone, investigators found property tax receipts in Kosovo worth 3.2 million euros. The family also bought huge plots of land in Montenegro, the Casa Grande hotel, which it used for a base, a restaurant in Sarajevo, an ice cream factory, as well as dozens of other houses and properties. Kelmendi also sold some properties to Avaz, the publishing company owned by Fahrudin Radoncic. Companies owned by his children had combined turnovers of nearly 4.5 million euros.

The indictment concluded:

"The core members of the Naser Kelmendi OCG had tremendous financial resources to hire highly experienced assassin Strahinja Raseta and a team of other criminals to execute a well-coordinated and extensive operation to murder Ramiz Delalic. This included providing living accommodations, food, special weapons, travel documents, transportation and the payment of at least 100,000 euros. Naser Kelmendi's extensive drug trafficking network and all the six specific drug transactions have been established through the corroborated statements of actual members of his Organized Criminal Operation."

At his trial in 2015, Kelmendi was acquitted of aggravated murder and eight other charges pertaining to organised crime and drug trafficking. He was found guilty of one charge of drug trafficking and jailed for six years. It means that he must be considered innocent of all allegations of murder and most of the specific drug trafficking allegations.

The EULEX prosecutor, Andrew Hughes, later spoke of his regret at the verdict in the Kelmendi case.

"I was disappointed that he was not convicted of the organised crime and aggravated murder charges against Ramiz Delalic," he said, "who was considered a great war commander and hero in Bosnia during the Bosnian war."

Hughes suggested there had been witness intimidation before and during the trial, adding, "One of them was even shot on two different occasions and almost died, but he still had the courage to come, and he was a close friend of the victim, and explained all the evidence related to this murder and what led up to the murder."

Fahrudhin Radoncic himself stood trial in May 2018 on charges of organising a criminal group and corruption, for allegedly intimidating witnesses in the Kelmendi case. He was cleared of all wrongdoing.

"We have stated from the beginning that we were innocent," he told reporters in Sarajevo. "I am so glad that a fair court process has shown there was not a single [piece of] evidence or legal reason for us to be tried, except for the wish to politically eliminate us."

Radoncic remains a member of the Bosnian parliament and the leader of the Union For the Better Future of Bosnia and Herzegovina party.

In August 2018, the Kosovo Appeals Court ordered a retrial for the single guilty verdict in the case of Naser Kelmendi. He was released ahead of new proceedings, which have still not been heard.

BALKANS BARONS

While the trials of Aldo Bare and Naser Kelmendi unmasked two of the Albanian mafia's most successful crime lords, they were far from the only Balkan-based criminals to exploit the opportunities presented by the new post-Communist world. Some were Albanian, but many were Serbs, Bosnians, Croatians, Slovakians, and Czechs, as well as Bulgarians, Romanians, and Russians.

For example, Baki Sadiki was an ethnic Albanian who had based himself in Slovakia since the early 1990s and obtained citizenship.[20] Sadiki was tried in absentia in 2011 and found guilty of running a heroin trafficking operation, with drugs from Turkey shipped through the Balkan Route hidden in, amongst other things, a consignment of flip flops. The drugs then went on to Italy, Poland and Switzerland.

The authorities identified at least six shipments of smack between 2007 and 2008, each of up to twenty kilos. At wholesale prices, it would have netted Sadiki around $3.5 million. Sadiki went on the run but was later extradited from his native Kosovo after being peacefully arrested in a Pristina coffee shop. He is serving a twenty-two year sentence.

Sadiki was not the only narco to base himself in Slovakia. One figure widely alleged to have headed a major trafficking syndicate was Dragoslav Kosmajac, a Serbian. Serbia's Prime Minister Aleksandar Vucic once described Kosmajac as the Balkan's version of Pablo Escobar, but he turned out to be more like Al Capone. Although he was arrested in 2014 and extradited to his home country after allegedly running a major drugs route which included shipping cocaine from South America, Kosmajac was cleared only to be later convicted of tax evasion.

The Balkan Route didn't just benefit criminals involved in the Class A drug trade. Ethnic Albanian Anton Stanaj, from Montenegro, made millions from smuggling cigarettes all over the region. A close associate of Naser Kelmendi, Stanaj set up dozens of front companies and invested in car dealerships and retail chains. He was charged with running a criminal organisation in 2008 and convicted in Belgrade, in absentia, in 2011. Stanaj was sentenced to six-and-a-half years in jail but never served a day because he was shot dead in Sudan in March 2013 by another Albanian gangster.

Then there is Bajrush Sejdiu, an ethnic Albanian from Macedonia, who became well known in Kosovo after marrying Hashim Thaci's

[20] The country became a haven for mafia figures from all over the region, including Italy, thanks to its largely peaceful divorce from the Czech Republic in 1993 and its border with Austria.

sister and for owning the Macedonian football club Milano. He was jailed for twelve years in 2011 for money laundering and other offences, but is also suspected of drug trafficking and is thought to be worth around £30 million.

Luka Bojovic was a Serbian gangster who took control of the country's leading narco trafficking organisation, the Zemun Clan, when its chiefs were wiped out in a wave of assassinations in 2003. Sometimes referred to as the "boss of bosses" as far as the Serbian underworld is concerned, he fled the country in 2010 and is suspected of at least twenty murders across Europe, including in Spain and Holland. He was arrested in Spain in 2012 and jailed for eighteen years for a range of offences, including possession of weapons and membership of the notorious Arkan's Tigers militia. An extradition request from Serbia was dropped. Since he's been inside, a number of his close friends and allies have been killed on the streets of Belgrade.

Another Serbian mob boss was Andrija Draskovic, also a former member of Arkan's Tigers. He was said to work closely with the Italian mafia and was involved in drugs and cigarette smuggling. Draskovic recently served time for the murder of a rival Surcin clan member, Zvonko Pleca back in 2000, but he was released early into a nine-and-half year sentence.

Meanwhile, Ferid "Fredi" Okic, a former Bosnian police officer, headed up one of the country's leading drug trafficking rings, shipping heroin from Turkey along the Balkan Route and ecstasy from Holland back East. He was suspected of several murders and later jailed for twenty-six years for his part in the crime syndicate. Another Bosnian network, headed by Haris Zornic and his brother Hamdo Dacic, allegedly worked with Turkish criminals to ship tons of heroin into Europe. However, in 2014 Bosnian prosecutors dropped the drugs charges and convicted him of money laundering, with a sentence of five years in prison.

One of the most successful Balkan-based narcos, until his arrest, was Darko Saric (see my book *Balkan Warriors: The Rise and Fall of Europe's Deadliest Drugs Cartel*). The Serbian, who also had Slovakian citizenship, was arrested after authorities in Uruguay seized more than two tons of cocaine on a yacht off the coast of Montevideo. The trail led back to Saric, who then spent several years hiding out in South Africa, protected by a well-established Serbian underworld. More on his case later.

A more recent case, which unfolded in Australia, illustrates the exceedingly violent and sophisticated killing methods employed by the Serbian mob in the country where Saric took refuge, as well as its global reach. It started on a normal weekday morning at Port Botany customs terminal in June 2019, where Border Force officers in the Sydney suburb made an extraordinary find that would have dramatic repercussions throughout the international underworld.

A tip-off had come in about a consignment of plant machinery from Cape Town which was believed to hold a substantial quantity of cocaine. The container in question carried a twenty-ton Caterpillar excavator — not a vehicle with an abundance of obvious hiding places. Nevertheless, the digger was x-rayed and the results stunned the watching officials. Inside the hollow steel hydraulic arm were dozens of small packages, far too many to count on the screen. But when the digger was opened up and the packages retrieved, they totalled 384 kilos of cocaine, with an estimated value of some £76m. "To put this in perspective," explained Border Force acting deputy commissioner of operations Sharon Huey, "in the 2017-18 financial year approximately 795 kilograms of cocaine were detected at the border. This 384 kilogram delivery represents almost half that."

The drugs were substituted for dummy packages and the excavator was repaired, resprayed and sent to its intended recipients. Armed cops later carried out raids in the Bungendore district, arresting two Australian men suspected of having links to the Rebels motorcycle gang. But investigators over in South Africa had good reason to believe the deal had actually been brokered by the Serbian mafia, with the aid of a British-Irish syndicate.

Two days after the arrests in Australia, on July 16, the former South African footballer Mark Batchelor was gunned down outside his home in the Johannesburg suburb of Olivedale.[21] Batchelor had been pulling onto his drive when two men approached on a motorbike and unleashed a volley of shots. Seven bullets smashed

---

[21] Batchelor was also a friend of Oscar Pistorius's victim Reeva Steenkamp and had testified against the athlete at his trial.

through the driver's side window, leaving the ex-sportsman dead at the wheel. Nothing was stolen and a gardener standing nearby was left unharmed. It had all the hallmarks of a gangland hit, not least because the dead man had notorious links with criminal Serbs.

Crime-watchers immediately pointed out that the previous October, a mobster named George Mihaljevic — known as Hollywood George for his movie star good looks and fleet of sports cars — had been killed in almost identical circumstances. Mihaljevic, a Serb born in Montenegro, was still mourning the death of his father Miso in 2013, after he had allegedly been kidnapped and tortured by men working for Czech crime boss Radovan Krejcir. By the time George was gunned down by a team of sicarios in the Dovedale suburb, Krejcir was serving a thirty-five-year sentence for fraud, attempted murder and conspiracy to murder, among other crimes (if he is ever successfully extradited to his home country, he will serve an eleven-year sentence for tax fraud).[22]

It's not known exactly who was behind the hit. Mihaljevic had publicly denied that Krejcir was involved in his father's death, although the Serbian had reportedly owed the Czech money. It was, in any case, the latest in a series of tit-for-tat shootings involving Eastern European gangsters across South Africa and back on their home territory, including the murder of corrupt South African State Security Agent George Darmanovich in Belgrade in 2018.

Another similar, high-profile killing had taken place in April 2019, with an even more prescient link to the Batchelor killing. Serbian Ivan Djordjevic, a business partner of the former footballer, was riddled with bullets after driving into a residential complex in Bryanston. Djordjevic was deeply enmeshed in the bitter political and criminal underworld of Serbia. He was friends with Dobrosov Gavric, also known as the Arkan Slayer, who was wanted for

---

[22] Kerjcir's story could fill a book by itself, but probably the most notable aspect of his career was the extraordinary assassination attempt he survived in 2013. Krejcir was behind the wheel of his Mercedes when the rear license plate of a parked car suddenly flipped down to reveal a dozen gun barrels, which opened fire by remote control. At least ten rounds struck his car but Krejcir emerged unscathed. The booby-trapped red Volkswagen burst into flames after the hit attempt, destroying all evidence. "All my life is like James Bond stuff," Krejcir joked with journalists. "That's how I live my life."

assassinating the warlord and Milosovic crony Zeljko 'Arkan' Raznatovic in 2000.[23]

The Arkan Slayer was associated with Krejcir, suggesting that he, Djordjevic and Batchelor were all in the same camp. Batchelor and Djordjevic had even gone into business together, starting up a debt collection company. At the time of their deaths, police were probing claims that both men had been involved in the theft of a ton of cocaine shipped into South Africa by a Serbian gang. But in the wake of Batchelor's assassination, it was also suggested that he could have been tied to the seized shipment in Australia and his death was in some way a punishment for the deal going awry.

South Africa's elite organised crime investigators, the Hawks, were also working on another theory about the excavator find. On August 30, 2019, Liverpool-born businessman John Burns was driving one of his luxury Range Rovers through Cape Town when the car was rocked by a small but powerful blast. Burns, then aged forty-nine, suffered horrific injuries to his lower back and bottom, although he escaped the explosion with his life. Hawks sources immediately linked the attack with the seized cocaine shipment in Australia. The drugs, they believed, had been shipped from Bolivia via Cape Town on behalf of a Serbian crime gang by a powerful group of British-Irish drug traffickers.

Police sources believe the Serbs fell out with the syndicate arranging the shipment and refused to pay a portion of the up-front fee. As a result, the middlemen tipped off the Australian authorities to ensure the drugs never reached their ultimate destination. The British-Irish cartel was also suspected of being involved in the killing of Serbian gangster Jugoslav Smiljkic, who had been gunned down in Johannesburg a few months previously. Smiljkic had been yet another associate of the Arkan Slayer. The Hawks were certain that the Serbs were behind the highly sophisticated bomb, which had been built inside a mobile phone and tucked into the crevice of the

---

[23] Gavric had been wounded while driving the SA crime boss Cyril Beeka during his assassination in 2011. Gavric, who is now in prison awaiting extradition, is dangerous to know — another associate, Milan Djuricic, was also killed in a separate shooting in 2018.

driver's seat. Sources believed the device may have been hidden, ironically, when Burns' £50,000 car was sent away to be fitted with bullet proof glass.

Precisely why Burns, who has no known criminal record in Britain or elsewhere, was targeted is not known and the attack could well be a case of mistaken identity. In any case, he spent nearly six months in hospital under the protection of a heavily armed security team, before leaving for Dubai. There seems little chance of the South African authorities solving either his case or the murder of Mark Batchelor.

Back in Eastern Europe, an equally bloody civil war is still raging between two Montenegrin clans, the Skaljari and the Kavac, both named after villages in the Kotor region (the full story of this feud is covered in my book *Balkan Warriors*). The twin organisations had spent years working together as the Kotor Clan under the leadership of Dragan Dudic, cooperating with the 'Ndrangheta to ship cocaine to ports around Europe, as well as to the Montenegrin port of Bar. But when Dudic was shot dead outside a café a Kotor in May 2010, the organisation began to split in two.[24]

In 2014, the senior Kotor clan member Goran Radoman 'lost' more than 200 kilos of cocaine in Valencia. The next year, he was executed on the street in Belgrade with twenty five rounds fired from a Kalashnikov. The attack came on the same day that his associate, Milan Vujotic, survived a car bombing. In October 2015, Skaljari member Goran Durickovic was shot dead by a sniper in Budva. The following year, fellow clan member Dalibor Djuric was killed by an audacious sniper while exercising in the yard of the high security state prison in Podgorica. A burnt out car was found nearby.

The violence is not restricted to Montenegro. Of the fifty two murders committed in Belgrade between 2012 and 2019, more than forty are thought to be in connection with the war between the two groups, including the murder of Aleksander Stankovic, the leader of

---

[24] Darko Saric had been a leadership contender, but he was on the run at the time of the killing, while his brother, Dusko, was also under arrest. The power vacuum eventually led to all-out war in 2014.

the Partizan Belgrade football hooligan group the Janissaries, which is allied to the Kavac.

Skaljari leader Jovica Vukotic was arrested in Turkey in 2018 and remains in prison in Montenegro, awaiting trial for the attempted murder of two Kavac members and the wife of one of the Kavac's leaders, Radoje Zvicer. He reportedly survived an assassination attempt himself while in custody, when four men posing as police officers stopped his girlfriend on the way to a visit in the hope of poisoning food she regularly bought to him in prison. He was only saved because, as they rifled through her belongings in the hope of adding cyanide to a drink or snack, they realised she had not yet collected his meal and was only carrying empty containers. Another Skaljari leader, Igor Dedovic, was shot dead in January 2020 while enjoying a meal with his wife and children in a restaurant in Athens. A leaked Serbian intelligence report showed how he had been splitting his time between Bosnia and Herzegovina, Croatia, and Brazil in the years before his death.

The bloodshed continued in May 2020, despite the coronovirus lockdown, when Kavac leader Radoje Zvicer survived a bungled assassination attempt in Kiev. Shocking CCTV footage released to the media showed two men accidently setting themselves on fire as they tried to burn a stolen Smart Car used in the attack, which left Zvicer with bullet wounds to the stomach. One of three men arrested attempting to flee the country was already wanted internationally for a contract killing, according to the Ukrainian news agency Interfax. "Having set a date for the murder, the defendants waited for the victim near his house," an official explained. "After firing five shots at the victim, the two perpetrators got into the car and left the crime scene. Hundreds of metres later they went and set the car on fire to destroy evidence."

Meanwhile, the most senior Kavac leader, Slobodan Kascelan, is also still alive and living on probation in Kotor. He survived a 2016 assassination attempt in Novi Sad, Serbia's second-largest city, and spent years on the run after being indicted on drug trafficking charges in Montenegro. He was arrested in Prague in December 2018 after hiding out in ten European countries under false identities, but was handed a remarkably soft sentence.

Despite the wave of killings taking place across Europe, including in Vienna and Marbella, very few people have been prosecuted. One theory has emerged that as well as the Montenegrin police being riddled with corruption, the gangsters have also installed their own network of CCTV cameras across the country which, in a twisted inversion of justice, they use to monitor the police. The Skaljari clan is also suspected of having close ties to the powerful, unnamed Serbian criminal organisation (formerly the Zemun clan) previously led by Luka Bojovic and which is now, according to a leaked Serbian intelligence report, led by a man named Filip Korac. Confusingly, the Zemun clan itself is also allied to the Skaljari and thought to be led by a man named Alan Kozar, credited by the Ukrainian authorities with ordering the attempted hit on Zvicer. At the same time, the Kavac clan is thought to have strong political connections.

Dozens of other major crime bosses have also emerged across the Balkans — these are only a few of the most notorious. Some have never been put before a court at all, while others were cut down in a hail of bullets before they could become dubious media darlings in their home countries, as some of the above-named gangsters are today.

But as powerful, fearsome, violent and successful as many of them were and are, most have lacked the Albanian mafia's truly global capabilities. And while the likes of Aldo Bare and Naser Kelmendi were enduring law enforcement pressure on their heroin empires in the early part of the century, their countrymen on the other side of the Atlantic were looking to expand.

BLOODY STATES

New York's wiseguys were unaccustomed to being on the receiving end of threats and intimidation. But their legendary status meant little to men like Alex Rudaj. Now, his upstart mob of Albanian, Greek and Italian-American gangsters had pushed their luck too far, in the view of Gambino family bosses, and they would have to pay the price.

Rudaj might have dressed like a Cosa Nostra mafioso — black sunglasses, leather jacket, black hair greying at the temples and slicked back over his head — but he could never become a made man, and according to the rules he couldn't lay a hand on one either. Trouble was, Alex Rudaj didn't give a damn about the rules.

The meeting was set for an out-of-the-way gas station in New Jersey. The Italians' plan: to ambush and execute Rudaj and his henchmen. But it quickly went wrong. Gambino capo Arnold Squitieri and his thirty mafioso vastly outnumbered Rudaj's six. When the Gambinos pulled out their guns and aimed them at their rivals' heads, there was no mathematical chance of survival for the Albanian-led crew. Except that when Rudaj aimed his shotgun in return, he didn't point it at Squitieri, or any of his goons, but at the gas pump.

"If this is what you want, then I'm ready to die," Rudaj snarled. "What about you?"

Squitieri didn't need long to come up with an answer. He ordered the Gambino soldiers to lower their weapons and back away, very slowly, and very carefully. Rudaj gang member Prenka "Big Frank" Ivezaj was later recorded on a wiretap recounting the confrontation.

"Everybody dies," he enthused. "Guaranteed. Nobody walks out of there alive. Either them or us." It was a humiliation for New York's Cosa Nostra, but it wasn't the first.

Alex Rudaj, known as Allie Boy or Uncle Rudaj, was an ethnic Albanian, originally from Montenegro. Arriving in New York sometime in the late 1980s, he soon drifted towards a life of crime and became an associate of the Gambino crime family, alongside his friend Nardino "Lenny" Colotti. Then, in the early 1990s, Rudaj and Colotti split from the Gambinos and set up their own illegal gambling operations in Westchester County and the Bronx. They even decided to give themselves a name loaded with chutzpah: The Corporation.

Both men were suspected of gunning down rival gangster Guy Peduto, an associate of the Bonnano family. Peduto survived and later gave evidence for the state, claiming that Alex Rudaj had been the triggerman in his 1993 shooting. According to Peduto, the row began over a stolen car scam, but ended in a crazy car chase through the Bronx, with Rudaj firing a 9mm handgun at Peduto's vehicle while hanging out the window of a car driven by Colotti. Peduto took five slugs to the head and body. Peduto eventually crashed into two parked cars and was left for dead, but he miraculously survived. Both Rudaj and Colotti were later cleared of attempted murder, meaning both men escaped a mandatory life sentence.

By 2001, The Corporation had encroached onto the traditional Italian mafia territory of Queens, which was ostensibly controlled by the Luchesse family. The Rudaj crew managed to turf out its rival mobsters, using a blunt and effective strategy of violence. As chief enforcer Nikola "Nicky Nails" Dedaj put it, "They make mistakes somewhere, we move in and take it."

On one occasion, a gambler was beaten to within an inch of his life, while a bar owner had part of his ear bitten off by Dedaj. And to make a further point, a fourteen-strong gang led by Rudaj stormed a Gambino gambling joint in Astoria called Soccer Fever with guns drawn, terrifying everyone present. "Gentleman, the game is over," one of the men declared. Tables were overturned, money snatched and at least one patron was pistol-whipped. That incident led to the confrontation at the petrol station.

By the end of the conflict with the Gambinos, The Corporation owned six gambling clubs in Queens, Astoria and the Bronx, and was involved in a whole host of other rackets, including loan-sharking and extortion. Bar owners were forced to install their gambling machines. If they didn't, violence was used to coerce them. Prosecutors later said a network of fifty machines raked in about $4 million a year.

When jailed Gambino boss John Gotti died of cancer in 2002, Alex Rudaj and his top lieutenants attended his funeral out of respect. Respect, not deference. Because they also now had the status to march into Rao's, the exclusive East Harlem restaurant frequented by mob figures, and claim Gotti's old table.

In 2004, The Corporation became the first Albanian-led mob to be brought down by the Racketeer Influenced and Corrupt Organisations (RICO) Act, legislation introduced to criminalise membership of organised crime gangs.

In total, twenty-two members faced charges including attempted murder, conspiracy to commit murder, extortion, loan-sharking, and illegal gambling. In court, assistant US attorney Timothy Treanor described The Corporation as "incredibly violent and incredibly feared on the street. They beat up made men and mafia associates. One man was shot five times in the back of the neck, but survived".

Prosecutor Jennifer Rodgers added, "This organization existed for one reason — greed and to make money. They didn't want to make money the old-fashioned way. They wanted to make it through violence, fear and intimidation."

Alex Rudaj and Nardino Colotti were both sentenced to twenty-seven years in prison, ordered to forfeit $5.75 million and hand over four properties. Other gang members also received hefty sentences. "Nicky Nails" got twenty-six years, and Prenka "Frankie" Ivezaj got twenty-two years.

While the Rudaj organisation might have been the first Albanian mafia group to openly challenge La Cosa Nostra on its own turf, becoming in effect New York's Sixth Family, Alex Rudaj was far from the first Albanian serious organised crime figure to make it big in the States, nor would he be the last. And while Rudaj was focused on becoming the biggest fish in New York, other mafia-style groups emerged with much grander international ambitions.

Heroin Kings

In 1985, the Queens-based Xhevdet (or sometimes Ismail) Lika, also known as "Joey", was given life without parole for being the boss of what prosecutors called a "group of Albanian-Yugoslavian drug dealers". Then aged thirty-four, tall, slim, handsome and with facial hair that wouldn't have looked out of place on one of the old-school "Moustache Petes" of La Cosa Nostra, Joey Lika was a truly international operator. He made personal journeys to Turkey and Yugoslavia to arrange heroin shipments, before distributing the drugs on the Lower East Side through a network of dealers, including Chinese clothing shops.

The evidence against him dated back to 1979. His erstwhile partner, Xhevdet Mustafa, also had a long criminal pedigree. Like many Albanians who made their way to the United States after Enver Hoxha's rise to power, both were living in exile from the Communist regime and were supporters of King Zog.

Mustafa even planned to assassinate Hoxha in 1982 but was himself killed in the aftermath of the failed plot while hiding out in Lushnje. He either shot himself or was crushed by a falling wall as an armored vehicle rammed into the property, depending on which version of events you prefer. Joey Lika contented himself with the comparatively safe world of the drugs business.

Lika's associate, another Albanian man called Skender Fici, was a legitimate travel agent, a business which he used to arrange flights to Turkey and Europe for Lika, and also to send mules abroad to bring back heroin. One of these mules was Albanian restaurant owner Duja Saljanin. He had agreed to import several kilos of heroin in 1981, but when it came time to hand the drugs over to Lika, he was one kilo short. It was a mistake he couldn't take back.

Joey Lika confronted Saljanin at his restaurant, with fellow gang members Mehmet Bici and Vuksan Vulaj, who allegedly fired the first shot. Bici later described what happened in court.

"Joey Lika had a gun, and he shot him too," he said. "I was there, and I shot him too. And then we just left, crossed the street."

Saljanin's body had been riddled with thirteen bullets. He died, but lived long enough to tell police what had happened. Vulaj was later gunned down himself, while Bici was also jailed for the attempted manslaughter of his wife in a separate incident.

After Lika and Fici were finally brought to justice, Lika reportedly offered $400,000 to anyone who would kill assistant prosecutor Alan Cohen, DEA agent Jack Delmore, US district court judge Vincent Broderick and his assistant William Tendy. Cohen, who was then working under US attorney for New York Rudy Giuliani, was given around-the-clock protection, and was even guarded when he went to the bathroom at court. While Lika was jailed for life, Fici was given eighty years. Bici got eight years for heroin trafficking and racketeering.

"After you have been convicted there is no rational reason to kill a prosecutor, except revenge," Giuliani later said.

Despite the sophistication of Lika's operation and his willingness to use extreme violence, he was a relatively small fish in comparison to his contemporary and fellow heroin kingpin Daut Kadriovski. Known as "The Grey Wolf", Kadriovski remains one of the world's most elusive and mysterious Albanian mafia bosses.

Born in Macedonia in 1949, Kadriovski moved to Istanbul, from where he oversaw a huge smuggling operation that resulted in thousands of kilos of smack being shipped to New York and Philadelphia. He was arrested in Germany in 1985 in possession of four kilos. He was jailed and the trappings of his luxury lifestyle, including yachts and villas, were confiscated.

But in 1993, Kadriovski managed to bribe the guards and escape, fleeing first to Turkey and then to the United States, where he already had an extensive criminal network. It was said that Kadriovski had plastic surgery before leaving the continent, and that his surgeon was later assassinated in order to cover his tracks. When the war in Kosovo began, Kadriovski reportedly used profits from his drugs empire to help fund the KLA.

His network stretched as far as Australia, where he was shipping heroin from Albania and Croatia to Sydney and Brisbane. At one point, he was sighted at an embassy in Athens, trying to obtain a Greek passport. Then he popped up again in Germany. Throughout the 1990s, Kadriovski was wanted in at least thirteen countries, and was said to have twenty different names and passports.

The Grey Wolf was arrested in Albania in September 2001, where he had been living for six years. A custody mugshot was released by the police, showing the crime boss looking disheveled and confused. But once again, he slipped the net. Some say he skipped bail, others say he's now dead. Another theory is that he was extradited to Italy but then released because of physical and mental health problems.

Despite his notoriety, remarkably little is known about Kadriovski's career. For a long time, he was described by the FBI as the head of one of Albania's "fifteen families", but as the concept of a finite number of Albanian crime clans, or *fis*, has today been shown to be largely a myth, his status might have been somewhat oversold.

However, it is certainly the case that law enforcement believed him to be an ethnic Albanian godfather and that other gangsters, such as Joey Lika, were in thrall to him. Furthermore, he was thought to be one of the first Albanian crime bosses to hit upon the idea of exchanging heroin for cocaine with South American cartels.

The Next Generation

Ethnic Albanian criminals who moved to America from the 1960s onwards often became entwined with La Cosa Nostra families, who mostly used them as triggermen or hired muscle. It was only in rare cases, such as that of Alex Rudaj or Joey Lika, where Albanians managed to establish themselves as crime bosses in their own right.

But with the political turmoil in the Balkans of the 1990s came a fresh wave of immigration, and with it a different breed of criminal. There was already a large Kosovar-Albanian community in America, while most Albanians from the Republic had for decades been prevented from leaving by the Communist regime. But with the fall of Enver Hoxha, then the pyramid crisis, and finally the break-up of Yugoslavia, ethnic Albanians found themselves more mobile. Many already had cousins or extended family in America. In some cases, those relatives were already involved in organised crime — providing an obvious opportunity for the new arrivals.

One such example was Kujtim "Timmy" Lika, a cousin of Joey Lika, the New York heroin kingpin. Lika formed a partnership with Myfit "Mike" Dika, a heavily tattooed thug with an Albanian eagle on one bicep, a dragon on the other and the words "Death Before The Sun" on his arm. The pair were based in New Jersey and New York, while their network extended to Chicago, Detroit, Texas, Macedonia and Albania.

Both men were big gamblers with long criminal histories, and Dika had already served ten years in Albania for heroin trafficking. And they both had one last bet to make — that the profits from a proposed multimillion-dollar heroin sale would generate enough cash for them to retire.

While they spent time in the States working in restaurants, behind the scenes they were putting together the deal of their lives. The only problem was that their customers were actually undercover FBI agents. Lika was described by the FBI as "very cautious, very sly" while Dika was also said to be "surveillance conscious". But neither man was careful enough.

Alongside a third man based in Albania, Gazmir Gjoka, the pair had built up a twenty-four-man mafia-style group that shipped heroin from Turkey, along the Balkan Route and then into Western Europe and the United States. In 2009, the FBI launched an operation to bring the network down, dubbed Operation Black Eagle.

FBI Special Agent Jim Farley later described their plans.

"They were involved in an international conspiracy to smuggle in over 100 kilograms of heroin from Albania and also were involved in actually selling us a kilo-and-a-half of heroin, which they cut on tape for us, showing how they could cut heroin and dilute it down, so you could make more money on the street," he said.

While Gjoka was arrested and extradited, the two ringleaders went on the run. Dika was eventually arrested in Toronto in 2010, while Lika was also held in the city in 2012. They both pleaded guilty to the conspiracy in 2013. Lika was jailed for five years and nine months, Dika was locked up for seven years and six months.

Another duo who left Albania to continue a criminal career in the United States were brothers Redinel and Plaurent Dervishaj, from Durres. Their gang had taken part in the carnage of the 1997 pyramid crisis with some considerable enthusiasm.

Plaurent was wanted for murdering four rival gangsters, including one who he obliterated with an anti-tank missile. He was also suspected of several other murders and had been charged with forming a criminal group, murder and illegally keeping weapons. On the day the warrant was issued, both men boarded a flight in Vienna destined for New York. Another warrant was issued for him in New Jersey a month later, but Plaurent remained a fugitive from justice and kept a low profile. Eventually resurfacing back in Albania.[25] Redinel on the other hand developed something of a high profile.

In 2007, he was convicted of grand larceny after trying to extort $20,000 from another Albanian man in Queens. The intended victim had pulled out a gun and opened fire, hitting Redinel in the arm, but killing his sidekick. Redinel served just a few months for the crime. Then, in 2012, he stabbed groom-to-be Antonio Lacertosa to death outside a Spanish restaurant in Staten Island. He claimed self-defence, and a grand jury declined to indict him.

The crimes that eventually brought Redinel Dervishaj down would shock the city, because they were carried out with the help

---

[25] Plaurent, a brother-in-law of drug trafficker Lulzim Berisha, was jailed for life in absentia in 2012 but avoided spending any time in jail thanks to legal wranglings. He survived an assassination attempt near Tirana in June 2019, when the car he was travelling in was sprayed with automatic gunfire.

of a corrupt ethnic Albanian NYPD officer. Redinel Dervishaj, new right-hand man Denis Nikolla, and cop Besnik Llakatura were not particularly sophisticated criminals. Their modus operandi was to strongarm their victims, usually other Albanians with their own businesses, into handing over protection money. One victim was a Queens restaurant owner, who was forced to make monthly payments.

Shortly after he had opened his restaurant in Astoria, Dervishaj demanded $4,000 per month, claiming he had opened it in "our neighborhood". The victim was a friend of Llakatura, an outwardly respectable cop based on Staten Island, and the victim asked for his advice. Llakatura told the victim not to report the incident to cops, in case Dervishaj made good on his threats of violence. He reminded him that Dervishaj was no ordinary thug and was related to the notorious Plaurent Dervishaj. When the businessman refused to make payments Nikolla and Dervishaj threatened him and chased him at gunpoint, before he managed to flee in his car.

Later that night, Dervishaj phoned him up and snarled, "You got lucky this time." In the end, Llakatura revealed his part in the plot, telling the victim, "Make sure you don't call the cops, because if you call the cops, you're done." In the end, the gangsters were handed around $24,000.

Between April 2012 and November 2013, Dervishaj and Nikolla also targeted an Astoria nightclub boss. After he refused to pay, Dervishaj and Nikolla confronted him at a bar in Queens. Nikolla took a gun from Dervishaj and jabbed him in the ribs. He said that if he didn't pay, Nikolla would go to his house and beat him in front of his wife and children, and then beat his wife and children for good measure. Dervishaj then gave the victim his phone number so he could make the demanded payments.

Finally, during 2013, Dervishaj, Nikolla, and Llakatura also tried to extort a man who ran two Astoria social clubs. Accompanied by Dervishaj, Nikolla demanded payments of $1,000 per week, once again for "protection." The victim refused to pay up and instead stopped going to his own social clubs. Wiretaps revealed that Llakatura helped to track him down and forced him to pay. In one instance, Dervishaj attacked the victim's friend, punching him repeatedly in the face, while a gun was held to the back of his head. The victim later fled abroad and sold his social clubs.

Dervishaj was jailed for fifty-seven years. A few months later Nikolla was sentenced to eighteen years in prison. Llakatura was sentenced to fourteen years and three months in prison. But as fearsome as Dervishaj and his thugs might have been, they were basic criminals compared with other outfits, who managed to combine brutal violence with more sophisticated conspiracies.

Like the Alex Rudaj Organisation, the gang led by Bruno and Samir Krasniqi could claim to rival any organised crime outfit in New York. From the early 2000s, the Krasniqi Group focused on trafficking and selling cannabis, importing large quantities of the drug from Canada.

Another Albanian immigrant, Parid Gjoka, had been running a separate outfit doing much the same thing, so it seemed natural for the two groups to join forces. However, in 2005 the underworld conglomerate suffered an acrimonious split.

During a bar brawl, someone pulled a knife on Gjoka. Rather than fight to the death, Gjoka retreated. The Krasniqi brothers decided their partner was weak and so they decided to stiff him on a shipment of cannabis. After all, they reasoned, if he had chickened out of a simple knife fight, he was hardly likely to strike back against the might of their organisation. And they were right. When Gjoka complained, Samir Krasniqi pulled a gun and threatened to blow his brains out. Gjoka backed down.

The Krasniqis later kidnapped a member of Gjoka's crew, beat him up and shoved a gun in his mouth until he told them where to find other gang members. Erion Shehu, one of Gjoka's henchman, was later killed in a drive by shooting.

Following that murder, Bruno Krasniqi was kidnapped and briefly held hostage by another Albanian cannabis smuggling gang. Then, in January 2006, Bruno and Samir executed a second man, Erenick Grezda, by shooting him in the head at point blank range while driving on the Brooklyn-Queens Expressway. His body was dumped from the moving vehicle and left by the side of the road. They believed he had been behind the kidnap plot.

Prosecutors later reasoned that the Krasniqi brothers' use of extreme violence came partly from their love of gangster movies, especially *Scarface*. One member of their crew even gave himself the nickname Tony Montana. As we shall see later, he was not the only Albanian criminal to do so.

The brothers, and members of their crew, were later found guilty of trafficking more than 100 kilos of cannabis, mostly from Canada, conspiracy to murder, kidnapping and other offences. Another gang member, Almir Rrapo, was later extradited from Albania and found guilty of taking part in Shehu's murder, kidnapping, and drug trafficking. By the time of his arrest, Rrapo had risen to become the senior administrative assistant to Albania's deputy prime minister and foreign minister. The Krasniqi brothers were sentenced to sixty years each. As a result of his cooperation, Rrapo got just six years.

But while all of these gangsters made a big impact on the North American underworld, especially in New York, it was the ability of Albanian organised crime to get its tentacles into South America that really pushed it onto the path to global infamy.

SOUTH OF THE BORDER

There will always be big money in trafficking heroin and cannabis, but there is something different about the allure of the cocaine trade. The drug itself has a more glamorous image, for a start. Perhaps that's why Hollywood films such as *Scarface*, with its glitzy discos and decadent piles of marching powder, are decidedly more popular with real-life villains than heroin flicks such as *Trainspotting* or *The Basketball Diaries*. Cocaine is associated with the rich and famous, movie stars, and big business. Smack is the drug of the layabout; the waster; the degenerate. Maybe if you're a drug trafficker, there's a little bit more kudos in cocaine than there is in heroin. Of course, such stereotypes don't always hold true, and in any case one of the major uses of cocaine is to be turned into crack, hardly a drug of the monied classes. But the huge profit margins offer a much more prosaic reason why serious organised crime gangs gravitate towards it.

Just like any illegal drug, it can be hard to put a price on the true value of cocaine. When the authorities make seizures, they tend to price them up according to how much criminals might make on the street, once it's been heavily diluted. Such methods ignore the fact that there is usually a long supply chain, with many individuals taking a slice of the pie along the way.

For example, to make one kilo of blow you need about 350 kilos of dried coca leaves, costing about $385. Once the leaves have gone through the process of being chopped up, mixed with chemicals to form a paste, then turned into powder by mixing it with acetone and hydrochloric acid before finally being allowed to dry out, a kilo of cocaine fetches $800. By the time it reaches the Colombian border, its value has hit $2,200. The price soars to around $14,500 once it enters the US, or a little higher for Europe. A supplier might take possession for $19,500 and then a street dealer could turn over anywhere between $78,000 and $122,000, depending on how many times it's been mixed with cutting agents.

Of course, the fewer links in the supply chain, then the higher the profits can be for the main players. It's why the Mexican cartels stopped acting as delivery guys for Colombian narcos and started moving their own coke across the US border in the late 1990s. It's why many major South American wholesalers also now have a tight grip on the retail market in their own countries. And it's also why the emerging Balkan mafias started making direct contact with the cartels in Colombia, Peru and Bolivia, where almost all of the world's cocaine is produced. For the developing Albanian mafia in the post-Communist years, it was a no-brainer.

At the turn of the millennium, European-based drug lords like Aldo Bare were supplementing their heroin businesses with an occasional bit of cocaine trafficking, but exactly how they were getting hold of the drug wasn't entirely clear. For the smack, they had a direct line to the poppy fields of Afghanistan, via Turkey. Anyone could get in a truck and drive there. But to source the blow someone had to transport it all the way across the Atlantic. When Aldo Bare wanted to buy cocaine, he would have to acquire it in Holland, or from the 'Ndrangheta in Italy. That meant he would pay somewhere in the region of \$15,000-\$22,000 or even \$40,000 per kilo.

No wonder that as the drug's popularity in Europe grew during the early 2000s, an increasing number of home-grown gangsters from the Balkans, as well from Britain, Italy, France, Spain and Holland, began dealing directly with South American cartels and negotiating their own rock bottom prices. Sometimes, meetings would take place with cartel representatives based in European cities such as London or Madrid, or on the Costa Del Sol. Other meetings took place in Aruba or in Greece.

As a result of this direct dealing, the price of a kilo purchased directly from South America has today dropped to around \$5,000-\$5,500. Factor in the opportunity that some networks have found to apparently retail the drug themselves, and the profits can be immense.

In his impressive history of Britain's decades-long fight against traffickers, *Drug War*, the journalist Peter Walsh chronicles the successes enjoyed by the British-led covert Operations Jezebel and Journey in the late 1990s. The investigative team, which included DEA and British intelligence agents, had managed to get a mole inside the organisation of Colombian narcos Ivan de la Vega and Jorge Garcia. Later, they would find the organisation was really run by Los Mellizos (The Twins) — identical brothers Miguel and Victor Mejia-Munera. They had previously worked closely with the Cali and North Valley Cartels before those organisations were torn apart.[26]

The team managed to make a number of massive seizures throughout 1999, including one destined for an Albanian mafia gang based in Greece. Although the group itself was never brought to justice, it was one of the first cases to show the increasingly global

---

[26] Overall, the organization was estimated to have shipped some sixty-eight tons to Europe and the US, estimated to be worth more than £3 billion on the streets. Later, agents would seize an eye-watering \$35 million in cash from two apartments linked to The Twins. Victor was shot dead by Colombian cops in May 2008, while Miguel was extradited to the US in March 2009. He reportedly decided to cooperate with the DEA.

reach of Balkans-based criminals. Still, it was far easier for criminal organisations already based in North America to make deals south of the border.

One New York-based Albanian outfit that was well aware of the huge profits to be made from the cocaine trade was led by Gjavit "Doc" Thaqi, and co-conspirators Arif "The Bear" Kurti and Gjevelin Berisha. Another important member of the cartel was enforcer Robert Rudaj, a cousin of Alex Rudaj. Prosecutors later described the network as having "hundreds of associated members, workers and customers spanning three continents".

For more than ten years, the Thaqi Network imported and distributed tens of thousands of kilos of cannabis from Canada and Mexico, as well as ecstasy from Holland and Canada and large quantities of prescription pills, such as oxycodone. Crucially, it also became one of the first Albanian-led organised crime groups to import hundreds of kilos of cocaine from South America, distributing to hubs all over the US, including to New York, California, Georgia, Colorado and Florida, as well as in Canada. Hundreds of kilos also made their way to Europe.

A four-year investigation found that the cannabis smuggled from Canada and Mexico was hidden in tractor trailers, usually in quantities of several hundred pounds, with some shipments weighing as much as 1,200 pounds. Drugs were stored in warehouses and stash houses throughout Brooklyn, Queens and the Bronx. The cocaine was exported directly to Albania and other European ports concealed in hidden compartments inside luxury cars. Although the cars were destined for outwardly legitimate dealerships, those businesses were actually controlled by syndicate members.

Right up until the network was smashed in July 2011, Doc Thaqi was negotiating to buy hundreds of kilos of cocaine from Colombia, which would then have been shipped through the United States to Canada and then onto Europe. Federal agents ultimately seized more than 1,200 pounds of cannabis, about $2 million in drugs money, twenty-two handguns, a military issue assault rifle and hundreds of rounds of ammunition.

In total, forty-nine members and associates of the syndicate were convicted. In 2014, Doc Thaqi, then aged forty-three, and Rudaj, then aged forty, were sentenced to ten years, and nine years and one month respectively for drug trafficking. Kurti was already serving time in Albania for heroin trafficking.

Syndicate members were prepared to use extreme violence. For example, Robert Rudaj, who was often used as an enforcer, brutally attacked a fellow inmate at the Metropolitan Detention Center in Brooklyn, New York, while the mob was awaiting trial.

Another man linked to the network was notorious hitman Bajram "Van Damme" Lajqi. In one case, Lajqi lost his temper with a fellow narco and ended up trying to gun him down. In June 2011, Lajqi and a friend, Carlos Alvarez, went to the Tosca Cafe in The Bronx, after tracking down their intended victim's car and puncturing the tyres. They watched the man for two hours, but Lajqi became increasingly irate. Eventually, he marched over to the restaurant and punched him in the face. Lajqi then whipped out a pistol and turned it on a bouncer, but didn't pull the trigger. However, the intervention gave the victim an opportunity to flee. As he ran away, Lajqi opened fire. Bullets tore through both his thighs, but the man was able to make it to a hospital. Investigators found that Lajqi and the victim had been partners in a cannabis-trafficking network. In 2014, Lajqi, then thirty-eight, was picked up and charged with drugs offences. He was eventually jailed for nine-and-a-half years.

As it turned out, the Albanians were not the only Eastern European mobsters sniffing around the coca fields of South America. The Serbian mafia is the main rival in this respect, with a number of traffickers basing themselves in countries where they have ongoing relationships with cartels.[27]

For example, Zoran Jaksic was a leading light in a Serbian and Montenegrin cartel known as "Group America". He went on the run in 2009, fleeing from Peru to Argentina, then onto Madrid, where he was extradited to Greece but later released. He was arrested again in 2016 trying to cross the border from Peru into Ecuador, where the

---

[27] The 'Ndrangheta is arguably the other main rival, although the Italian crime network is more generally though to co-operate with the Albanians than work against them. 'Ndrangheta chiefs are thought to work closely with Brazil's First Capital Command (PCC), using well-established smuggling routes to move cocaine from Bolivia to European ports.

group bought cocaine, turned it into liquid and transported it across the Atlantic in wine bottles. Jaksic is now serving a long sentence in Peru.

Another major player in Group America, which has been known to use private planes to ship drugs across the Atlantic to Europe, was Darko Saric, one of Serbia's leading narcos. He was thought to be making an eye-watering $1 billion a year buying cocaine directly from Colombian cartels and selling it on to European crime syndicates. In October 2009, Uruguayan cops seized more than two tons of cocaine from a British registered yacht named Maui in the port of Santiago Vasquez, west of Montevideo. One Uruguayan and one Croatian national were arrested. The trail led to Saric who was then accused of smuggling nearly six tons of the drug to Europe. He went on the run for four years but turned himself in to avoid what he said would be a "bloodbath" and was jailed in Serbia for twenty years, later reduced to fifteen on appeal.

Other Group America members were also based full-time on the continent. Goran "Scarface" Nesic, was the cartel's man in Brazil, one of the main trafficking thoroughfares to the Atlantic. According to some reports, he ranked even higher in the organisation than Darko Saric and lived in a fortified compound in Baurau surrounded by dozens of heavily armed guards. In the surprisingly peaceful operation that led to his eventual arrest in 2011, police recovered 620 kilos of cocaine and nearly one million euros.

Other notorious Serbian drug traffickers, such as the gangster and murderer Sreten Jocic, known as Joca Amsterdam, as well as numerous mafioso who have never been convicted, also made huge profits shipping blow from South America to Europe.

Albanian mafia figures have also based themselves in South America full time, although at least a couple have been caught up in gangland feuds in recent years. Ilir Hidri, originally from Vlora, had three bullets pumped into his head as he ambled down the street wearing flip flops in Guayaqil, Ecuador, in May 2017. The assassin was a traditional South American *sicario* who made off on the back of a motorcycle. It was later alleged that Hidri had been a DEA informant who was recruited shortly after arriving in the country three months previously, and that the hit might have been ordered by his own people.

Then, in November 2017, Kosovan-Albanian Remzi Azemi, Hidri's nephew, was shot in the same city as he travelled in an armoured car with his wife and three-year-old daughter. The attack was again carried out by motorcycle-riding *sicarios* who pulled alongside the car and fired through the window as Azemi's wife wound it down to smoke a cigar. Authorities said that Azemi had been under investigation since 2014.

According to journalists from the Organized Crime and Corruption Reporting Project (OCCRP), Azemi was himself charged with kidnapping a fellow narco based in Ecuador in March 2018. Montenegrin national Fadil Kacanic had been at home preparing to start a ten-year jail sentence for drug trafficking when six uniformed police officers turned up with an unsigned warrant. Needless to say, the boys in blue were gangland imposters. The sixty-four-year-old Kacanic was later found dead alongside his wife Elsa. Kacanic was killed with three bullets to the head, while Elsa was bludgeoned with a rock.

Other Albanian traffickers based in South America have been successfully brought to justice. A report on one case published by the United Nations Office on Drugs and Crime set out how a syndicate that shipped cocaine from Bolivia to Durres was smashed in 2010.

It named the ringleader only as "EP", but said that he had lived in Bolivia and established close ties with a cartel there. Cocaine was typically shipped in quantities of ten to twenty kilos, hidden in consignments of rice. The rice was ordered by a company registered to another syndicate member, "DB", who had it delivered to Durres via Rotterdam and Malta. Another member, "ES", dealt with the shipment when it arrived in Albania, escorting it from customs to Tirana and overseeing the unloading. The rice was taken to a market and sold at a knock down price to keep up the pretense of running a legitimate enterprise.

Dutch and Albanian authorities working in tandem brought the network down. Customs agents in Rotterdam found eighteen kilos hidden in the rice pallets and swapped eight of them for a substitute that could be traced. Once "ES" had finished unloading the rice, the Albanian police swooped. On this occasion, "EP" had returned from

Bolivia and cops arrested him at his apartment in Tirana seconds later.

In a separate case the following year, police in Spain put a tracker on a truck laden with 200 kilos of Colombian cocaine dissolved in palm oil. It was traced to southern Albania where two Macedonians and one Albanian were arrested. It was a massive seizure, but much larger shipments were still making it through. The Albanian mafia had gone truly global.

PART TWO: MAFIA UK

MURDER CITY

Life comes at you hard and fast on the Gascoigne Estate. "I've been stabbed and shot at," says Jermaine defiantly, as he lifts up his t-shirt to reveal a short, thick, pink scar on his lower back. "And I've done bad things myself, not gonna lie. That's how it is round here." For this low-level former street hoodlum, "round here" covers not just the sprawling 1960s collection of tower blocks and warren-like alleyways that make up the notorious concrete jungle in Barking, East London, but the wider deprived environs of Newham, Tower Hamlets and the capital's other gang-infested boroughs, where life is getting cheaper by the day.

Tilbury docks, in the neighbouring county of Essex, are just twelve miles away to the west, while the gleaming towers of the City of London, The Shard and its fellow megastructures dominate the skyline from the upper floors of the estate's east-facing flats. The toxic fumes from the A13, which connects Essex to London like a main artery constantly pumping traffic in and out, waft over the estate. A shipment of cocaine could, in theory, be ashore in Britain for less than an hour before being hoovered up the noses of affluent City workers.

The significance of the estate's geographic position is not lost on this still relatively young, surprisingly polite, ex-drug dealer. Now aged 26 and with a trail of convictions and prison sentences in his wake, Jermaine insists he's going straight. His naturally soft facial features, which only seem to harden when he talks about his former life of violence, would be sure to help him in that regard. But Jermaine knows that as long as he stays in the badlands of Barking, a major hub for drug dealing gangs, he can always jump back into the game.

"I'm an old man now," he insists. "If I stay on the road I'm dead. People don't give a fuck, they'll kill you over nothing. But it's hard to get out."

Sometimes it feels like London is in freefall. Politicians are distracted by Brexit and the police have been badly hit by spending cuts prompted by the 2008 financial crash. But there is now a full-blown murder crisis that simply can't be ignored. This is no media-propelled moral panic. There were 132 killings in the capital in 2018, an average of two-and-a-half a week. By the end of the first two weeks of January 2019, when I first meet Jermaine, the Metropolitan Police has already opened six new homicide investigations— nearly one every two days.

Street wars are raging across the capital. Killings are chronicled in YouTube rap videos featuring young men who brag about "splashing" their rivals, slang for stabbing. Most of the growing number of gangs— at least 200 of them— are making significant profits from the sale of heroin, cocaine and crack cocaine, adding dangerous intensity to any sort of feud, even when the original cause of the beef is minor. For them, large amounts of money and, more importantly, status is at stake.

The youngest victim is a fourteen-year-old boy, Jaden Moodie, who dies in the street about seven miles away in Waltham Forest, North East London. He is rammed off a moped by up to four men in a Mercedes. Three jump out and stab him seven times in the back as he lays helpless. Jaden had been dealing drugs for a rival gang.

Another victim caught in the literal crossfire of a war between North London gangs in Tottenham and Wood Green is seventeen-year-old Tanesha Melbourne-Blake. Tottenham's Northumberland Park Killers (NPK) gang claim responsibility for her shooting on Instagram, with a post that says, "If your (sic) chilling with my ops I ain't gonna adjust my aim for you." The words are accompanied by a laughing emoji and the hashtag #NPK.[28]

Back in Jermaine's main stomping ground of Barking, gang-related violence and murders have been steadily increasing since 2006, but the phenomenon is getting worse. He shows me the streets where he says young men have been stabbed and shot. Some attacks were fatal, but there is no longer anything to mark the spot — no police cordon, no flowers, no memorials. Just cold, ordinary pavements.

One recent case is that of Hasan Ozcan, nineteen, who was stabbed to death by youths riding bicycles. Although the family says Hasan was not involved in gangs, his Facebook profile suggests otherwise. Multiple profile pictures show him making gang signs and in one, the word "gang" has been superimposed over his photo.

***

The London-wide death toll in 2018 had reversed a twelve-year decline in the capital's murder rate, from the previous high of 174 in 2006. Scotland Yard's murder squad had lost more than a quarter of its 1,208 officers in that time, making the task of bringing the spiraling violence under control that much harder. And as cold as it may sound, in some ways the dead bodies were just the tip of the iceberg.

---

[28] A month earlier, NPK gang member Kelvin Odunuyi, nineteen, known as Lampz, was shot dead outside a Wood Green cinema, just weeks after apparently taking part in the murder of former Tottenham gang member Kobi Nelson, twenty-two. Kelvin had appeared in YouTube videos bragging about stabbing and shooting his enemies from the other end of Lordship Lane, the long thoroughfare that connects the two areas. "Most of these killings are being fuelled by a huge spike in the movement of drugs, particularly cocaine," says local MP David Lammy in reaction to the crime. "Young men, particularly in communities like mine, become footsoldiers for gangsters and McMafia bosses much further up the tree."

Knife crime was at an all-time high, with nearly 15,000 incidents recorded in the capital in 2017/18. Acid attacks were way up, from fewer than two hundred in 2014 to nearly five-hundred-a-year by 2018. Although still relatively rare, the number of shootings also appeared to be on the increase; nine of 2018's murder victims were shot to death and 2017 statistics showed that gun crime in London was up 42 per cent on the previous year.

And these were just the recorded figures. As Jermaine says, when you have to survive somewhere like the Gascoigne Estate you tend to keep away from the police as much as you can.

"Lots of people get stabbed in the leg or arm. Or the arse," he tells me with a grimace. "Sometimes it's a punishment, sometimes it might just be for fun or gang initiation."

In other words, many victims will not to go to hospital unless they really need to, so the true number of violent incidents across the capital is probably far higher, "It's not like everyone who gets stabbed is going to die. You don't go to hospital if you cut yourself shaving. That's all it is sometimes. You know when it's really bad because it won't stop bleeding."

There was also plenty of anecdotal evidence that stabbing victims involved in gangs, many of them as young as fourteen, were going to backstreet doctors or vets to get sewn up. And if you accept that most street violence can in some way be traced back to the drug trade, whether directly or indirectly, then you have to look at who's supplying the drugs.

Back in the early 2000s, Barking's self-proclaimed guvnor was gold-toothed Jamaican gangster Delroy "The King" Lewis. He'd already served a sentence in New York for guns and drugs offences, but he dodged deportation on his release by voluntarily shipping himself off to London.

Lewis ran his new venture from two flats in the Gascoigne Estate's Cobham House block, where he processed and packaged hundreds of thousands of pounds worth of cocaine. He installed his lover in one flat, while another girlfriend and the mother of his child was left to run the day-to-day, twenty-four-hour drug dealing operation. Most of the action took place in the building's stairwells, where his dealers could earn up to £400 for a twelve-hour shift. In total, police believe he made £12,000 a day and sold £3.4 million of

Class A drugs in one year alone. Eventually, Lewis was arrested on a wounding charge and given bail.

Realising the game was up, the drug dealer ordered his £80,000 Lexus to be shipped to Jamaica and with £50,000 in cash strapped to his body and suitcases stuffed with designer goods, he planned to flee the country. When police stopped him on the way to the airport in December 2002, they found he had a one-way ticket to Kingston. He ended up getting 16 years in prison.

Delroy "The King" Lewis had been doubly unlucky. Not only did he get caught, but soon after he was locked up, Britain's drugs market boomed. Cocaine became not just a drug for the rich and famous, but something that was socially acceptable at middle-class dinner parties and among students. Whereas in the past these recreational drug users might have shared an after-dinner joint around the kitchen table, now they were passing around a £20 note and a mirror or CD case covered in white lines.

Crack cocaine, while less socially acceptable, was also becoming more popular, especially with heroin users. A single rock can cost between £10-£20, and it's just as profitable as powder cocaine. By 2018, Public Health England was warning that the number of people seeking help for problems related to crack cocaine use had soared in under two years. Not only were more people using the drug, but it was of stronger, purer quality. The same went for powder cocaine. Government minister Ben Wallace warned the country was "fast becoming the biggest consumer of cocaine in Europe". Metropolitan Police Commissioner Cressida Dick also weighed in, saying middle-class cocaine use was driving the bloody gang wars.

Statistics show that more than ten percent of adult Britons have tried cocaine at least once, while the average across the EU is just 5.4 per cent. Part of the reason is the price. Back in the 1980s, a gram of blow could cost as much as £250. Today, the average price is £50, with dealers offering half gram deals and a range of prices depending on the quality. While it was once a drug destined only for the nostrils of high earners, now it can be snorted by anyone who has enough ready cash to spend on an average night down the pub.

The boom wasn't only happening in Britain of course — across Europe as a whole the increased popularity and purity of the drug was causing more deaths. Yet in 2018 the UK accounted for about 34 per cent of the continent's 7,929 fatal cocaine overdoses. Increased demand was driving production in South America, and the increased purity was in turn driving demand.

It wasn't just the big cities where demand was surging. The same inner-city gangs that were chopping each other to pieces in London started running 'county lines'— essentially drugs hotlines operated by junior gang members or franchises in smaller towns and cities further afield. Each line could have hundreds of customers and generate millions for the gang. At the start of 2019, the National Crime Agency warned the number of these lines had more than doubled in a year, to 2,000. This nefarious franchise system was also bringing rivalries, violence and murder out to these satellite towns.

One major catalyst for the cocaine boom, and thus the ensuing violence between street gangs, was the influx of Albanian crime syndicates.

As Jermaine explained, "It was a gradual thing. You used to deal with Yardies or Turks. Then you started to get more Eastern Europeans. They pretty much took over. To be honest, I couldn't really tell the difference, Romanians, Albanians or whatever. But what I did notice was that the Albanians had more of an identity, if that makes sense, in that you would start to know who was Albanian by the way they acted. They earned the reputation as the ones to go to and they were able to elevate themselves above all the street gangs."

By late 2018, some law enforcement sources estimated that the majority of the cocaine being sold on the streets of Britain — at least in the South East, London and the Midlands — had at one point passed through Albanian hands. Whether they were trafficking the drug through European ports or road networks, importing directly from South America, or distributing to wholesalers or street gangs, Albanians had a presence at every level of the trade. Whoever their customers were — British crime syndicates, street gangs, other Albanian outfits or end users — cost savings were usually passed on, further driving demand.

The apparent ubiquity of the Albanian cocaine connection came down to the mafia's ability to cooperate with other criminal gangs, including some of Britain's traditional crime families, but most importantly the Italian 'Ndrangheta, which controls much of the criminal activity at Europe's ports, where corrupt workers can earn up to 125,000 euros for giving shipments a smooth passage. In addition to controlling the port of Durres, Albanian crews were working with the 'Ndrangheta to achieve a stranglehold on the largest port in Europe, Rotterdam, which deals with eight million containers each year. The aforementioned Tilbury docks are a forward destination from Europe's second busiest port, Antwerp, similarly infiltrated by Albanian and 'Ndrangheta operatives.[29]

By the end of 2019, London had seen a total of at least 149 murders, exceeding the number for the previous year. The very last killing took place on Christmas Eve.

Flamur Beqiri, thirty-six, an Albanian with Swedish citizenship, was returning with his wife, Debora, and their young child, to his £1.5 million home in Battersea, South West London. It was dark, just after 9pm, and before he could get his key in the door, a lone gunman approached and fired several shots, hitting Beqiri in the back. As he lay bleeding on the pavement, the assassin fired a coup de grace into his head. Neighbours frantically gave first aid while his wife's screams rang out, but it was to no avail. Beqiri died at the scene.

At first, it appeared to be a robbery gone wrong. After all, Beqiri was clearly a wealthy man. He ran a record label representing a handful of minor Swedish pop stars. While the label was generating only a modest income, his sister, Missé, was a model and reality television star who was engaged to Jake Hall, from The Only Way Is Essex, and who had previously been married to Manchester United and Sweden footballer Anders Lindegaard. But while her life was certainly interesting, Flamur's past was even more intriguing.

---

[29] In 2018, the authorities seized a combined seventy-three metric tons of the drug at Rotterdam and Antwerp, a thirty-five percent increase on the fifty-four tons seized in 2017. To give some idea of the scale of the discoveries, back in 2013 Belgian police seized just four tons at Antwerp during the entire year. Nevertheless, the seizures are nothing compared with what probably makes it to the streets — a general estimate from police forces is that seized drugs account for around ten percent of what gets smuggled across the border.

In 2008, Swedish police had named him as one of the country's most wanted men over his involvement in a £2 million cannabis smuggling plot. He had fled from a police bust at the Swedish border and later beat the drugs charge by claiming he had not known that a man from Holland who he was meeting had 340 kilos of cannabis in his car. Beqiri managed to convince a court that as far as he knew, he was only doing a deal for illicit alcohol and cigarettes. Beqiri was handed a suspended sentence. He later left Sweden, living for a while in Amsterdam before moving to London, where he met glamorous Debora Krasniqi through his sister.

The pair married in a lavish ceremony at Lake Como in Italy in October 2018, where he paid for guests from around the world to stay at the luxury five-star Grand Hotel Imperiale. Debora gushed about the fairytale romance to a luxury goods website.

But back in Sweden, some of Beqiri's old friends were down on their luck. Convicted robber Naief Adawi had once taken part in a $9.2 million (62 million Danish kroner) cash-in-transit robbery in 2008, carried out by a 20-strong gang. While he was jailed for eight years, most of the gang got away and the majority of the loot was never recovered. Adawi and Beqiri were close friends and there were rumours that some of the cash might have been laundered through the record company.

In August 2019, Adawi was out shopping in Malmo with his doctor wife Karolin Hakim, thirty-one, and their two-month old baby. A gunman approached the family outside a falafel shop, where Adawi handed the youngster to his wife and ran for his life. Rather than give chase, the Syrian killer turned the gun on Karolin and riddled her with bullets. As she lay dying on the pavement, her child still in her arms, the assassin finished her off with a bullet to the head. In the aftermath of Beqiri's similar killing in London, Metropolitan Police detectives confirmed that they were looking into possible links between the two murders.[30]

Flamur Beqiri was far from the first Albanian immigrant to London to be murdered. Nor was he the first to have lived an outwardly normal family life while hiding a serious criminal

---

[30] At the time of writing, a Swedish kickboxer named Anis Fouad Hemissi, aged twenty two, had been charged with murder.

past. Jermaine said that on the streets of Barking, the Albanians "came out of nowhere," but that couldn't be further from the truth. As we've seen, the pyramid crisis and the war in Kosovo sent tens of thousands of citizens fleeing to safer countries. And while most were genuine refugees hoping for a better life, some were trying to erase their violent backgrounds and establish a new criminal empire.

TONY MONTANAS

"**H**E LOOKED LIKE a cut-price Tony Montana," says Chrysoulla Michaels, recalling the moment she first laid eyes on her eventual husband-to-be. It's clear that despite everything that's happened since, she doesn't mean that as an insult. Even though Ardian Rragami would go on to become her tormentor, and be unmasked as a criminal and murderer, there is still some residual affection there.

At the time of their meeting, at a North London pub back in 2002, the beautician thought he was handsome and still remembers those early days fondly.

"He was dressed in a black suit and shirt and had this kind of aura," she says. "We didn't actually speak for a long time. When he came in everyone would stand up and shake his hand and he never walked up to the bar himself, everyone would buy him drinks. He later told me it was because of how he fought against the Communists. He was this kind of amazing figure."

It has to be said that Chrysoulla was easily impressed at the time. She was working behind the bar of her local pub in Turnpike Lane. The shifts helped to top up her modest salary as a mortage arranger for a high street bank. A newly single mother-of-one, she was desperate to provide for her daughter. There wasn't much time for her to meet men, and in any case most of the Albanians who hung around in the pub looked like low-rent gangsters or straight-up losers.

Ardian had genuine charisma, good clothes, a warm smile and the respect of his peers. He became a regular and their eyes often met across the bar. For a while, Chrysoulla assumed nothing would happen, but he eventually introduced himself as Ardian Gashi, a refugee from Kosovo. Ardian had already been in the country for two years, he said. But he hadn't really had time to meet anyone, what with his long hours working as an electrician.

Chyrsoulla admits that she fell "head over heels in love" with this exciting new man in her life. Everything seemed to be coming together. She started doing so well at the bank that she could afford to drop the bar work. Ardian never seemed to be short of cash, so the pair wasted no time in going on regular dates — touring the capital, eating out, enjoying several drunken nights of passion. She even got a heart-shaped tattoo on her arm with the words 'Ardian' and 'ti je jeta jeme,' which means 'you are my life' in Albanian. Soon, Ardian had proposed marriage.

In 2003, the couple got hitched in a Greek Orthodox ceremony in North London. Ardian, a non-practising Muslim, even got baptised so that he could marry into his lover's faith. By the end of the year, they had a child on the way. Then the careful facade that Ardian had built around himself began to crumble.

During the couple's whirlwind courtship, Ardian had explained that the respect shown to him by other Albanians was because of the way he had fought against Communist rebels during the country's civil war in 1997. It didn't really make much sense, because Ardian said he was from Kosovo, rather than Albania. But Chrysoulla wasn't particularly knowledgeable about or interested in

Eastern European politics. To her, one distant conflict was much the same as another, so she brushed her doubts aside.

Of more immediate concern was the drastic change in her new husband's behaviour. Just one week after they married, Ardian punched her for the first time.

"It shook me," she says. "I felt like I was quite a high-powered person, I had stopped working in the pub and I was getting promoted and working longer hours at the bank. But at home I was living on eggshells. He would taunt me and call me names, he would punch and kick me. At first I thought maybe it was a phase he was going through because he was worried about having a baby."

But the beatings didn't stop. It was only now things had turned sour that she started to question Ardian's mysterious source of income. Why did he always have so much ready cash? Where did he disappear to for days at a time? But asking questions would always end in an argument, or worse.

"In the end," she says, "I didn't ask him where he got his money or where he went because he would just snap. Then he'd put his jacket on and I wouldn't see him for another three days."

The situation led to Chrysoulla's father and brother distancing themselves from her, unable to witness any more abuse. Yet she didn't know how to break it off, and by 2007 Chrysoulla had given birth to another child, with the family moving to Wickford, in Essex. But another big shock was just around the corner.

Ardian was suddenly arrested and remanded into custody, accused of stealing money from parking meters in the West End. It sounded crazy to her. It seemed a bizarre and minor crime, not the sort of serious offence for which it was necessary to withhold bail. Chrysoulla was even more astounded when Ardian received an eleven-month prison sentence after standing trial with a number of other men.

But she shouldn't have been surprised. For some Albanian criminals living in London, the parking meter game was big business. For a few, it was even worth killing for. Around a year earlier, in October 2006, London had been the scene of an Albanian-on-Albanian mob hit. But the dispute was not over drugs, vice, or protection, but parking meters.

It is a classic organised crime ploy, which appropriately enough features in another Al Pacino movie, *Donnie Brasco*. In the film, a crook is seen cracking a meter open with a hammer in a desperate bid for cash to feed up the chain of command. Each meter might net only a few hundred pounds, which is usually not enough to trouble the local CID, let alone Scotland Yard. But when parking meters are broken into as part of a systematic effort, the losses for the local authority can run into the millions, while providing a fantastic low risk income for organised crime gangs.

Back in 2006, Westminster Council, home to MPs, high-flying lawyers and titans of industry, was writing off more than £1.2million a year as a result of repeated attacks, mostly by Albanian gangs. The profits were being distributed among the members, but some were agitating for a bigger slice of the pie. The only way to increase profits was for competing gangs to stick to their own territory, and that's what the meeting in the Albanian Club, in Park Royal, was supposed to resolve.

Nightclub doorman Herland Bilali, a man with a fearsome reputation for violence, and his sidekick Kujtim "Timi" Spahiu, arrived at the bar in the early hours of October 14, 2006. They rang the buzzer, the door opened and they walked down a flight of stairs into the bar. But instead of pulling up a chair to open talks with the rival gang members, Bilal pulled out a pistol and began firing. Two men were wounded, but innocent bystander Prel Marku was shot in the head and died. Marku had been in the club playing cards and had nothing to do with the parking meters dispute.

Spahiu, a thirty-two-year-old refugee from Kosovo, later claimed he had no idea what Bilal had in mind.

"It was all over in a matter of seconds," he insisted. "I turned and ran down the stairs. I'd never seen anything like this before. I felt shocked, really bad."

Bilali later told him why he had started shooting. "They wanted to kill me, they had guns," he claimed.

Spahiu fled to Manchester, while Bilali escaped to Denmark. Both men were eventually tracked down and jailed for life for joint enterprise murder, and ordered to serve a minimum of thirty-three years.

With her husband in prison, Chrysoulla was torn. On the one hand, Ardian's absence from the family home came as a relief. It gave her respite from his violent urges. On the other, the domestic abuse had not extinguished her love for the father of two of her children, or at least that's how she saw it at the time. When Ardian was eventually released, he came back home.

But Chrysoulla's world imploded again in 2009 when police with an Interpol warrant crashed through her door.

"It was like something out of a movie," she recalls. "They were searching the house as if we were major criminals. They told me that I wasn't married to who I thought I was. Ardian had a different last name and he was wanted for murder. It was then that I started to remember bits of stories that he had told me right at the beginning."

Little is known about the murder itself. The victim was a neighbour from Ardian's apartment block in the Albanian — not Kosovan — city of Shkodra. The murder weapon was a Scorpion submachine gun, which he had cold-bloodedly used to spray the man's body with bullets as he drank in a nearby bar.

Ardian had told Chrysoulla parts of the truth, but he'd dressed it up as yet another tale from his supposed Communist-fighting days, claiming to have acted in self-defence after he was shot at. As far as Chrysoulla was concerned, there had been no suggestion that Ardian was in the wrong, or that he had skipped the country to dodge a murder trial.

"I realised I was married to somebody I didn't really know," Chrysoulla says. "I tried at that point to get a divorce but the solicitor told me that I couldn't divorce him because Ardian Gashi didn't exist. But as the police took him away, I did think: 'Thank God, I've been saved from this man.'"

Ardian was quickly deported to serve a fifteen-year sentence back home, but that was far from the end of the saga. He managed to get the sentence knocked down to just four years, and made contact with Chrysoulla again in the final twelve months. The pair reminisced about their first happy days together and against her better judgment she told him she would think about taking him back.

After his release in 2014, Rragami was smuggled back into Britain in the back of a lorry. He only came to the attention of the Home Office again after contacting a solicitor about officially changing his name to Rragami by deed poll in June 2015. He was arrested and released, before once again being held and released in 2016. It was a farce that was soon to hit the family in an unexpected way.

The *Daily Mail*, as part of a campaign against the British government's allegedly lax immigration rules, publicly identified Ardian, his conviction for murder and the two occasions he had conned his way past border control, the first time by claiming to be a refugee from Kosovo. Reporters were at the door, Chyrsoulla's local paper picked up on the story, and the kids had to be taken out of school.

The publicity intensified Ardian's rages, often made worse by booze, and the couple officially separated in July 2017. Police went on to open a domestic violence probe in January 2018, but the case came to nothing.

"He just became a crazy person," Chyrsoulla says of those difficult months.

The nightmare only came to an end in January 2019, when Ardian attacked Chyrsoulla with a knife, resulting in a court case that ended up on the front page of *The Sun*. The knife attack had come about because by then, Chrysoulla had been made homeless and her daughters needed to stay at Ardian's flat in Wickford so they could attend school. Chrysoulla also stayed there occasionally, while Rragami slept on the sofa.

"The night he held the knife to my throat he had been drinking. He was just in a rage," she says. "He grabbed my hair and was pulling me about, screaming in my face, calling me a bitch. He was shouting nonsense, just noise. I was frozen to the spot. Then he let go of my hair and went into the kitchen, coming back with a knife in his hand. I thought: 'You can't be serious.' I can remember his face being twisted up with hate as he held it to my throat. I thought I was going to die."

Ardian appeared at Basildon crown court the following month. Chyrsoulla was there, for once not to support her husband, but to see justice being done. Ardian had made no comment in police interview, but he pleaded guilty to causing actual bodily harm and also to the common assault of a young girl, who he pushed out of the house during his rampage. Despite everything — the murder, the two illegal crossings into Britain, the years of domestic abuse and now a guilty plea to an incident that could easily have led to more serious violence — Ardian was handed just a ten-month suspended sentence.

Chrysoulla was incredulous. But thanks to the national attention given to the case, the Home Office moved in. Ardian was rearrested by border agents before he could be turned loose by prison authorities, and he was on a plane back to Albania by the end of the month.

Like many domestic abuse victims, Chrysoulla blames herself for sticking by her violent husband and enduring years of torment at his hands.

"I am learning not to," she says, "but I still feel like I let it escalate to that stage. I was too trusting because I thought: 'He's got a tag, he's under curfew and is fighting the Home Office, is he really going to jeopardise all that?' I'm just one of those people, I trust too much. It's like being brainwashed. I was just beaten down so badly by him."

There is no doubt that in addition to being a criminal in the domestic setting, Ardian Rragami was also on the fringes of organised crime in Britain. Chrysoulla later learnt that Ardian had been involved in a prostitution ring in Germany before coming to London, where he also made money from vice. She says he frequently carried a gun and was well-known in London's Albanian underworld. As well as his role in the parking meter war, Ardian had also been investigated for his part in a people smuggling ring, which saw his cousin, Gentian Rragami, forty-four, from Wandsworth, convicted, in the same court, on the same day, in front of the same judge.

The court heard how the removals man had been followed by Metropolitan Police officers on October 12, 2017, to a layby on the M20 in Kent. Gentian parked between two lorries and two men were seen to emerge and get into his car, before driving back towards London. Then, on December 14 that year, he was stopped after another two men were seen getting into his car at a layby in

Kent. Gentian Rragami initially claimed he had pulled over to use the toilet and the men asked for a lift to London, but he could not explain the £1,296 in cash he had on him and later admitted two counts of facilitating unlawful entry. The judge accepted the dad-of-three was only a driver in the plot and jailed him for ten months, meaning he would not face automatic deportation proceedings and is probably still in the country. Ardian never faced charges for people smuggling.

Ardian Rragami's story may be horrifying and at times farcical, but it is hardly unique. The fallout from the chaos of the pyramid crisis and the Kosovo war had sent ethnic Albanians seeking new opportunities across the globe. Most of them were of course honest and law-abiding people, but many were criminals and, like Rragami, fugitive murderers escaping the prospect of prison or death through blood feud.

Britain was perceived to have a weak immigration system and almost anyone declaring themselves to be a refugee from Kosovo was likely to be assured of safe passage. It was easy to slip into the country hidden in the back of a lorry, living standards were high, there was free healthcare and cash-in-hand work was not hard to find.

It's important to recognise just how rapidly the Albanian diaspora grew in Britain. Unlike New York, there had been next to no history of Albanian immigration until the pyramid crisis. In fact, the first Albanian immigrants to Britain of any significant number came after World War Two, when Enver Hoxha seized power. But even then, only about 100 political refugees and intellectuals sought sanctuary.

Even by the time of the 1991 census, there were just 338 registered Albanians in England. By 1993 the number had increased to around 2,500. The influx was officially due to ethnic Albanians in Kosovo fleeing persecution. In 1996, the High Court made their persecuted status official, and in 1997 around 30,000 people claiming to be from Kosovo applied for asylum in Britain. Of course, as in the case of Rragami and countless others, many were actually from Albania and were fleeing the chaos caused by the collapsing economy.

Thousands of Albanians also fled to Greece, Italy, and other places in Western Europe.[31] As European Union integration increased, any immigrants who obtained European citizenship then automatically gained the right to live and work in other EU countries. This mobility would perfectly suit the loose-knit Albanian mafia model of cross-border criminal networks.

Today, the exact number of Albanians living in Britain is unclear. The 2011 census recorded 13,415 Albanian-born residents. Of that number, nearly fifty-three per cent were living in London, with twelve per cent in the South East and another ten percent in the East of England. But the International Organisation for Migration puts the nationwide figure far higher, at up to 100,000. Of those, as many as 18,000 are now thought to live in Barking, East London, with up to 60,000 in the capital in total. Another 12,000 Albanians are thought to be based in the West Midlands.

Of course, the vast majority of ethnic Albanian immigrants to Britain were, and are, good people doing nothing more than trying to improve their lot in life. But there is no disguising the fact that Britain, with its strict gun laws and generally unarmed police force, was an attractive prospect for organised crime gangs originating from one of the most heavily armed regions on Earth.

The Psycho

Back in 1997, a violent young man, Mane Driza, committed his first known murders in Albania, shooting dead father and son Lavdosh, seventy-one, and Elmaz Kannani, thirty-three, in a blood feud linked to people trafficking in Fier, near Tirana. Fearing both the police and reprisals from the family of his victims, Driza fled to Britain, claiming to be a Kosovan refugee called Sokol Drenova.

By June 1999, Driza had married a Brazilian woman called Rosie and was ostensibly working as a stonemason in Watford. He had introduced himself to Rosie in a Leicester Square club as "Simon", but almost as soon as the ink was dry on the wedding certificate

---

[31] The mass displacement of ethnic Albanians didn't stop there. In 1999, Albania took in about 440,000 Albanian Kosovars fleeing the civil war in Kosovo. Another 400,000 fled to Montenegro and Macedonia. Thousands more also ended up in the United States and Western Europe, including Britain.

from Barnet Registry Office, Driza told her the truth. His name, age, place of birth, even his religion (Muslim, not Christian), had been lies.

But Driza kept other truths to himself. Although he did earn an honest wage as a stonemason, it was not enough to pay for the designer clothes, numerous mobile phones or flash cars he liked to drive. Rosie also wondered why he used false names when speaking to contacts, including the decidedly unsubtle moniker "Tony Montana".

In fact, Mane Driza was deeply embedded in the capital's fledgling Albanian underworld, earning his keep as muscle for criminal gangs seizing control of vice in Soho. The marriage broke down after Rosie learned the truth about his identity and he moved in with a fellow Albanian stonemason, Stefan Mone. This apparent Good Samaritan was to become Mane's third murder victim.

During his later police interview, Driza claimed that Mone had once been in prison with Elmaz Kannani, the first man he had gunned down back in Albania. This was apparently enough to convince him that Mone was now on a contract to kill him in revenge.

This was demonstrably untrue, not just because there was no evidence of Mone's involvement in crime, but because colleagues at the stonemasons recalled Driza loudly complaining that Mone had stolen his wedding ring and presented it to his own girlfriend, Zoe Blay, who was six months pregnant at the time. It sent Driza into a violent fury. "I'm going to kill him," Driza loudly declared, over and over again. Nobody took him seriously.

Driza also insisted that on the day of the attack, Mone had come at him armed with a knife and a baseball bat and that he "lost control" while acting in self-defence. Again, this seemed unlikely. Mone's body was left almost unrecognisable as a result of at least 120 injuries, inflicted with a pickaxe handle, lock knife, cheese knife and a screwdriver.

Mone's girlfriend found his body the next day, but by then Driza had already started making his way to Italy. Six months later, in a bar in Catania, Sicily, Driza shot and killed two more Albanian men, Maskaj Artan and Blushaj Albert. A third man, Maskaj Lufter, escaped with his life when Driza's gun jammed. All three were allegedly involved in prostitution and extortion rackets in the town, and the shooting was assumed to be part of a gang war.

Driza was arrested the following day and he was eventually handed a thirty-year sentence for conspiracy to murder and one count of attempted murder. After the conviction, an Italian police officer said, "Mane is a homicidal maniac. He has been convicted of murder here in Italy but is suspected of at least three others elsewhere. Medical reports show that he has two pieces of shrapnel lodged in his skull from an attempt on his life and doctors believe this triggers his murderous rage."

Driza was ultimately extradited to face trial in Britain and jailed for twenty years in April 2019, to be served after his sentence in Italy.[32]

The cases of Ardian Rragami and Mane Driza provide colourful insights into how those on the lower rungs of the first wave of Britain's Albanian organised crime gangs lived their lives, but they are far from unique. For example, another villain who claimed to be a Kosovan refugee, Hektor Mahmutaj, was deported to Albania in 2019 to serve a twenty-five-year sentence for the 1997 blood feud murder of a farmer. Mahmutaj had racked up a string of convictions for fraud, theft and firearms in Britain before he was finally kicked out of the country. A similar case reported in February 2020 involved Leke Prendi, an Albanian murderer who likewise had arrived in Britain posing as a Kosovan refugee called Aleks Kola.

While Ardian Rragami was involved in organised crime to a lesser extent and appeared to fade in and out of the criminal world as and when necessary, Driza was a different story. He gave the appearance of having legitimate work, but was undoubtedly

---

[32] As a somewhat bizarre footnote, Driza's erstwhile wife Rosie went on to live a colourful life herself. A few years after splitting from Driza, a second Albanian lover was gunned down in Plaistow, East London. Then, after taking a job as a cleaner for a judge, she was later convicted of blackmailing him over their affair. The conviction was later overturned on appeal.

involved in serious organised crime. Newspaper reports have at various times described him as a "mafia member" and a hitman. Certainly, the men he killed in Italy were involved in prostitution and drugs, and it is entirely possible the murders were contract killings. The same could be said about the murders back in Fier. The London killing was entirely different; the ferocity of that attack would suggest a crime of passion.

In any case, the stories of Rragami and Driza shed light on the world inhabited by Albanian criminals who sought a life in Britain. Common to each case was the use of false names and bogus asylum applications citing Kosovo, not Albania, as their homeland. Both lied about their religion to marry women living in Britain. Both lived secret lives away from their married homes, bringing back large amounts of cash not in keeping with their official jobs. More importantly, both cases show how it is possible for Albanian criminals to play an ad hoc role within organised crime groups, shifting loyalties from one to another much as any normal employee would change jobs.

For example, Driza clearly had some involvement in organised crime back in Albania, probably worked for another group in London, and then another in Sicily. Rragami was highly respected by London emigres for his activities during the civil war and had even killed a man, but once in Britain he found himself on the fringes of the underworld, robbing parking meters and operating as a cheap pimp. No doubt he was involved in the people smuggling business, most probably fulfilling the British end of a criminal enterprise with its roots back home.

But while footsoldiers like Rragami and Driza were scrabbling around for a place in the mafia's pecking order and bringing nothing but chaos to their personal lives, serious and disciplined criminals were taking on London's established underworld — and beating it at its own game.

TURF WARS, PART ONE

Edmund Gulhaj flung himself into the cold North London night. In his haste, the twenty-two-year-old left his jacket behind, but that was the least of his worries. As shots rang out, he knew the threats had been real, the firearms inside equally genuine. His heart pounding, all Edmund could do was run. But something stung him on the hip and he lurched forwards. Then, almost in slow motion, the pavement came rushing towards his face.

The young man would have had no idea what happened next. But anyone watching would have seen another Albanian approach and loom over his prone body. Calmly, the executioner raised his handgun and without hesitation fired three more bullets into Edmund's head.

It was a scene that could have come straight from *Scarface*, the inspiration for so many wannabe kingpins. But these were not the harsh streets of Lushnje, Pristina or the Bronx, or even 1970s Miami, where the mob classic is set. Instead, the killing took place in Palmers Green, North London, in January 2002.

Two other men received critical injuries in the shooting, but pulled through. Two gunmen fled the scene, later resurfacing in Albania. Detectives soon determined the catalyst for the carnage. Two rival groups of Albanians had arranged to meet for talks, either to discuss a drug deal or to carve up territory. Nobody was exactly sure which.

But The Fox public house had been an ideal meeting place, because it was under the radar of other gangs in nearby Haringey, which was controlled by the feared Turkish mafia clan of Abdullah Baybasin. Both Albanian outfits were in the same business as Baybasin and they preferred to keep out of his way when possible. The Baybasin mob wasn't afraid to direct its street soldiers, the Bombacilar, or Hackney Bombers, to liquidate anyone taking liberties on its turf. Yet despite the relative safety of the meeting place, there was nothing the Albanians could do to protect themselves from each other.

The finer details of what happened that night remain shrouded in mystery, because detectives could not get anyone to talk. As hard as they tried, neither the victims nor the other men rounded up near the pub were willing to give up the shooters. In the end, police used mobile phone technology to work out who had been at the scene and who was now missing.

The phone numbers were tracked to Albania — where there was no extradition treaty with Britain — and to the homes of Ermal Sinani and Florian Metalla. By the time the British police located the pair in 2004, they were both already in custody for separate offences. At the time, the country's chief prosecutor was taking a hard line on Albanian gangsters who brought blood feuds among the diaspora back to their homeland, so when the call came through from London that the two men were wanted for murder, he was only too happy to help.

In what was something of a first, the Albanian authorities used evidence gathered by their English counterparts to bring a prosecution. The mountain of evidence stacked up against Sinani and Metalla proved so overwhelming that the two men pleaded guilty, and in February 2008 they were each sentenced to twenty-one years for murder and two counts of attempted murder.

The murder of Edmund Gulhaj was just one violent incident among dozens of gangland clashes as Albanian mafia groups fought to establish themselves in London's underworld and beyond. Eventually, open warfare would erupt between Albanian gangsters and the Baybasin mob. But drugs were not the only cause of turf disputes as Albanians also sought to muscle in on another lucrative criminal industry— vice.

The unrest in the Balkans throughout the 1990s didn't just open the region up to drug traffickers and arms dealers. One of the more profitable businesses and one which was decidedly safer for gang bosses was prostitution. Vulnerable girls from places such as Romania, the Ukraine and Moldova were brought to towns in Bosnia and Serbia, as well as in Albania, Montenegro and Macedonia, usually after being either kidnapped or tricked.

The growth of brothels thinly masquerading as cafes or social clubs became a Balkan-wide problem and was by no means an exclusively Albanian mafia-run affair. But it was the Albanian mob that gained the most sordid reputation for violence and rough treatment of the women. Typically, the girls would spend only a limited time in each location, before being transported to the next venue. Increasingly, as the power of the mafias grew, they found new destinations in Western Europe.

According to the researcher Jana Arsovska in her book *Decoding Albanian Organised Crime* many of the Albanian people trafficking groups in Europe in the late 1990s and early 2000s came from the southern city of Berat, with up to 400 girls and women from the region traded and put to work as prostitutes in Europe between 1992 and 2007. At least fifteen percent of them were underage. At one point, there were estimated to be 30,000 Albanian women working as prostitutes in Europe, again around thirty per cent of them minors. According to Arsovska's research, one typical prostitution ring was active in Belgium. Albanian gangsters recruited local women and told them they would earn "big bucks" working as escorts in Holland. However, they soon found themselves being sexually abused by their masters. To add insult to injury, they were never paid what they were promised; in one case a pregnant girl earned 500 euros in a single day, but was only paid twenty euros. She confronted the two Albanian brothers in charge and as punishment they raped her, killed her unborn child and left her with life-long facial scars. They were ultimately convicted in France.

Other pimps were well known for luring women into slavery with promises of marriage, before turning on the girls, and beating and raping them. Girls would also be trafficked by members of their own families, and there was also evidence that in the fallout from the war in Kosovo armed gangs prowled refugee camps looking for the most attractive females to kidnap. Some of the girls, many aged just twelve to fourteen years old, were destined for slave markets where pimps bought them up like cattle and kept them in similar conditions.

A separate prostitution ring in Italy hit the headlines in December 1997 when five people, including a five-year-old girl, died in a boat accident off the coast of Brindisi. The human cargo was being shipped across the Adriatic from Albania on a well-known smuggling route.

In the aftermath of the disaster, the Italian pimp was heard on a wiretap saying, "Dammit, a little girl died. But the four girls who survived were prostitutes. That's a relief."

It transpired that the girls were bought from their families for £800 each, raped by the gang members and then sold on to pimps for as much as £1,500. Two of the women who survived the capsize later vanished from their hospital beds.

Another disturbing case was uncovered in Germany in 2000, when police were told an Albanian mafia group was shipping pregnant prostitutes to the country, where the children were then sold on to Western couples for as much as £20,000 each. The allegations had been made by a prostitute in Italy who escaped from her pimp's clutches.

A more recent case in Italy showed how some Albanian pimps are linked to other forms of crime. In November 2016, police arrested fourteen Albanians as part of a people smuggling ring that brought Eastern European women to Milan for the purposes of prostitution. They then used the proceeds to buy cocaine from Holland to import into Italy.

Like most major cities, London already had a well-established vice district by the time Albanian gangs were forming in the capital in the late 1990s. Soho had traditionally been run by an alliance of Maltese and English villains, dating back to the 1930s and the reign of the notorious Messina Brothers. The area's various strip clubs, clip joints and brothels were taken over in the 1960s and 1970s by the likes of "Big Frank" Mifsud and Bernie Silver, who ran the day-to-day operations while paying protection money to English gangsters such as the Kray Twins. Although Mifsud and Silver ostensibly got out of the vice game after being handed hefty prison sentences, many of the seedy properties have remained in Maltese hands until this day.

Albanian criminals inevitably drifted towards the district. Some found work as bouncers at legitimate clubs and bars; others were hired as muscle at less salubrious establishments. Once they'd had a close-up look at the Maltese operation, they decided they could do better. As the journalist Ben Judah wrote in his book *This Is London*, it was relatively easy for the violent Albanian mobsters, many of them killers who'd gunned down rivals during the 1997 crisis, to wrest control from the Maltese:

> "The Albanians disdained them as weak Soho bisexuals in pink bow ties and floral shirts selling only ugly girls from Newcastle upon Tyne. Barely warm in their leather jackets, smoking cigarettes at four in the morning outside the Maltese brothels on Greek Street, they hatched a plan. They would conquer Soho. The first Maltese to fall went on his knees when the bouncers pointed a gun at his head. Quivering and pathetic in his purple jacket he agreed to sell up. But now they needed girls. Girls who were better and cheaper. One Albanian got in a truck and drove to Moldova. They trundled around the peasant villages promising glittering careers in waitressing and modelling. Then they raped and trafficked them."

It was a simplified retelling of events, but the essence of the takeover was true enough. The psychopathic killer Mane Driza was one of the muscle men who beat the Maltese into submission. But while there probably wasn't one single gang member who "got in a truck" to source the girls, there were a number of high-profile pimps.

One such figure was Mustapha Kadiu. In 2002, he was convicted of enslaving a fifteen-year-old girl trafficked across Europe from Romania. She was brought to London on false papers, raped, threatened with a knife and forced to work for up to twenty hours a day in numerous brothels. She eventually escaped with the help of a sympathetic brothel maid. Kadiu was jailed for ten years for one count of rape, two counts of indecent assault and two counts of living off prostitution. His cousin, Edmond Ethemi, was jailed for a total of six-and-a-half years for possessing cocaine with intent to supply, and for living on his wife's immoral earnings.

By the end of 2002, Albanian organised crimes gangs had seized around seventy-five per cent of vice, not just in Soho, but around the country, including in Liverpool, Glasgow, Edinburgh, Hull and Telford. Police raids in Soho found that about seventy per cent of the girls were ethnic Albanians. The reason was two-fold. Besides their propensity for violence and fearsome reputations, the Albanians could source the most beautiful girls from Eastern Europe and ensure that punters never got bored by shunting them around the country through their wider criminal networks.

One pimp in particular became a master of the system. Luan Plakici arrived in Britain as a Kosovan asylum seeker in 1996. Needless to say, Plakici was actually from Albania. In any case, he soon found work as an interpreter for a solicitor specialising in immigration cases. That job enabled him to become an expert on Britain's immigration laws. At one point, he even appeared on a BBC documentary on the subject as a talking head. In 1999, Plakici obtained British citizenship and then a passport, which would become the key to his empire of vice.

Travelling around Eastern Europe, Plakici sought out "poor, naive and gullible" women, mainly from Romania and Moldova. Using the well-honed 'lover-boy' method of recruitment, Plakici seduced and then persuaded them to return with him to Britain. He destroyed their passports and issued them with fakes to get past immigration. But once they were back at his lair in Golders Green, North London, they were coldly informed that they would now be working as prostitutes to repay their £8,000 travel bill. Any disagreement was met with violence, rape, and threats against their families back home. Plakici later admitted to "helping" at least sixty women into the UK, but admitted trafficking only a handful.

Plakici's enterprise was only brought down after two kidnapped Romanian sisters, aged seventeen and twenty-four, managed to escape and alert the police. They had been told that they would work as waitresses, but were instead trafficked through Europe and forced to work in brothels. At trial, another woman, aged twenty, from Moldova, told the court how she had been just sixteen when she was taken first to Italy on a precarious boat with thirty other people, and then flown to Heathrow and escorted through customs with fake documents. She was later sent by Plakici to claim asylum as a Chechen refugee.

"He just said to us that whatever we thought we were going to do, we were not going to do it. We are going to work for him as prostitutes. He is going to be our boss," she explained. The woman earned up to £500 a day, giving half to Plakici and half to the brothel maid.

Seven of Plakici's victims bravely gave evidence at the trial. Most of the girls told similar stories. They were forced to service up to twenty men a day, seven days a week. The women were supplied to brothels in North London, Bedford, Luton and Reading. In a demented twist, it emerged that Plakici had even married one teenager, before brutally ordering the girl to spend her wedding night working as a prostitute. He later forced her to have two abortions, making her return to 'work' within hours of each one. She earned him £144,000 in two years.

Plakici spent his profits on designer clothes, a string of luxury homes across Europe — including a "palace" in Albania — sports cars and at casinos. When he was arrested, he had splashed out on a Ferrari Spider just twenty-four hours earlier. He also had £200,000 stashed in various bank accounts, although cops believed he made at least £1.2 million.

After three weeks of deliberations, a jury found Plakici guilty of three counts of kidnapping, one of procuring a teenager to have unlawful sex and incitement to rape, and three of living on prostitution. Another man, Ismet Islami, twenty, of Palmers Green, north London, was found not guilty of one count of rape.

Sentencing Plakici to ten years, Judge Robert Winstanley said, "The idea of selling human beings is one of the most repugnant. You took cynical advantage of the fact that these young women led lives of considerable hardship in their own countries. Young women in these circumstances were easy prey to you and your false promises to better their lives."

Speaking outside the court, Detective Chief Inspector Mark Holmes described Plakici as a "violent and unfeeling pimp". His sentence was later increased to twenty-three years, after the Court of Appeal found it had been "unduly lenient".

By the summer of 2004, it was being reported that Albanian mafia-led operations in Soho were worth at least £15 million a year, and that Albanians owned at least eighty per cent of the trade there. In total, police believed at least 12,000 Eastern European women were working in Britain as prostitutes.

The takeover of Britain's sex trade was described as a "bloodless coup" by some reporters. But that only seemed to be as far as the competition — the Maltese and East London gangs — were concerned. Hundreds, if not thousands, of women suffered and the profits were re-invested in other areas of crime, such as drugs and weapons trafficking. Meanwhile — elsewhere in London — there was open warfare between new Albanian arrivals and established organised crime gangs.

TURF WARS, PART TWO

Britain's underworld has no secret ceremonies, *omerta*, or codes of honour, unless you count the Masonic handshake. There is certainly no Commission overseeing it all. In fact, like the Albanian mafia, British crime groups are often small, autonomous and family-based. And their bread and butter activities are no different to those of any mafia-style organization, namely extortion, robbery, fraud and drug trafficking, the latter an industry which only really emerged in the late 1980s.

By the late 1990s, when both Albania and Kosovo were in a state of flux and spewing organised crime networks into Western Europe,

London's serious organised squads were already dealing with dozens of native family-based crime syndicates.

One particular investigation narrowed in on eight East and North London families, each with close ties to corrupt police officers, who were accused of frustrating investigations and even murder probes by destroying evidence or tipping gang bosses off about surveillance. Only a handful of charges were ever brought, but we know about the cases because of a leaked report, dubbed *Operation Tiberius*, which identified the gangs and the corrupt officers. Many of the deeply disturbing allegations are too libelous to print, although the report can be found on the internet. But equally interesting — for the purposes of this book — was the level of detail provided about the gangs' drug trafficking operations.

For example, one firm based in East London was suspected of importing large quantities of cannabis, cocaine and amphetamine. The drugs were hidden inside lorry loads of flowers from Holland.[33] The trucks would arrive at Dover having crossed by ferry from Rotterdam. They would then be taken to a front business at the New Covent Garden market, but would be diverted *en route* to a service station on the M2 to be unloaded into another vehicle and then driven to a safe house in Loughton. The gangsters would then arrange a sale and deliver the drugs to the buyers.

The highly sophisticated and violent group was also heavily involved in lorry hijacking, a sideline that helped them develop contacts with qualified HGV drivers, who they then recruited to traffic drugs. On one occasion, police in Scotland believed a three-kilo consignment of cocaine had been delivered to a major drug dealer through one of their men recruited primarily for the robberies.[34] When one deal went wrong, an enforcer allegedly

---

[33] In June 2001, the head of the crime family organised a shipment of one ton of cannabis from Thailand. It was set to arrive in the UK from Holland, hidden in a container load of Oriental vases. The firm owned a legitimate furniture business which had imported ceramic pots and vases from the Far East for years. It was managed by a man who'd already served nine years in France for drug trafficking.

[34] Sometimes, the hijacking and cigarette businesses could be combined. The Tiberius report detailed the aftermath of one such hijacking, where a tense armed operation was launched to try and catch the gang as it ambushed a Spanish lorry

blinded another man in a vicious attack. The gang also diversified into counterfeit cigarettes and alcohol, with one of its key leaders personally travelling to China to place orders.

One of the eight syndicates mentioned in the report was run by the notorious crime lord John 'Goldfinger' Palmer, who was gunned down at his home in Brentwood, Essex, in 2015. A crew led by his chief money launderers was said to be involved in shipping cannabis and cocaine from Spain and distributing it across North East London and Essex, with their main areas of activity being centered on Chigwell and Buckhurst Hill. Another member was said to have done a deal with Turkish criminals to import forty kilos of heroin.

Three of the crime syndicates had ethnic Turkish or Greek bosses and appeared to be even more deeply involved with drugs. One had enlisted the help of a number of corrupt detectives, two of whom had themselves stolen a kilo of cocaine and sold it to gang bosses for £12,000.

In one case, a villain looking after several kilos of heroin in a stash house for one of the Turkish gangs had his fingers chopped off with garden sheers after becoming the victim of a "robbery". The head of the group was eventually jailed for eighteen years for drug trafficking.

One of the Greek gangs, based in Green Lanes, North London, had links with some of the same corrupt officers, and two of the cops even part-owned two racehorses with the gang's leading members. They were also involved in property deals together. The Greeks were labelled significant players in "large scale importation and distribution of heroin". All of the gangs were linked to dozens of murders and other violent attacks.

At around the same time, Albanian mafia groups began very quietly organising their own importation and distribution networks. As we shall see, the scale of their operations would go on to dwarf

---

carrying fags and booze valued at £850,000. The driver was attacked, tied up, and driven away in a van. The robbers were traced to a yard in Dagenham but escaped when a cop's radio was picked up by their counter-surveillance equipment.

those of the traditional families who, at the turn of the millennium, were some of Britain's most sophisticated criminals.

The Albanians saw that most of the heroin being trafficked by the London families, and those in Britain's other major drugs hub, Liverpool, was being obtained through Turkish godfathers. Cannabis was coming from Asia or Holland, and cocaine was coming from Spain or Holland via traditional smuggling routes favoured by the South American cartels. Only a few of the English gangs (usually from Liverpool) had any direct dealings with the cartels, so most were paying huge mark-ups to middlemen.

Indeed, one former lorry driver who made thousands working for some of East London's most notorious organised crime groups, told me he often only went as far as Holland to collect shipments and then returned on the ferry.

"I didn't always know who I was working for," he said. "There were people who would tell you where to pick [the trailer] up from and where to bring it back to. Then it gets unloaded, you get paid, and you're on your way. I did it hundreds of times and never got caught. I usually never knew what was in the load."

It wasn't his concern, but the gang bosses were paying huge mark-ups to the criminals who arranged the shipments to Holland.

The Albanians figured they could do better. With the collapse of Communism across Eastern Europe, the Balkan Route became a major pipeline for heroin coming into Europe. Albanian drug barons were beginning to rival the Turkish godfathers and could move their heroin inside Britain through their own distribution networks. In Albania, in places such as Lazarat and Lushnje, farmers were growing vast quantities of cannabis for export. Meanwhile, crews based on the other side of the Atlantic, such as the Thaqi Network, were making deals with the South American cartels and having huge consignments of cocaine shipped to European ports. Thousands of kilos of blow could now be unloaded by Albanian gangsters, driven through Europe by Albanians and then sold on the streets of London, Birmingham and Manchester by Albanians. If the whole operation could be conducted by one single network then all the better, but in any case the all-Albanian trafficking model was saving millions.

Just like vice, it was another almost silent takeover. There was very little conflict with the London crime families, because the firms didn't really twig what was going on until it was too late. If anything, the Albanian connection was beneficial to the home-grown mobs.

In 2001, one of the crime syndicates named in the *Operation Tiberius* report — an Irish-led crew with some of the country's most corrupt police officers on its books — began working with an Albanian gang based in Italy. The report detailed how the crime boss's "right-hand man" had been scouring Europe for new contacts and was arranging a shipment of 100 kilos of cocaine from Albania concealed in a shipment of metal pipes. The lorry was stopped by the Italian authorities but they were unable to find the drugs and the shipment was sent on its way.

In truth, while the major British syndicates were widely feared, Albanian organised crime groups looking for inroads into Britain had few reasons to come into conflict with them. For one thing, the leaders of some of the groups were beset by legal problems. These included the Adams Family, from North London, the John Palmer Syndicate and the Turkish and Greek outfits. Others organisations, principally a notorious Essex-based family, were increasingly distancing themselves from organised crime and shifting into the legitimate worlds of property and entertainment. There was also the fact that while the syndicates were all involved to a certain degree in drug trafficking — as well as their core businesses of protection, extortion, money laundering and fraud — they were all minor players compared with the true kings of the heroin world — the Turkish mafia.

The Godfather of Green Lanes

From the 1980s to the early 2000s one name was synonymous with the heroin trade across the whole of Europe — Baybasin. This Turkish-Kurdish clan, while partly based in London, was organisationally worlds apart from Britain's traditional crime families. The clan oversaw not just the trafficking of heroin and cannabis to almost every major European city, but also controlled the refining process in Turkey of raw opium harvested in places like Afghanistan and Iran. While there were many other players in the heroin market, such as the "Grey Wolf" Daut Kadriovski, none were as big as the Baybasins.

The clan originally hailed from the Kurdish village of Lice, in the south east of Turkey. They had family all over the world, many of them involved in organised crime, but its leaders were undoubtedly Huseyin Baybasin, born in 1957, and his brother Abduallah, born in 1960. By the late 1970s the pair were overseeing opium refineries set up in villages close to their hometown. By the early 1980s, they were making millions exporting the drug to Europe. At the height of their powers, the Baybasins were thought to control up to ninety percent of Britain's heroin market, worth as much as £10 billion.

Huseyin described his early years in Istanbul in an extraordinary interview with researchers Frank Bovenkerk and Yucel Yesilgoz in 1997, for their book *The Turkish Mafia*.

"We formed a group and everyone started to get scared of me," he said, "because I was unusual. 'Spider', they called me, because I was involved in everything...I always visibly carried a weapon, the police could see it and everyone on the street: a gun."

Huseyin hinted that he had used his gun more than once, disposing of it once a year in a town that did not do ballistic investigations for Istanbul. He went on to claim that he helped traffic drugs for the Turkish state, organised false flag attacks for the right-wing government that allowed left-wing activists to be rounded-up, and even took part in plots that resulted in activists being slaughtered. On another occasion, he said, he helped to murder four people, including two child molesters, in prison. Eventually, Huseyin said he saw the error of his ways, politically, and started to fund the Kurdish PKK.

In the early 1980s, Huseyin set up a travel agency with twenty-eight coaches at its disposal. They were not used to smuggle drugs, but to transport huge bundles of cash back from England, Holland, Germany and Belgium. Baybasin didn't use the Balkan Route at all. Instead, the drugs were mostly flown from Turkey to Azerbaijan, or to Uzbekistan, Turkmenistan and then onto Russia. The substances needed to refine the opium, "thousands and thousands of tonnes" of water, calcium and other chemicals, were flown in the opposite direction. Everything was allegedly done with direct government involvement.

In 1984, a British court sentenced Baybasin to twelve years in prison for drugs offences, although unknown to the authorities he was living under an assumed name. After five years, the Turkish government engineered a prisoner exchange and he was then sent to a prison in his homeland. However, Huseyin claimed that he refused to work again for the state and was tortured, before being released and made the target of a hit squad. He fled Turkey to live in Holland where, in 1998, he received a twenty-year sentence for drug trafficking and conspiracy to murder. The sentence was increased to life in 2002.

It then fell to his brother Abdullah to take control of the family business. Even though the drug lord was left wheelchair-bound after being shot in the spine during a shootout in an Amsterdam bar in the 1980s, he never let it hold him back. Abdullah settled in Edgeware, North London, in 1997. In addition to the drug game, Abdullah also set up a vast protection racket targeting cafes, kebab shops and other businesses on the six-mile stretch of Green Lanes and the surrounding areas.

Abdullah adopted the nickname Uncle and controlled his empire from the back room of a scruffy shop in Haringey, which he visited twice a week. He was caught on surveillance footage there behaving like Don Corleone in the *Godfather* as he beckoned local businessmen to lean forward and kiss his ring finger. He also spoke in a malevolent whisper, forcing his followers to lean in attentively as he spoke. Cops dubbed him the "Godfather of Green Lanes".

Another occasion caught on film was much less comical — a man was dragged to the floor, stripped, and threatened with castration by machete. Just a year after setting up home in London, police raided his £1.2m seven-bedroom home and found a gun next to Abdullah's bed. He served some time in jail, but his organisation was barely affected.

In every industry there is always a younger generation, keen to take the place of their more experienced colleagues. But Abdullah was clever. He co-opted hordes of young Kurdish thugs into a new gang, the Bombacilar, or Hackney Bombers, and used them as his enforcers in an extortion and robbery racket that victimised the Turkish community across North London.

Some business owners paid up to £10,000 a year in protection, and for good reason. On one occasion, a mob of twenty armed Bombacilar raided a café in Stoke Newington armed with Samurai swords and a gun, where they fired shots and then chopped a man's finger off.

The Bombacilar soon came to the attention of London's branch of the Kurdish PKK, which vowed to protect the Kurdish victims. On November 9, 2002, a mass brawl erupted between the two groups in Green Lanes. One man, Alisan Dogan, forty-three, was stabbed to death and four others were shot and injured. Dogan, an innocent customer in a nearby café who had earlier dropped off his disabled son at a respite centre, had nothing to do with either group.

The Baybasin organisation also faced other enemies. On July 12, 2002, London's detectives found themselves investigating a direct shootout between Albanian and Turkish gangsters. The Albanians had been gradually encroaching onto Baybasin turf, wholesaling heroin shipped to Britain along the Balkan Route from Turkey but bypassing the godfathers' organisation.

Back in January of that year, Edmund Gulhaj had lost his life during a gun battle with other Albanian gangsters in Palmers Green. It had brought the issue into the limelight, and the Bombacilar were ordered to send a message. The two groups faced down outside a car showroom in Wood Green, next to the Nightingale pub and just two doors down from the police station.

It's not known who drew their weapons first, but at least thirty-five shots were fired, sending passers-by diving for cover. One man was injured in the shootout, but he fled the scene, leaving a trail of blood, before anyone could work out whether he was Albanian or Turkish. Police were there in seconds, but they were all unarmed so there was little they could do. They recovered thousands of pounds in cash, two handguns, including a .45 Magnum pistol, and arrested nine men. The rest fled in a car.

One copper described it as "like a scene out of Gunfight At The O.K. Corral or the St Valentine's Day Massacre. There was a gang of men inside the garage shooting out and a gang outside shooting in".

139

By now, the Albanians had allied themselves to the Bombacilar's natural enemies on the other side of North London, the Tottenham Boys, another Turkish-Kurdish street gang fronting for a rival cartel of Turkish godfathers.[35] This was not a simple postcode war, of the type common today among London's street gangs. Between 1997 and 2006, a series of turf disputes involving the Bombacilar and Tottenham Boys resulted in twenty-five murders, with dead on both sides.

One former Tottenham Boy agreed to meet me far from the Turkish mafia's usual North London stomping ground, at a café in Hither Green near Brixton, South London. He spoke to me on condition of strict anonymity, and didn't even want to be identified by a pseudonym in case his former colleagues went after someone else.

"I don't want a mistaken identity on my conscience," he said.

The man described how Albanians arriving in London at the turn of the century had been "easy to get along with" even though they were simultaneously trying to muscle in on Turkish turf.

"They weren't about being big men, but they let you know they could handle themselves if they had to" he said. "They were into the same things as us, heroin and weed. Everything seemed to be easy for them, or they made it seem easy, so they were good people to deal with. Fair. Never any problems. We started dealing with them [for drug supplies], because we knew the feds were watching our people but not the Albanians. It was safer. They could also supply guns. They helped us out with a lot of problems." When I asked whether that meant committing murders or supplying weapons, he smiled. "Problems turned into no problems," he replied.

In December 2003, the Metropolitan Police raided fifteen addresses in a bid to smash the Bombacilar and the Baybasin

---

[35] The Tottenham Boys were also involved in large-scale drug trafficking. One 1998 case had seen two gang members unable to drive their oversized lorry through the Blackwall Tunnel, blocking traffic for miles. When police came to investigate, they found sixty-six kilos of brown worth an estimated £7.2 million hidden in the load. They were also involved in other high profile cases in which heroin was distributed to places such as Liverpool, Birmingham, Leeds, Manchester and Dublin.

organisation. They seized guns, drugs, fake passports and uncovered a torture chamber hidden behind a reinforced door in a bedsit off Green Lanes. The grim cell included two meat hooks on the ceiling and lengths of electric cable for stringing up prisoners. Around 300 people were arrested and at least six members were jailed for a total of sixty-eight years, including two men for the attempted murder of another Turkish man on a garage forecourt in Tottenham in October 2003.

Abdullah Baybasin was also brought to justice after a painstaking case put together by cops probing a 2001 heroin deal. Six people were initially arrested, but it took several years to gather enough evidence to nail the Godfather of Green Lanes.

On May 15, 2006, Abdullah Baybasin, then aged forty-five, was sentenced to a total of twenty-two years in prison for conspiracy to supply 2.2 kilos of heroin, a drop in the ocean compared with the vast quantities he'd dealt in over the years, and a separate charge of blackmail, or demanding money with menaces. It emerged during the trial that his brother Huseyin had been an informant for Customs and Excise, to whom he supplied information about Turkish politicians tied up with the heroin trade. It was a murky business and lead to speculation that the entire Baybasin clan had been given special treatment by the authorities.[36]

---

[36] Abdullah later won a retrial on the drugs charges after the Court of Appeal found the original judge's summing up had been unfair. A judge at Woolwich crown court then ordered the new jury to find him not guilty, because of a lack of evidence. Abdullah was moments from being released from Belmarsh Prison when the then-Home Secretary Theresa May ordered deportation proceedings to begin. He was released after a habeas corpus writ and later won a £20,000 payout from the Home Office over the discriminatory treatment he received during the total of six years he spent inside. Abdullah said other inmates had to bathe and clothe him because there were no facilities for disabled prisoners.

Despite winning his freedom, and subsequently being deported, Abdullah stayed in the drugs game. In 2011, he was arrested alongside his son Cagdas and thirteen other people after a boat was impounded in the Ambarli docks in Istanbul. Police found 281.5 kilos of cocaine on board, hidden among wooden pallets. The boat was reportedly owned by Baybasin and had sailed from Bolivia. It was Turkey's biggest ever blow bust. Baybasin was jailed for forty years, a sentence later knocked down on appeal. He was released from prison in 2017, but he is still barred from Britain.

Another Baybasin brother, Mehmet, then forty-eight, was jailed for thirty years in 2011 for running a major heroin pipeline up to a bunch of Liverpool drugs barons. The group had also planned to import cocaine worth around £4 billion directly from Colombia.

The fall of the Baybasin clan sparked an all-out war between the next generation of North London's Turkish gangs, which were less well-organised and more prone to bouts of extreme violence. In January 2009, members of the Bombacilar and the Tottenham Boys got into a fight at the latter's Manor Club pool hall in Wood Green. The Bombers' leader, Kemal Armagan, was given a literal slap in the face, and vowed bloody revenge. Two months later, innocent shopkeeper Ahmet Paytak, fifty, was gunned down in a case of mistaken identity by a Bombacilar hitman. That October, a Tottenham Boy was shot to death at the wheel of his Range Rover in front of his five-year-old stepson. Then, three days later, a man fired dozens of bullets from an automatic weapon into Hackney's Clapton FC club, where Bombacilar members were hanging out. An innocent bystander, Cem Duzgun, aged twenty-one, was shot eleven times while playing pool. He died at the scene. A leading Tottenham Boy was later jailed for a minimum of thirty-three years. Then, in February 2012, Kemal Armagan's brother Ali, thirty-two, was shot dead as he sat in his Audi near Turnpike Lane Tube. More shootings followed in both London and Turkey.

A report by the National Criminal Intelligence Service in 2003 outlined the roles being taken on by Albanian criminals in Britain at the time, detailing how they had "successfully established themselves as significant suppliers of heroin in several parts of the EU, including Switzerland, Italy and parts of Scandinavia". But, it added:

> "Thus far, these groups have not been seen to play a significant role in UK heroin importation or wholesale distribution. Instead, some ethnic Albanian criminals have been acting as enforcers or security for Turkish trafficking groups, following a pattern that was established in those European

countries where ethnic Albanians now dominate the heroin trade. The potential threat in the UK from ethnic Albanian criminals is therefore considered to be significant."

By the end of the Turkish gang wars and the fall of the Baybasin clan, Albanians had indeed become much more significant. It wasn't quite the case that they hadn't fired a shot during those early years in Britain, and we might never know exactly how 'hands on' some had been during the carnage in North London.

But now, in the aftermath of the Turkish gang war, they found they had a unique advantage. There was more room in the heroin market, and everyone knew they could move tons of the stuff through the Balkans. And unlike the Baybasin mob and the English crime families, the Albanian gangs based in Britain had no need to travel to South America to arrange huge cocaine shipments themselves. By now, they only had to hit up their contacts back home in Albania to agree huge multi-kilo deals — something the established families in Britain simply couldn't do. Instead of paying upwards of £22,500 a kilo, like many of their competitors, each kilo could cost them as little as £4,000.

What followed can fairly be called a torrent of Albanian-sourced cocaine, flooding almost every major city in the country. And in the years to come, one gang based in Barking would gain particular notoriety — The Hellbanianz.

HELLBANIANZ

The morning of January 25, 2016, began just like any other for Renaz Ameen. The mother-of-two woke up early, at about 5.30am. She roused her children and packed them off to school. Then she headed to work at Mr Dweeb Computer Repairs in Park Road, Crouch End, North London. After exchanging early morning pleasantries with her manager, she settled down to her work. Moments later, the Albanian mafia literally came crashing into her life.

"I couldn't see the car," she later told London's *Evening Standard* newspaper. "The glass was coming towards me in waves and it was all going in my face. It was like something out of The Matrix. It wasn't stopping so I just dived over the counter, landed on some boxes and hit my head on the wall. I hid behind some boxes because I thought it was a bomb. I didn't know when it was going to stop."

Fortunately for Renaz, the dramatic crash into the shopfront was the end — not the beginning — of a major gangland incident. Just minutes earlier, undercover cops had observed Tristen Asllani, aged twenty-nine, a senior member of the Hellbanianz gang, as he stood outside a property in nearby Avenue Road. They watched as he handed a suitcase to another man, Arber Beqaj, twenty-four. The younger man then climbed into a red Toyota Prius, with another gangster, Ndricim Musaj, also twenty-four, and the pair left the area. The Toyota was pulled over by police nine minutes later. In the boot, they found a blue suitcase with twelve bricks of cocaine, weighing a combined thirteen kilos.

Asllani knew nothing about the traffic stop. He went into the address, where he was seen taking a lift to the sixth floor, up to a flat leased in his name. He stopped to speak to a maintenance man — who was in fact an undercover police officer — and emerged from the building fifteen minutes later with another suitcase and a rucksack. He put the bags in the back of a six-year-old black Volkswagen Passat, registered in Northern Ireland, and drove away. When cops turned on their blue lights and sirens and sped up behind Asllani's motor, he slammed his foot on the accelerator.

It wasn't really much of a car chase. Less than two minutes later, Asllani lost control as he turned a corner into Park Road, smashing head first into the computer shop. Although he was battered and bruised, Asllani somehow managed to walk free from the wreckage and stumbled down a side street close to the scene. Cops scrambled the helicopter and Asllani was soon cornered by specially trained police dogs.

Police found twenty-one kilos of cocaine in his car and £1,281 in cash on his person. When officers searched his flat, they found another six kilos of cocaine, 16.5 kilos of cannabis and a Scorpion submachine gun, fitted with a silencer, as well as around £6,000 in cash. Luckily, Asllani had decided not to take the gun with him in the car, because it was fully loaded with the safety catch off.

Asllani also had photographs of two other men seen leaving the flat earlier in the day, suggesting that they were buyers who Asllani needed to be able to recognise. It was clear that Asllani, Beqaj and Musaj were part of a major criminal conspiracy. Documents in the flat suggested that the gang had actually been involved in handling at least sixty-four kilos of cocaine with an estimated street value of more than £6.4 million.

Following their convictions, Scotland Yard described Asllani as the ringleader, saying his "reckless attempt to avoid capture endangered the public in the area and caused damage to private property. This dangerous network has been convicted and that their stock will not be sold on the streets of London."

But how exactly did these three men fit into the pattern of Albanian organised crime in Britain?

Facing the prospect of a lengthy trial at Kingston crown court, Asllani pleaded guilty to conspiracy to supply drugs and dangerous driving. After a short trial over the Scorpion submachine gun, he was found guilty of possession of a firearm with intent to endanger life. Beqaj also pleaded guilty to the conspiracy, while Musaj was found guilty after a trial.

Giving evidence, Asllani admitted working for the gang as a driver since September 2015, and said he had previously worked alongside Beqaj in other criminal enterprises. The working relationship was clearly close — mobile phone evidence showed 180 contacts between them in the six months leading to the operation.

None of the men had previous convictions, in Britain at least. Asllani was the son of a policeman, and he had two children with his former wife back in Albania, as well as a three-month-old child in Britain. He maintained that he was only a driver, and evidence showed that he received text messages on his phones containing various postcodes. But the judge didn't buy it.

Sentencing Asllani to eleven years for the drugs offences and fourteen years for the gun charge, to run consecutively, giving a total of twenty-five years, the judge provided a long list of reasons as to why Asllani was a major player in the gang, including his name being on the lease for the flat where the drugs were stored; his supervision of the delivery and distribution of the drugs; possession of keys to the flat when arrested; his possession of photographs of other people involved; and "close links to the source of the cocaine" as evidenced by the purity of the powder, meaning that it hadn't yet been watered down by street dealers.

The other men had lesser roles. Musaj had been brought over recently from Albania to act as muscle. Musaj's lawyer described how he had left school aged seventeen and went to work in a wine factory, earning around £200 a month. He came to England to earn enough to send money back to his family. He didn't really know, or care, what he would be doing. Indeed, Musaj had only been in the country for three or four days when the raid took place.

As for Beqaj, he too claimed to be nothing more than a runner, although he also admitted to working with Asllani in a drugs gang in the past. His lawyer went on to describe how Beqaj became involved, claiming there had been "an element of him being engaged by pressure and coercion, and to some extent he has been exploited". He said Beqaj had been living in Britain as an Albanian national when he was approached in a café.

"He was invited outside by two large gentleman who knew of him, knew of his family, and told him that he had a debt through his father regarding the sale of land in Albania," the lawyer said. "He doesn't in any way suggest that there was duress or that anyone pointed a gun at his head or that there was a significant threat to life, but he was intimidated and he was in effect recruited by these two men, who told him that he would be doing jobs for them to repay the debt, and that is how he came to be involved in this offence."

Beqaj, he added, came from a "good family," had no previous convictions and had "found being in custody extremely difficult, it is a wholly alien environment to him and certainly the attitudes of many that he finds inside are wholly alien to him".

In the end, Beqaj received eight years, while Musaj was sentenced to nine years behind bars. Two things that the court case didn't establish was where the drugs had originally come from and where they were destined to go. But the high-profile nature of the case did put Asllani's wider associations with the Hellbanianz in the spotlight.

ADDICTED TO ACTION

As Britain's Albanian population grew in the post pyramid crisis and Kosovo war years, Barking's criminal contingent coalesced around one gang — the Albanian Troops. They were nothing much to write home about. The Troops weren't the biggest mob in Barking, or even on the Gascoigne Estate. But somewhere along the line the next generation morphed into the Hellbanianz— a wholly different proposition. By the end of 2018, the gang was making serious money by supplying other dealers in the area with cocaine and cannabis smuggled into the country through extended mafia networks.

The nature of Britain's Albanian street gangs can be hard to get your head around because they frequently work together, unlike other postcode crews. There are the Albanian Boys, in Bromley, South London. Then there are the Real Albanian Gangsters (RAG) and Young Albanian Gunnerz (YAG) based in Wood Green, North London. Further afield, Albanian drug dealing gangs are known to operate in Bournemouth, Norwich, Birmingham, Manchester and Northampton, among other towns and cities. Most don't have a name as such, but thanks to the fame achieved by the Barking mob, locals often refer to them as Hellbanianz. And if the originals don't like their name being appropriated then tough — that's the price of fame.

Unlike most street gangs and criminals in general, the Hellbanianz have worked hard on social media to convince the general public of their central role in London's new underworld. For example, despite his long sentence, Tristen Asllani re-remerged into the public sphere unexpectedly in early 2018.

His image had appeared on an Instagram account called "My Albanian in Jail". The gangster was shirtless, his chest and shoulders massive, as if he'd set about his sentence with a determination to eventually emerge from prison bigger and stronger than when he went in. He was grinning and making a 'devil horn' gesture with fingers on both otherwise clenched fists. The photo was captioned with the phrase, "Even inside the prison we have all conditions, what's missing are only whores." It caused a minor media storm.

The computer shop worker who he'd nearly killed, Renaz, spoke about Asllani's brazen disregard for the rules of prion, where mobile phones and social media accounts are supposedly banned.

"He doesn't care, he looks really happy in prison," she said. "He looks like he has just been in the gym the whole time and is having fun in there."

The photo received predictable opprobrium in the British tabloid press, with the *Sunday Express* leading the charge. As a result, the Instagram and YouTube antics of Asllani's numerous gang colleagues in Barking also came under greater scrutiny.

In some ways, there isn't much to separate the Hellbanianz from other typical Rich Kids of Instagram — those brash, moneyed youngsters who use social media to flaunt their lavish lifestyles, usually only made possible because of their wealthy parents. Their Instagram accounts are envy-inducing — Hellbanianz members wear £20,000 watches on their wrists, sometimes more than one at a time. Their stories feature selfies taken on helicopter rides and private jets, and meals at exclusive five-star restaurants. There are also images featuring stacks and stacks of cash, supercars — including a gold-plated Mercedes Benz — and other trappings of wealth that might make even the most overpaid Premier League footballer jealous.

The dozens of young men posting under the hashtag even share a logo— two pistols placed barrel-to-barrel and facing upside down, mimicking the double-headed eagle of the Albanian national flag. The symbol is emblazoned on sports jackets, fashioned into gold jewellery and tattooed onto members' skin. Then there are the real-life handguns and automatic weapons spread over tables already teeming with banknotes, bullets, and gold rings. In another snap, huge bundles of £20 and £50 notes are lined up in a pattern on the floor, snaking across the room for several feet. And if there was any doubt about the dubious activities of these young men, some of their accounts show other members of the gang, like Asllani, posing in their prison cells, the initials "HB" scrawled in marker pen on the walls.

The Hellbanianz also produce slick and admittedly catchy rap videos. Performed in Albanian but filmed on the streets of London, most non-Albanians would need a translator to know for sure that the lyrics are about drug dealing and violence. But the visual tropes are no different to those seen in the genre for decades — gang and gun signs, plenty of bling and voluptuous women. One track, called Hood Life, was shot in front of their former Rookwood House base on the Gascoigne Estate and features lyrics boasting that the "gango" is "taking over" and "addicted to action". Their YouTube videos, which contain the disclaimer that the makers "do not condone violence of any kind," have raked in tens of thousands in revenue.

The two main rappers performing under the Hellbanianz umbrella are Ervin "Vinz" Selita and Fatjon "Stealth" Dibra. Some of their lyrics include references to jailed gang members such as Azem "Ziro" Dajci and Fabion "Gucci" Kuci.[37] By June 2019, the videos on the branded Hellbanianz YouTube account had received more than

---

[37] According to the Sunday Express (8.12.19) Dajci, Kuci and another gang member, Ardi Sheta, armed themselves with a gun and machete and raided a Romanian cannabis factory in Hendon in November 2018. Dajci was tasered by cops, but managed to pull out the wires and flee in a car, ramming a police vehicle as he made off. According to the report, Dajci is the owner of a gold-plated Mercedes with the number plate HE11 BOZ, which features in many of the gang's videos.

twenty million views and the account had 90,000 subscribers. If the group earns a conservative $3 per view 1,000 views, the gang could be pulling in hundreds of thousands of dollars through legitimate musical efforts alone.

Many of the Instagram accounts were closed down following the first wave of publicity, although new ones soon appeared, with fresh updates as members continued to flaunt their wealth and gangster lifestyles. Months later, some members had apparently relocated to Tirana where they appeared to be living in luxury accommodation and playing gigs to adoring crowds. But after the publicity had died down, locals in Barking and East London were still living in fear of the gang.

After their headquarters at Rookwood House was demolished at the end of 2018 as part of a council regeneration scheme, the Hellbanianz became more thinly spread across the borough and dispersed into North London. But the gang didn't need to actually reside on its main territory to keep the business thriving. It was still the borough's main supplier of cocaine and gang members had adopted a meeting spot outside the King's Lounge public house in Barking town centre.

When I paid a visit on a rainy Friday afternoon, one local business owner pointed out two members standing next to the pub, apparently street dealing.

"There you go," he said. "They are doing it out in the open, under a CCTV camera, but the police do nothing." Later on, more hoodlums gathered in luxury cars to rev their engines, openly smoke cannabis and intimidate passers-by.

"They don't give a fuck. It's like the law doesn't apply to them," another local told me. "They throw bottles, smoke, stab people. Even people just walking past can get stabbed," she said. "The pub is losing business because people won't walk past them to get there."

When I approached the group for an interview, I was forcefully warned to leave the area.

Eventually, I did arrange to meet two gang associates after messaging them on social media. One of the men, a skinny, hard-faced young man in his early 30s who I'll call Fatjon, barely spoke

English so we conducted our chat through his friend, Gentian. The interview took place in a white BMW parked in a supermarket car park in Beckton. Fatjon, who gave off an intentionally menacing air throughout, sat in the back alongside Gentian, while I sat in the front passenger seat. A third man, the driver, stood chain-smoking nearby. Fatjon explained why some gang members were involved in low-level dealing while others, such as Asllani, were moving much larger quantities.

"Albanians never have a boss," he said. "We are a family and we support each other. Some people can make the arrangements [for big deals], so maybe they are higher up. Maybe I do not have such friends, but I do business and also make money [street dealing]. It is a way of life and one big family."

He went on to explain that what started out as a gang has morphed into a powerful brand across Western Europe and Albania.

"Not every Albanian in London is the same," he said. "But now, everyone thinks all Albanians are Hellbanianz. It is funny, but also a very good time to be an Albanian and making money because there is a certain reputation [that we have]. It has spread because of YouTube."

Those videos, he says, now act as a recruitment tool attracting youngsters back home to sign up with criminal gangs sending street dealers and footsoldiers to Western countries.

"They see the money we are making and then it is easier to find people who want to work. Everyone benefits from the [Hellbanianz] videos, really the chiefs should be paying us [to make them]."

Another young man living in the borough gave me a different perspective on the capital's Albanian organised crime scene. Besmir (again, not his real name) had paid smugglers to bring him to Britain in the back of a lorry aged nineteen. Tall, good-looking and softly spoken, Besmir had high hopes. But he ended up in Dublin, where he found himself living with several other men in a crowded flat, cleaning cars by day for a pittance.

After a few weeks, two "big men with big black beards" arrived at the flat.

"They made me hand over my ID card and told me that from now on I would be working for them. I said nothing because they said they knew who I was and that my family would be hurt if I caused trouble," he said.

From Dublin, Besmir was trafficked to London, where he was quickly installed in an East London cannabis factory set up in a gutted residential home.[38]

"I have instructions to look after the plants, keep them growing well and to make sure the neighbours or police don't interfere. I do get some money but it's not much. I can't leave because I fear for my family," he said.

When I asked him whether the Hellbanianz were responsible for his predicament he shrugged and smiled.

"When I tell people I'm from Albania, they say *I'm* in Hellbanianz. It is something that people expect, I think," he said.

I later heard that the property where Besmir was living had been raided. I don't know what happened to him, whether he was arrested or simply moved to another part of the business, but I never heard from him again.

In March 2019 the National Crime Agency announced the result of a huge operation that saw raids on ten East London businesses, including car washes, restaurants and bars, and resulted in nine arrests. A thirty-seven-year-old woman was also arrested on suspicion of fraud and accused of falsifying around 500 UK passport applications for Albanians involved in organised crime. I couldn't help but think that Besmir had probably been one of them.

---

[38] A similar operation was uncovered in Chigwell, Essex, in January 2020. Albanian national Valmir Beqiri was found with 196 plants and jailed for twelve months. A much larger farm was found in Gateshead, Newcastle, in May that year. Three Albanian men were arrested in a warehouse the size of a football pitch, where more than 2,000 plants were being grown. The men claimed they had been brought to Britain by gangsters and forced to work for them.

CRACKDOWN

While the Hellbanianz use social media to boast that they oversee the entire London drugs supply, that isn't strictly the case. In truth, Britain's Albanian-led cocaine crimewave began well before Barking's most notorious gang was exposed in the tabloids.

One of Britain's first high-profile Albanian drugs cases actually unfolded in Glasgow, Scotland, in 2013. Arben Dumani and Albert "Diti" Memia headed up a four-man syndicate supplying cocaine to drug dealers across the country and the north of England. The case made headlines because of photos on Diti's phone that showed him snorting lines of cocaine laid out in his own nickname. The gang was nicked with a suitcase stuffed with cocaine worth £1.2 million and hydraulic presses for packaging the powder up into kilo deals. Dumani was jailed for twelve years, while Memia got ten years. He became something of an inspiration to other Albanian wannabe drugs lords, as evidenced by Hellbanianz members wearing "Free Diti" t-shirts in some of their videos.

A Birmingham-based crew led by Asmirald Miraka was busted in 2015. He brought millions of pounds worth of cocaine into Britain from Albania in specially adapted cars. Interestingly, two of his couriers were named Desar Asllani, and Aleks Asllani. It's not known whether they are related to Tristan. The syndicate was also tied to the network overseen by another major drug trafficker, Klodjan Copja. More on him later.

Miraka distributed to dealers in the city, as well as in Wolverhampton and Nottingham. Although police suspected hundreds of kilos had been smuggled into the country, they were only able to seize ten kilos. The Miraka network was not only vast, it was ethnically diverse. Wolverhampton dealers Levi Watson and Richard Chapman were part of the conspiracy, as well as Adam Whiteley, from Oldbury. Thirteen people were jailed in total, with Miraka getting sixteen years and the Asllani brothers ten years each.

Another gang of suppliers, based in Brent, was busted with £4 million worth of heroin and cocaine in 2015. Part-time model Olsi Beheluli, Besim Topalli, and Azem Proshka, were jailed for a total of thirty-one years. Beheluli had posed online with more than £240,000 in cash, money which he claimed was earned from gambling during the World Cup.

Cops in the capital broke up another large-scale operation in 2016. Gentian Cuka, Skender Toci, Abdul Tocu and Besnik Mansaku, were all involved in a plot to supply sixteen kilos of blow. At least six other members of the network, some of them British, were also jailed.

In 2017, police in Oxford disrupted a cocaine supply network run by Erald Mema, who frequently travelled between Britain and Albania. When he was nicked, cops found ten kilos of blow, a hydraulic press and £560,000 in cash. The network is thought to have supplied millions of pounds worth of cocaine in multi-kilo deals throughout the Midlands, Oxford and Bracknell. In total, nineteen members were convicted, including British-Indian Khalad Uddin, Mema's chief lieutenant and "national coordinator" who ensured drug dealing gangs got hold of the gear. He was jailed for sixteen years. Mema got twenty-five years.

At least one network broken up in London in 2017 had political connections back in Albania. Amarildo Fufi was the son of Democratic Party MP Mhill Fufi. He worked alongside Basmir Berberi and Mario Xhafa, both former professional footballers who played for the Albanian national team and Italian Serie C outfit Benevento Calcio respectively. Fufi, who also previously played for Partizan of Tirana, lived a luxury lifestyle, with access to a private Cessna jet, yacht and supercars.

The three men, alongside a fourth, Kamado Dishan, admitted being part of a conspiracy after a surveillance operation caught them transporting twenty kilos of cocaine, worth an estimated £2 million, from Peterborough to a house in Finchley. It appeared that they were not involved directly in the importation, but were buying large quantities from other Albanian nationals, then selling the drugs on to street dealers, with a purity of about eighty per cent.

Fufi was jailed for sixteen years, Berberi twelve years and Xhafa and Dishen to eight years each. Another man, Marius Paul, who was caught trying to buy a kilo from the gang, was jailed for five years. Surveillance also recorded the gang distributing kilo packages to other, unnamed, drug dealers.

These are only some of the most notable cases. Between 2013 and 2019, scores of other Albanians were caught in cocaine plots involving hundreds of kilos worth millions of pounds. But not every Albanian narco in Britain is on the supply side — plenty of sophisticated outfits also serve up drugs to the public.

One case that perfectly illustrates how street dealing Albanian gangs operate across territories and with a high degree of sophistication was uncovered in leafy Tunbridge Wells, in Kent. The town became famous in the nineteenth century as a resort favoured by royalty, including Queen Victoria and Prince Albert. Later, it established itself as the epitome of British middle-class suburbia, with a nearly ninety-eight percent white population of around 55,000 people. In the 1950s it found satirical fame as the bastion of Middle England after "Disgusted of Tunbridge Wells" was used as a sign off by a fictional letter writer to national newspapers. But in a twelve-month period in 2018, its residents did something unusual. They spent an estimated £4.2 million on cocaine.

The police described the operation as a "Deliveroo for drugs". The model was similar to any number of county lines running across the country, except for one ingenious twist — a "call centre" based forty miles away in South London.

This is how it worked: The gang operated two burner phones which were used only to receive and confirm orders at their base in Deptford. Once an order was received, a separate phone was used to tell the street dealers in Kent where to go. The call centre then replied to the customer to confirm that the delivery was on its way. It meant that even if the street dealers were picked up by cops, the order lines would remain active and the leaders would be insulated. It also afforded a degree of protection to the street dealers, because they would have no incriminating texts from customers on their phones.

The scheme began to unravel when one of the dealers, Ervish Dervishi, gave a lift to two undercover police officers posing as drug users. He told them to be quiet while on the phone to a boss because he wasn't allowed to have people in the car. This led to the officers buying from a number of the dealers and tracing the call centre numbers to London, where one of the gang, Rigels Hadashaj, was based. At other times, the numbers had been operating from an address in Romford, or from Surrey Quays, near Rotherhithe. Top-ups were purchased mainly in Tunbridge Wells by the street dealers, despite the phones never visiting those locations, again helping to insulate the top bosses.

Perhaps the scheme's turnover was overestimated by police (they based their numbers on 1,500 orders made to just one of the phone numbers in a single week) but there is no doubt the gang members were making vast profits. One member, Arlind Palushi, had more than £8,000 in cash and £2,000 worth of cocaine on him when he was arrested. In court, Dervishi was described as a "big time Charlie" who filmed himself throwing cash at an Albanian singer in a nightclub in Palmers Green, North London. Another conspirator, Nelson Aliaj, used profits to buy his mother-in-law new teeth and bought land and businesses in Albania. He also sent a 2017 Range Rover Sport back home to a pal. It was a pattern of behaviour seen time and time again from Albanian gangs in Britain.

157

But what stood out was the geographic spread of the operation. Clearly, it had bases in East and South London, while members also hung out in popular Albanian nightspots in North London. The street dealers were mostly living and working in Kent, while one of the men had an address eighty miles away in Colchester, Essex. Two of the gang members had even been stopped by police in Staffordshire, during an incident in which another Albanian man was arrested on suspicion of supplying cocaine following a car chase. What's more, at least five gang members were either not identified or failed to answer bail.

Clearly, what prosecutors called the "24/7 network" was part of a much larger, more complicated and geographically diverse criminal syndicate. Most gang members admitted being in Britain illegally. But Nelson Aliaj, Fitim Sadrija and co-defendant Fatos Metalia all claimed they had been coerced into taking part in the scheme, after gangsters threatened their families back home.

Extreme violence was also a feature of the case. The network was suspected of being involved in a stabbing that left another Albanian man with a punctured lung. Abedin Hoxhaj was a passenger in a silver VW Golf travelling along Forest Road, Tunbridge Wells, on July 16, 2018. Another car, a blue Vauxhall, crashed into it head-on. Four men, including Hoxhaj, got out of the Golf, while two got out of the Vauxhall. A fight ensued and shortly after a silver Range Rover pulled up. Two more men got out of that car and proceeded to attack Hoxhaj. No charges were brought, and it was never clear whether Hoxhaj was a part of the 24/7 network or a rival.

In any case, the order line briefly went down after the stabbing. When one of the undercover officers asked why, they were told by Arsid Metaj, "The phone was turned off due to some trouble." Another dealer explained, "There were too many police around."

Nine men were jailed for a combined fifty-eight years for conspiracy to supply cocaine. Sadrija was found not guilty. The jurors believed his claims that he had been coerced.

Whether they are on the supply or retail side, one thing common to most Albanian drug cases in Britain are claims that defendants have been coerced into leaving Albania. It's almost impossible to determine who is lying and who is telling the truth.

In June 2019, an investigation by the journalist Lindita Cela for the website *Balkan Insight* found many young Albanians, most from remote areas in the North such as Shkodra, Diber and Kukes counties, were indeed being recruited by mafia gangs. She focused on one case from Brighton, similar to the Tunbridge Wells cell, which had seen eight Albanians jailed in 2018. One of the men, Kadri Dema, was among 6,200 Albanians sent home between 2015 and 2019. Both he and his brother Izmir had been sentenced to three-and-a-half years in prison, but were returned nine months before the halfway point under the British government's Early Removal Scheme, which meant they also got a £1,500 payoff from the UK government.

Dema's family claimed that several young men from their clan had paid smugglers around £1,000 to get to Britain, where they thought they would work in car washes. But they were not exactly forced into the drug dealing gang.

As one family member said of Kadri, "He is in England; he left as soon as he came back [after being freed from jail]. He says he is OK and we talk time after time on Skype."

Details about how one trafficker claimed he was recruited at gunpoint emerged in a court case in February 2020. Emanuel Jella, twenty, said he fled Albania after being threatened in a bar, but soon found himself in further trouble upon arrival in Britain. Jella claimed he was cornered in a bar in Kingston and led out to a Mercedes at gunpoint, before being told to start earning £15,000 a week. Later, when police pulled over his VW Golf and found eleven kilos of cocaine, the determined that the haul had been smuggled into the country inside frozen chickens. Jella's tale of hardship stretched credulity — besides spending most of his time in London living it up in the city's bars and nightclubs, he also had at least two girlfriends.

Another key aspect of Britain's Albanian drugs gang phenomenon is the relatively restrained use of violence. While the postcode gangs of Barking, Tottenham and elsewhere might be stabbing and shooting each other on a daily basis, the Albanians try to keep out of the fray. It's not that they are unprepared to dish it out. As the Tristan Asllani case showed, Albanian criminals in Britain still have easy access to high powered weapons. Meanwhile, some other

Hellbanianz members have been convicted of carrying out raids on rival gangs. But the simple fact is that violence is usually unnecessary.[39]

For one thing, the Albanian gangs on the supply side are offering cocaine at cheaper prices than almost anyone else, creating a monopoly situation in which there are few, if any, direct competitors. On a practical level, there is also the fear factor — it's just as difficult for rival villains to work out who's truly in charge of a particular Albanian-led crew as it is for the police, making them difficult to target.

There also isn't much competition between the Albanians themselves. There is some circumstantial evidence that many apparently autonomous suppliers are actually part of extended networks, for example, some clan names, such as Asllani, have cropped up in multiple cases. It might also be because otherwise unconnected mobs are buying from the same original sources back in Albania, and they don't want to upset the apple cart.

Because the truth is that the real kingpins rarely, if ever, set foot in Britain. There will always be another Hellbanianz-style gang ready to buy from them and chance their arm on the supply or retail market. Most young dealers are willing to risk a few years in jail if it means they can use their profits to buy up property, businesses and cars back in Albania — or even a new set of teeth for the mother-in-law.

---

[39] An underworld source told me the 2015 fatal shooting in Waltham Abbey, Essex, of Paul Simmons-Turner, a drug dealer who was friends with reality television stars Joey Essex and Mark Wright, was linked to Albanian gangsters. To date, nobody has been arrested. There are plenty of similar anecdotal accounts of Albanian organised crime gangs using violence to enforce their will, and it may well be that many victims and witnesses refuse to come forward. At the time of writing, I am aware of at least three other London murder cases linked to Albanian criminals that are still sub judice. In one case, twenty-seven-year-old barber Grineo Daka was shot dead outside a snooker club in Leyton, East London, in July 2018. Fellow Albanians Edison Brahimi, twenty-nine, and Liridon Saliuka, also twenty-nine, were charged with murder. Saliuka died in Belmarsh Prison in January 2020 before the case had come to trial. Brahimi denies murder. Another man, Jeton Krasniqi, was later arrested and charged with murder, as well as the wounding of another man. Brahimi's brother, Mirsad, was also wanted over the attack.

PART THREE: MAFIA STATE

FAMILY MISFORTUNES

The cops should have been diligently guarding the front door, but they melted away as the two assassins approached. It was late and all signs of movement from within the apartment had long-since ceased. Nudging the door open, silenced pistols in their hands, the men flicked on the light. The old man was dozing in an armchair. He stirred with the sudden brightness but kept his eyes closed. There was no sign of their main target.

Motioning towards a room at the end of the hallway, the pair approached in single file. As they crept closer, they could hear the sound of a man snoring on the other side. Gently pushing the door, they peered into the room where Gentian Beqiri was sleeping. They stood over him for a minute, transfixed by the power they now held, the power of death over life. Then, as Beqiri soundly slept, they peppered his head and body with bullets. It was an easy kill, almost unreal. The dead man hardly flinched as they unloaded their clips. But as they turned to leave, they found the old man, Nezir Beqiri, was blocking the hallway.

"What have you done?" he demanded. They could have shot him too, but instead one of the killers simply punched him in the chest. The old man collapsed to the floor. Later, when they heard that

162

Nezir had died from a heart attack, the killers couldn't stop laughing. When the police eventually attended the scene, they found Gentian's brother, Sajmir, shot to death in a nearby car. The assassins had all but wiped out the Beqiri family. For them, justice had been served. Welcome to Albania's mafia wars — Elbasan style.

No region illustrates the working model of modern Albanian organised crime quite like the central industrial heartland of Elbasan, which also contains the country's third largest city of the same name. Although landlocked and bordering Macedonia to the east, Elbasan is just thirty miles away from Tirana, thirty-six miles from Lushnje and fifty-six miles from Durres. So it's easy enough to get the cocaine into the city, where it is processed, cut and funneled directly to capitals across Europe. Even South American cartel operatives are here, helping to process the drugs. And while the blow is being sold on the streets of places like London and Berlin after changing hands in Western Europe quite peacefully, the gangsters back home are blasting each other to pieces.

Take the blood feud that claimed the life of Gentian Beqiri and his family. He was no angel, to say the least. The reason the killers had to bribe their way past the armed guard was because the forty-year-old was being held under house arrest on suspicion of shooting dead an Elbasan crime boss called Sokol Capja, seven years earlier on Boxing Day, 2005. Beqiri had already been convicted and sentenced to twenty-five years in prison for the crime, but in a move typical of the eccentric Albanian justice system he was out on appeal ahead of a retrial, freed because an old bullet wound left him with mobility problems.

Beqiri's victim, Sokol Capja, had owned a luxury hotel complex and a range of other legitimate businesses. But his assassins knew he was in the habit of visiting a friend's café near the city's university most nights, instead of patronising his own joints. On the fatal night, Capja was in the company of two women when three masked gunmen burst in and ordered staff and customers to lay on the ground. All except Sokol Capja that is. The killers opened fire, at least two with pistols, one with a Scorpion submachine gun. Capja was taken to hospital but later died. The gunmen fled in a car with

Italian license plates. They were later named by cops as Dritan Schembri, Armando Hasani and Gentian Beqiri.

Schembri was the nephew of a police officer, Fadil Mema, who had previously offered to adjudicate a quarrel between him and Capja, which started when the crime boss failed to pay up for the contract killing of an Albanian named Rezart Cela, a front man for an Italian mobster who was trying to control gambling and other rackets in the region. It was a messy situation. The Capja clan suspected Mema, who was also related to a rival crime family, of orchestrating the murder plot.

In the aftermath of Capja's slaying, Mema was subsequently shot and injured near his home. His brother-in-law, Ardian Ibrahimi, was killed. Beqiri was caught by police attempting to flee to Greece, while Schembri was gunned down by gangsters in Tirana. The other suspected assassin, Hasani, went to ground and is still thought to be living under an assumed identity. Later, when Beqiri himself was assassinated, it would be a grandson of Sokol Capja, a hot-headed young gangster called Florenc Capja, who was one of two men arrested. He was never charged.

By March 2015, Mema was no longer on the force and was working as a newspaper seller in Italy. But the Capja clan had not forgotten the blood debt. Two gunmen approached him at his stand in Turin and fired six bullets into his head and body. His son, Elton, later said, "We know who the ordered the murder, but not who the killers are. They are probably Albanians."[40]

Then, in March 2016, the Capja family became the victims once again. Agron Capja, his grandson Ardit Sinakolli and another man, Eno Badelli, were shot dead in a bar in Krasta, Elbasan. Florenc Capja was also sprayed with bullets, but survived. Five other people were wounded in the shootout.

And it didn't stop there. In December 2017, Agron's brother Ardian Capja survived an audacious assassination plot when gunmen used a car that had been re-sprayed and fitted with false plates to look identical to his neighbour's vehicle, pulled up and unleashed dozens of rounds from a Kalashnikov as he emerged from his own

---

[40] Florenc Capja was re-arrested in July 2019 and charged with organising the murder. He was awaiting trial at time of writing.

driveway. Ardian had also previously survived a grenade attack, after the explosive failed to detonate.[41]

Meanwhile, as the Elbasan gang wars raged, police in London were linking another man from the Capja clan with a major cocaine supply operation in Britain.

***

Detectives from the Metropolitan Police had found their target to be a bit of a puzzle. For two years, between 2013 and 2015, cops had eyes on Klodjan Copja and his gang, and had taken plenty of photographs.[42] But they didn't know his name and he somehow kept slipping the net, even as they gradually dismantled his network.

Even when they finally extradited the gangster from Greece, they didn't know his real identity until they got him back to take fingerprints, thanks to his use of fake passports and ID cards. What isn't in doubt is that Copja's drugs supply operation was massive. Not only was he dealing in multi-kilo packages of cocaine, he was directly overseeing their entry to Britain, liaising with teams of smugglers and the couriers who would then distribute the packages to gangs and street dealers across the country.

Copja was first spotted by police in April 2013, when he was seen moving between several London safe houses with two other Albanian men who were later found delivering five-and-a-half kilos of coke to three dealers. When cops raided their stash house in Earl's Court, they found a further eleven kilos of blow and seven kilos of smack, as well as three kilos of cannabis. The drugs had been sourced in Kent from a man named Stephen Hall, a courier for the syndicate. He was later jailed for twenty years, while nine

---

[41] The latest attack on the Capja clan had come just a month after another family member, Besnik Capja, had been arrested on suspicion of drug trafficking in Italy. He was previously convicted in absentia in Turin and sentenced to six years and four months.

[42] Klodjan would ultimately be convicted under a variation of his clan name, Capja. It's common to find Albanian surnames spelt differently in Western countries, not least because they often use pseudonyms and provide fake IDs.

members of his gang were also jailed. The other two Albanian men seen with Copja got thirteen and eleven years respectively. But at the time of the raid, as police were smashing their way into the flat, they watched in dismay as Copja was driven past in the passenger seat of a car. Their mystery kingpin had slipped the net for the first time.

Quickly realising that he'd had a lucky escape, Copja fled the country. However, no international arrest warrant was issued because the police still didn't know their suspect's name. As a result, Copja eventually felt it was safe to start rebuilding his network. When he resurfaced in 2014, he was working with a man called Edvin Gjoka and two Romanian lorry drivers. The drug transfers were done out in the open in a layby in Kent. On one occasion, in July that year, cops stopped a lorry on the French side of the tunnel and seized forty-three kilos of cocaine hidden amongst the load. Evidence from traffic cameras and Eurotunnel records showed it had entered Britain and met with members of Copja's mob on at least twelve occasions. On three other occasions, Gjoka was tailed back to an address in North London, where he passed the boxes onto a variety of couriers.

Copja always seemed to be in the background, pulling the strings. He would turn up at safe houses, associate in a friendly but authoritative way with Gjoka and give orders over the phone about prices and locations. He also took care of the more mundane decisions. On one occasion, he suggested that a member of the gang who needed to be put on the car insurance could have his costs deducted from his "debt". On another, he was heard discussing where a courier should meet a customer. The police knew they had to tread carefully because it also seemed likely that the group had access to firearms.

On one occasion, Copja told Gjoka, "Take the cousin."

Gjoka replied, "Obviously." Police believed "cousin" was code for a gun.

They also discussed prices, which weren't always cheap. At one point, the gang sold one kilo for around £41,7000. Sums of up to £90,000 were frequently changing hands as other members of the network were followed trafficking the drugs onwards to Birmingham, Nottingham and Kettering.

Gjoka was eventually nabbed in the back of a Honda taxi with twelve kilos of blow. He had just done a deal in Wembley with another man in a Vauxhall. Cops found twenty-eight kilos in the boot. The purity was high, around eighty-five percent. In 2015, Gjoka pleaded guilty and was jailed for twelve years. Another member of the network, Birmingham-based Asmirald Miraka, who was mentioned in the previous chapter, was jailed for sixteen years.

Copja again went on the run. He was eventually arrested on the border of Greece and Albania on his thirtieth birthday, and later extradited on a European Arrest Warrant. The operation to smash Copja's network had seen a total of 204 kilos of cocaine seized, although cops believed at least 800 kilos had made it through. They placed a value of some £150 million on the drugs. Dozens of men were jailed with sentences totaling hundreds of years for the multiple conspiracies. And when Copja was handed seventeen years and four months he was hailed by cops as the undisputed ringleader.

But as ever, the headlines didn't tell the full story. In fact, as Klodjan Copja's lawyer Paul Hynes QC argued in court, the gangster was nowhere near the top of the chain.

"Mr Copja does not have a mansion in Surrey. He does not have £10 million available to him," he said. "It is, as a practical proposition, impossible to suggest that this was Mr Copja's operation, or indeed that of Mr Gjoka. They were in a very real sense employees."

Copja insisted that he had only arrived in Britain shortly before the first sighting of him in April 2013, after being recruited by a mafia group back home (no mention was made in court of his notorious clan). Copja said he was told that because he wouldn't actually be handling the drugs, he would get off lightly if captured.

"Mr Copja is not so trusted that he effectively runs the United Kingdom end of this operation," Mr Hynes went on. "He is not Chief Executive Officer in charge of Western Europe, he is someone who is trusted and a manager and he comes in, effectively to ensure that deals that have been arranged and negotiated at a much higher level, go through effectively and painlessly and profitably for those above him the organisation...He knows what's going on below him. He knows what's going on above him and he doesn't necessarily know what's going on to the sides. He certainly doesn't have a business overview. That is all resident it would seem, certainly as far as he is aware, in Albania. One can see from the lifestyle that he is living, the surveillance evidence where it exists, the telephone patterns where they can be relied upon, none of those things suggest in any way, shape or form a Mr Big." Of course, the police publicly took the polar opposite view.

The lawyer also pointed out that Copja did not even have a mansion back home in Albania where he could flee to when the heat got too much. And when asked by the judge whether Copja had handed himself in voluntarily, the reply was remarkably candid.

"He disappeared for exactly the reasons that one might imagine. He was scared. He realised that what he had been doing had come to the attention of the authorities. He anticipated that things would not go well for him and he had some small idea of what had gone on before and the sort of sentences that had been passed.... He hadn't made a new life for himself as a sheep farmer on some Grecian hill, but he was trying to keep his head down and do the best he could because he appreciated that, to put it colloquially, there was quite bad news waiting for him here. He now appreciates just how bad the news is."

Copja insisted that he had known little about the drugs game before he got involved in 2013. He said he had just divorced an Italian woman and was unhappy in his personal life. He decided to take a punt on this "seductive" and "fairly easy" new opportunity that had presented itself.

"For what it's worth," Mr Hynes added. "He told me how much he was being paid and it was 200 euros per kilo handled by any dealer of which he aware and facilitated. So, that may well explain the absence of the Surrey mansion."

Whatever the truth about Copja's position in the famous Capja crime family (perhaps he really was just a minor cog in the machine), it was certain that he was a major player in the drugs game, simply from the quantities involved and his obvious position of authority in the gang. But at the same time, he was not so big that he could remain in the relative safety of Elbasan and orchestrate the operation from there. Exactly where he fitted into the extended network — and who he was working for — was never quite clear.

168

What can be reasonably deduced is that the cocaine Klodjan Copja was supplying to dealers in Britain had most likely transited through Elbasan.

THE COLOMBIAN
CONNECTION

It was a shocking drugs conspiracy, even by Albanian standards. Not just because of the quantity of cocaine involved— at least 120 kilos smuggled from South America to Europe over the course of one year— but because one of the main players was the grandson of former Communist dictator Enver Hoxha. It was hard to believe, but even one of the country's most illustrious families was tied up in the cocaine game.

Ermal Hoxha, a forty-year-old grandson of the former dictator by his eldest son Ilir Hoxha, was an unlikely narco. A dad of three and a businessman involved in a high-profile and long-term relationship with the Albanian singer Rezarta Shkurta, common sense might dictate that someone like Hoxha would have too much to lose. But as ever, the lure of huge profits was too much to resist.

While Hoxha's arrest grabbed the headlines, the true significance of the case was in the detention of two Colombian cartel operatives. According to prosecutors, the early morning raid on January 14, 2015, was based on intelligence provided by the authorities in Germany. Cops smashed down the door of the former state reserve stores in Xibrake, Elbasan, where they found nearly twenty kilos of high-grade blow, guns, processing equipment, and two rather sheepish South Americans. Ermal Hoxha had also been filmed at the premises and was one of a total of eight men quickly arrested and charged.

It was another man found at the scene, Ilir Hyseni, who was initially thought to be the head of the network.

"I had my affairs at the place where I was caught by the police," Hyseni later insisted. "But I have no connection with cocaine traffic. I do not know the other arrested people. It does not tie me to anything."

He denied knowing any of the other men, in particular the Colombians. He also denied knowing a woman in Germany, Pranvera Ebeling, who was part of a separate case being brought by the Hanover Prosecutor's Office. She was said to be Hyseni's lover.

The Germans had been investigating the network as it shipped vast quantities of cocaine from South America. Hyseni was watched for weeks, and monitored as he travelled from his love nest with Ebeling to the cocaine lab in Elbasan. The purpose of the lab had been to extract cocaine from cement and other ostensibly innocent liquids. The whole network had been operational for at least one year, police believed. It was hard to say whether the conspiracy was Albanian-led with Colombian assistance, or the other way around. The two Colombians, Cezar Avila and Valter Moreno, had arrived in Greece on November 8, and were tracked as they crossed into Albania later that month. After they were arrested, both men claimed they were only there to help process the drugs. Still, the Greek authorities believed a third Colombian, named only as "Carlos," was based in Greece as part of the network.

Either way, it was a truly international operation. Prosecutors went on to allege that while Hyseni was the group's chief organiser in Europe, overseeing the trafficking from South America and then onwards into Albania and Western Europe, Hoxha was the main financier. Meanwhile, the group's overall leader was said to be a man called Genic Xhixka, who had based himself overseas. He was sentenced to thirteen years in absentia. Xhixka is still thought to be hiding out either in Cuba or elsewhere in South America. Interestingly, in October 2019, a police raid in Brazil uncovered 617 kilos of cocaine on a truck, packaged in blocks featuring the logo of the Elbasan football club. The authorities made the obvious link with the Albanian mafia.

Hoxha was initially jailed for ten years. But following an appeal, the sentence was reduced to six years and eight months. In the end, Hoxha was released in September 2018, after serving less than two years. The rest of his sentence was suspended. Hyseni also saw his sentence reduced, from twelve years to eight. Even Genic Xhixka will serve less time if he ever returns. Judges ruled that his new sentence should be just eight years and eight months. The two Colombians ended up getting eight years each.

It was a case that underscored the truly international nature of the Albanian mafia and its ability to cooperate with other criminal groups. Not only did the Xhibraka network have a leader based in South America, but bases in both Germany and Albania, and Colombian operatives working directly with the network processing the cocaine in Albania itself. Without doubt there would also have been members of an extended network who would have taken delivery of the drugs in Western Europe.

DRUG WARS

While the Xibrake network made headlines because of its scale, high-profile conspirators and the presence of Colombian cartel operatives, it was not exactly unique. Huge international Albanian mafia syndicates and drugs seizures have become increasingly common in Albania and Western Europe. For example, in October 2018 Albanian cops found six men, one of them Turkish, in a similar processing lab in a village near Tirana. Again, the raid was sparked by an investigation in Germany. In fact, work done by EU countries is usually crucial in bringing down or disrupting the networks.

Back in 2012, French authorities arrested forty-two members of an "Albanian-Kosovar" mafia gang trafficking drugs into France and Germany. Prosecutors said "hundreds of kilos" of cocaine were seized. More recently, in January 2019, Spanish police in Valencia raided another drugs lab staffed with Albanian, Colombian and Spanish villains. Again, the lab was being used to extract coca paste from a liquid base. As part of the same operation, the authorities also seized around 400 kilos of coke and 8,500 chemical agents at the Galician port of Marin. In April 2019, Europol announced that it had smashed a huge Albanian crime syndicate operating in Belgium, France, the Netherlands, Italy and the UK. In total, 600 law enforcement officers took part in raids that saw sixty-four people arrested —fifty-five of them in Belgium, including the leaders. The operation also saw twelve large cannabis factories across Northern France and Belgium closed down. In addition, the group had been involved in human trafficking, mostly in France.

Another Europol and Danish-led investigation, dubbed Operation Goldfinger, in July 2019, took down a sprawling drug trafficking gang that was transporting cocaine across Europe from Albania, via Slovenia, Sweden, Denmark, Germany and the Netherlands. In total, thirty-one people were arrested and fourteen charged in Denmark with trafficking around 1,650 kilos of blow and smack using hidden compartments in specially adapted cars. Prosecutors said the gang had made at least fifty-five trips to Copenhagen since March 2018. The alleged leader of the gang, a fifty-one-year-old man, was arrested back home in Shkodra.

One of the biggest seizures of all was made in Durres, where this book began. In February 2018, port authorities found a staggering 613 kilos of high purity Colombian marching powder hidden underneath a shipment of twenty tons of bananas which had transited through Malta and Italy and was destined for a fruit company called Abri Garden. Cops believed the drugs would be processed in Albania and once mixed the cocaine would equate to about 1.8 tons and reach a value of about 180 million euros, or $219,000,000. It was the biggest cocaine seizure ever made in Albania.

The drugs themselves where thought to have come from the Clan del Golfo (the gulf's clan), previously known as Los Urabenos, a drug cartel that emerged from the ashes of the right-wing paramilitary group Autodefenses Gaitanistas de Colombia. It is one of the country's most powerful and violent drug cartels, with about 3,000 members and the blood of thousands on its hands. According to prosecutors, the Colombian navy had instigated the probe, warning the Albanian authorities about the illicit load before the ship docked in Durres. As a result, the shipment was held for eighteen days. Even so, this apparently wasn't enough to spook the mafia bosses, and cops followed the drugs to the fruit company's warehouse once the load was collected. It was suggested that the shipment had cost the gangsters around six million euros, with the cost split between four Albanian mafia groups. There was some speculation in the press that the two Colombians previously arrested in Elbasan had belonged to the Clan Del Golfo. Therefore, some reasoned, it was possible that one of the groups that had taken part in the purchase was also led by the fugitive Genic Xhixka.

Meanwhile, in Germany, police arrested the owner of Abri Garden, an Albanian businessman named Arber Cekaj. Germany at first refused to extradite Cekaj to Albania and was reportedly successful in getting him to flip. He was later extradited, despite saying that he feared for his life.

An investigation by the Organized Crime and Corruption Reporting Project (OCCRP) found that Cekaj had personally travelled to Ecuador to arrange more than 130 exports of bananas and was already known to the authorities at the time of the seizure. The well-educated entrepreneur had registered his company in 2012 after living in Germany for several years. In 2015, he was observed by plantation workers adding four boxes to a shipment, each marked with a monkey logo. As the container moved out, he was said to have excitedly exclaimed, "The monkey has left! The monkey has left!" Suspicious workers reported the incident to police and they uncovered 28 kilos of cocaine hidden in the load. Cekaj fled the country, but even though the Albanian authorities were notified, he allegedly went on to receive a $152,000 EU loan administered by the government to build a massive refrigerated warehouse. He continued to import thousands of tons of fruit before his arrest.

In October 2018, police in Albania carried out a series of nationwide raids, most linked to the Durres seizure. The reputed leaders of the Avdyli clan of Shijak were held, along with fourteen other alleged mobsters and two former Socialist Party MPs. The authorities hailed it as a successful joint operation, although to date nobody has been charged in relation to the coke.

In November the same year, police in Italy smashed a 'Ndrangheta operation that saw at least 1.7 tons of Colombian blow smuggled into Calabria in the space of two years, with a further 800 kilos going through Antwerp. More than 200 people were arrested across Europe. According to evidence revealed by Italian investigators, the 'Ndrangheta was selling the coke on to Albanian traffickers.

BODY COUNTS

With such high stakes involved, it's no surprise that Albania's internal mafia wars have become increasingly bloody, and not only in Elbasan. Most law-abiding people in Albania are still relatively safe, unlike narcostates such as Honduras or Mexico, where cartels and armed gangs have engaged in widespread kidnapping and massacres. But it's always worth remembering the example of those Latin American countries where violence has increasingly been directed towards the general population. Things can go downhill fast when the rule of law is fatally subverted.

The long-term murder rate in Albania is skewed by the extraordinarily high number of killings in 1997, when there were fifty murders per 100,000 of the population. In recent years, it has gone down from 5.38 in 2012, to 2.7 in 2016. But it's listed as the

128th deadliest country in the world, and ranks about eighth or ninth in Europe, with around 80 murders a year. In 2014, Tirana had the third highest murder rate of European cities, at 6.7. Using the same measure, the murder rate in Britain as a whole is just 1.2 per 100,000.

Some gangland slayings— such as those linked to the Capja clan — are more notable than others. For example, one murder in 2014 was carried out by Konstandin Xhuvani, the son of a Socialist Party MP, Luiza Xhuvani, and a famous film director, Gjergj Xhuvani. Four men, Edison Jaho, Enea Xhaja, Arber Demiraj, and Italian national Paolo Azzolo, were all gunned down during an early hours party in a Tirana nightclub (ironically located in Elbasan Street). Xhuvani was one of three men arrested. He had only recently been released from prison for killing another man just three years previously and going on the run. Quite why Xhuvani had received such a light sentence is not clear. However, on the second time around he was given thirty years.

Another notorious mob set itself up as an Albanian version of Chicago's famous Prohibition-era Murder Inc hit squad. Admir Tafilaj was a convicted murderer who was serving life for killing two brothers and attempting to murder a police chief. He had subsequently managed to break out of prison not once, but twice. On one occasion, another jailbreak was foiled by guards who found explosives in his prison cell. Even after he was safely back behind bars, Tafilaj continued to head up a gang of at least thirteen hitmen who charged between 20,000 and 50,000 euros to take out rival gangsters, orchestrating the plots from his cell. The gang committed at least four gangland murders, in Shkodra, Durres and Tirana. They were also involved in gun-running and drug trafficking. At a trial in 2017, Tafliaj was given a while life sentence, while nine other members of the gang were jailed for a total of 104 years, two of them for thirty-five years each.

Over in Durres, a bloody gangland war that began in Vlore has played out for years. In November 2018, Edison Harizaj, known as El Padrino in homage to Pablo Escobar, was gunned down as he travelled through the city in an Audi A8. Harizaj was a drug trafficker, extortionist and convicted murderer who was friends with fellow notorious gangster Emilianjo Shullazi. A few months previously, back in Vlore, three members of a rival family had been shot and injured, sparking a spate of kidnappings and shootings. The hit on Harizaj was thought to be in retaliation for the violence. The feud is still ongoing.

And back in Elbasan the bloodshed still hasn't stopped. On December 29, 2018, three people were shot dead as they travelled through the streets in a black Range Rover. The victims were Endrit "Tarzan" Alibej, Arben Dylgjeri, and Erdal Durnay, a Turkish citizen. Alibej, who was a native of Elbasan, was said to be the boss of a cocaine trafficking ring based in Italy. In addition to occasionally using his mother's maiden name, Dylgjeri, he had also posed as a Romanian citizen, Gabriel Manu, and a Greek, Dimitrios Kriporis. His home in Asti had been covertly raided in 2012 and police found around 400 grams of cocaine, hidden in a box of whiskey. The items were photographed and an operation began to bring down the rest of the gang. But as things gathered pace, Tarzan fled the country. In 2014, he was jailed in absentia for five years and four months, but he didn't officially resurface until his death.

One of the country's most disturbing underworld hits took place in Elbasan on March 22, 2019. Mob lawyer Ravik Gurra, fifty, who lived in Britain, was executed with three bullets to the head from a silenced pistol as he sat outside a café. He was well-known for representing members of the Capja family and another notorious gangster, Emiliano Shullazi, as well as an allegedly corrupt judge and members of the Revenge for Justice organisation. The killing sent shockwaves through Albania's legal community. Why had Gurra been killed? Who had been responsible? There was some speculation that he could have been whacked because he'd lost a case, or because he'd been critical of Albania's justice system.

All this goes to illustrate the vast difference between the behaviour of the mafioso in Albania and the emissaries sent abroad to work at the sharp end of the narcotics industry. While outfits like the Hellbanianz might occasionally stab or even shoot at their rivals, the gangsters in places like Elbasan and Tirana are blowing each other up and spraying nightclubs with AK-47s like it was still 1997.

Another difference is that clearly the quantities of cocaine being handled within the country are massive. So far, nothing approaching the 613-kilo cocaine seizure in Durres has been made in Britain. Instead, if the Klodjan Copja case provides any indication, it appears that Albanian mafia gangs prefer to offload the drugs in Albania where they can deal with corrupt officials, and then ferry them across Europe and then the Channel in lorries. And that arrangement doesn't look like slowing down any time soon, not when the friends of some of the county's most powerful politicians — and allegedly some of the politicians themselves — are making money hand over fist.

BALKANS ESCOBAR

The world has an unofficial unit to measure the power of drug barons — the Escobar. The only trouble is, it's not exactly scientific. The Escobar's namesake, Colombian drug lord nonpareil Pablo, had an estimated net worth of about $3 billion at the height of his powers; controlled about eighty per cent of the worldwide cocaine market through the Medellin Cartel; and is thought to have killed about 4,200 police officers and civilians, not to mention hundreds of fellow narcos, during his nearly two-decades-long reign. No other individual drug trafficker has come close to wielding power in quite the same way as El Padrino, even if some contemporary South American cartels do make more money and murder more people. But that hasn't stopped the widespread use of the label "Escobar" to describe high profile narcos in other parts of the world.

For example, a man called Andrew Deamer, from Leicestershire, was dubbed "The East Midlands Escobar" for allegedly helping to run a £350m cocaine ring based in Colombia that shipped drugs out to Europe. At one time, Turkish godfather Huseyin Baybasin was hailed as "Europe's Escobar," even though his principal business was in heroin. Prada Alava, nicknamed Gerald, is known as "Ecuador's Escobar". It seems that almost every region or country has a crime lord who has at some point been bestowed the dubious honour. Perhaps not surprisingly, the Balkans has at least two Escobars. The first "Escobar of the Balkans" was Darko Saric, the Serbian cocaine king now serving fifteen years for overseeing a massive criminal empire that stretched from South America to Western Europe. But in recent years a new "Balkan's Escobar" has emerged, and he is Albanian.

In some ways, Klement Balili fits the Escobar mould better than most, because aside from being a major drug trafficker he also has the kind of political connections that helped Pablo transform Colombia into the world's first narco-state. Balili was handed the moniker by the Greek police, who originally arrested him in 2006 after intercepting 750 kilos of cannabis worth about 1.5 million euros on the island of Zathynkos. The weed had been shipped from Albania and five Albanian men, including Balili, as well as two corrupt Greek police officers waiting on shore with a truck, were arrested. At the time, the prosecutor's office took the unusual step of quashing Balili's charges and ordering his release. The other four men were jailed for up to ten years each. Something wasn't quite right about the decision, but the case didn't make major headlines back in Albania.

In fact, in October 2013, just seven years after his arrest in Greece, Balili was handed political office as transport director in his home city of Saranda. It was a move that— with hindsight — was a mistake comparable to Pablo Escobar's election to Colombia's congress in 1982. It brought Bailili into the public eye, and when things began to go wrong it invited scrutiny of those who had appointed him.

At the time of the appointment, the Socialist Party was in a new coalition government with the Socialist Movement for Integration (LSI), a breakaway party. The SP's Edi Rama was Prime Minister and Saimir Tahiri the Interior Minister. Former SP President and Prime Minister Ilir Meta was by then the leader of the LSI and Chairman of Parliament. It was later alleged that that Balili had donated funds to the SP's election campaign, although that was denied by officials. But he was also said to have made donations to the LSI. After all, his brother and business partner Rigels Balili was the LSI mayor of nearby Delvina.

Klement Balili was also a construction boss who had recently completed work on a three million euro luxury resort in Saranda called Santa Quaranta. The ribbon-cutting ceremony in August 2015 was attended by Rama, Meta and former Socialist Party deputy Koco Kokedhima, as well other top officials. Footage showed them all smiling and taking an active part in the celebrations. The Balili brothers also owned the Hotel Olivia on the coast of Butrinti, another popular resort, as well as an insurance company in Vlora and a travel agency, which specialised in booking holidays to Greece. But while Balili had built up his legitimate business empire since his 2006 arrest, the authorities back in Greece had continued their investigation into his other activities.

A decade after Balili was first arrested, on May 9, 2016, Greek police swooped on fifteen people it said were part of a major drug trafficking network. They called a press conference and unveiled a raft of evidence. Their dossier was extensive, damning and showed the syndicate to be comprised of a number of nationalities.[43] Initially,

---

[43] For example, on January 25, 2014, in Patra, a Bulgarian was arrested with 451 kilos of cannabis. In April 2014, another 678 kilos were intercepted on the border of Greece and Macedonia. In April 2015, police in Britain seized twenty-three kilos of cocaine. The same month, another 531 kilos of cannabis were seized in Bulgaria. In May 2016, a Tanzanian man who arrived in Greece from Brussels was arrested with 1,060 grams of heroin, while the following day a Brazilian citizen who arrived from Sao Paulo was found with just over 1.5 kilos. In addition, the Italian police had arrested fifty-nine people, and seized more than three tons of cannabis, ninety-six kilos of cocaine and sixty-five kilos of hash in three years.

the Greek police said the syndicate's leader was a forty-four-year-old Albanian citizen who they dubbed "The Balkan Baron" or "Balkan's Escobar" and named only as "KB". Meanwhile the "brains of the operation" was said to be a Greek man who oversaw the actual logistics of the smuggling. Another key member was an Albanian man based in Brussels. He owned several front companies which facilitated the smuggling. The network was distributing hundreds of kilos of cocaine and cannabis all over Western Europe and had amassed a bank balance roughly equivalent to Greece's national debt, which may have been some exaggeration. But there was no doubt the crew was awash with cash.

The Greek police claimed KB had millions of euros in various banks, and homes and luxury cars stashed away in at least ten countries across Europe. The police file said one gang member received a 10,000 euro-a-month salary just for coming up with creative new ways to hide the drugs in lorry loads. And the seized drugs were only the tip of a very large iceberg. As an example of the kind of deals the police had failed to intercept, they said that in 2015 the network had been planning to smuggle sixty kilos of cocaine into Belgium, but the operation was called off after the Paris terror attacks, with bosses sensing that there might be heightened security.

It had been a painstaking international investigation, but bringing Balili to justice proved to be equally hard work. In the days that followed the announcement a huge scandal erupted in Albania. Opposition MPs had taken the decision to out Klement Balili as "KB".

Balili was forced to speak publicly on the matter, claiming, "I am not related to the accusations of the opposition, I have a clean record. Anyone who mentions my name will see me in court."

Of course, no lawsuit ever materialised. But the opposition also publicly accused Edi Rama, Interior Minister Saimir Tahiri and other high-level public officials of protecting Balili. They were incredulous that someone of Balili's ilk had been appointed to public office.

All were linked to the same sprawling organisation. The seizure that had sparked the announcement involved 678 kilos of cannabis in Greece.

Democratic Party Secretary General Arben Ristani raged, "That's why drugs have exploded everywhere. Because the Prime Minister not only opened the way for traffickers, but also handed over important state offices."

Former DP PM Sali Berisha weighed in, accusing socialist politicians of being in bed with a narco trafficker. Balili again denied that he was the man wanted by the authorities in Greece and threatened to sue anyone who repeated the allegations.

"I have nothing to do with these allegations and clearly understand that they are political," he insisted. As proof, Balili offered the fact that he had visited Greece in recent years and had not been arrested. Three days after the allegations emerged, Justice Minister Ylli Manjani announced that Balili had been relieved of his position and was under investigation. Meanwhile, Greece issued an international arrest warrant. Then, something entirely predictable happened — Balili vanished.

The DP issued a strongly-worded statement accusing Interior Minister Samir Tahiri of helping Balili escape and being involved in drug trafficking himself.

"The connection and defense that Klement Balili has, is called Saimir Tahiri," it said. "Saimir Tahiri's ties with criminal gangs and drug trafficking organizations are now well-known by our European and US partners. It is urgent that he leave an hour ago from office, and a comprehensive and thorough investigation of his criminal ties [is opened]."

Further investigations found that Balili's electronic criminal record had been wiped. Gone were the details of his 2006 arrest in Greece, as well as a complaint about the "illegal construction" of the Santa Quranta complex. It was also found that a local judge had acted as a legal advisor for two companies owned by the Balili brothers at around the time Klement was involved in the first trafficking case in Greece. At the time, the judge was suspended pending a separate corruption investigation and was working as a lawyer. He had received at least $47,000 from the Balili brothers and failed to declare it, although in the end no criminal charges were brought and he was able to keep his job.

Meanwhile, the fugitive Balili continued to enjoy the high life. In August 2016, the DP published a photo of Bailili on his yacht off the coast of Saranda, in the company of the deputy general director of the state police, claiming it was taken after the arrest warrant was issued. The following month, another video emerged, this time showing Balili at the wedding of a niece of the head of the SP in Tepelena.

By November, the authorities in Greece had grown so frustrated with the lack of progress that they had their 10,000-word dossier on Balili translated into Albanian and sent to the government, accusing officials of dragging their feet. In December, the United States heaped on the pressure with a personal visit to Tirana by CIA director John Brennan. It was never publicly stated, but Balili's outstanding arrest was believed to have been top of the agenda. On December 10, the Albanian police launched a large-scale operation to find Balili, but to no avail.

A few days later, US ambassador Donald Lu launched a scathing attack on the government. "The delay in the arrest of Klement Balili, former official in Saranda, represents a great failure of the police and the justice system," he said. "For seven months I have encouraged the police, the Minister of Interior Affairs, the General Prosecutor, to arrest Klement Balili. It's seven months ago that the Greek police arrested drug traffickers linked to Balili in Greece. [Balili] freely walks the street of Tirana, because until last Friday the Chief Prosecutor hadn't ordered his arrest. Albania would be a better place if the governments would turn their ear to the People's Advocate. Instead, left and right-wing politicians have paid attention to the powerful interests of corrupted businessmen, big criminals, and even drug traffickers. If Albania cannot capture Klement Balili, how can it go after the other big fish? Who would want to work with Albania, who would believe that this is a country that's serious about fighting drug trafficking?"

In May 2018, Saimir Tahiri resigned as an MP (having already quit as Interior Minister) to fight his own corruption and drug trafficking charges. Pressure from the West finally kicked the Albanian government into gear. But it was too late. Balili was a ghost. It wasn't until January 2019, after nearly a dozen failed operations designed to snare the kingpin, that he finally gave himself up. While the new Interior Minister Sander Lleshaj was busy setting up a staged press conference complete with balaclava-wearing police officers, it was Sali Berisha who spoiled their party with an announcement on social media.

"Klement Balili hands himself over! He has set off for Tirana along with Rigels Balili," he wrote.

When later asked what Balili had been offered to get him to surrender, Lleshaj, having wisely decided against the mock show of force, told reporters, "The assurance of a fair legal process."

Even so, the government was still at pains to make Balili's arrest look like a heroic success. Edi Rama called the surrender "one of the most sophisticated police operations," suggesting that it hadn't all been on Balili's terms. But one thing was made clear — Balili would not be extradited to face the charges against him in Greece.

In May 2019, Klement Balili was sentenced to ten years in prison after being found guilty of charges including drug trafficking, membership of a criminal organisation and money laundering. The total sentence was knocked down from the eighteen years sought by the prosecution, after he took the well-worn drug trafficker's route of asking for an abbreviated trial, which meant the full facts of the case were not explored in court. The Prosecutor's Office also requested the confiscation of his assets including some twenty apartments, luxury hotels and several plots of land.

NARCO-STATE

There are few places in Europe where the Klement Balili scandal would have been possible. Whether or not the official inertia following Greece's arrest warrant was down to corruption or incompetence, the fact that Balili, with his previous arrest on drug trafficking charges, could have risen to high political office in a democratic country was beyond belief for most citizens. But Albania is no ordinary democracy.

By July 2017, as the Balili affair rumbled on, Albania had a new government — just about. A June election had been called in December 2016, but the DP claimed the SP was planning huge electoral fraud and began boycotting Parliament. In the end, the election was delayed by a week and only went ahead after mediation from the US and EU. As a result of the negotiations, the DP was guaranteed several government positions, including one deputy prime minister, six ministers, the chair of the Central Election Commission (CEC), and directors of various agencies. The election result gave the Socialist Party a majority, so it formed a solo government again under Edi Rama, while Ilir Meta, still chairman of the LSI, became President.

Edi Rama is a painter and former basketball player who entered political life in 1998, becoming Minister of Culture, Youth and Sports in the new Socialist government under Fatos Nano. The brash, colourful and outspoken politician later became mayor of Tirana, then opposition leader and finally Prime Minister for the first time in 2013. The following year, he was hailed for instigating a huge operation aimed at smashing the cannabis industry of Lazarat. He also shepherded a new "vetting law" through Parliament in 2016. The law required judges and prosecutors to explain their sources of wealth, as well as any past verdicts which may be open to allegations of corruption. If they cannot do so, they face disqualification. The law was said by the European Union to be essential if Albania had any hope of joining. At least 160 judges have since been dismissed after falling foul of the law, around one fifth of the country's judiciary. A similar law to be applied to politicians has so far been resisted by those in power. Rama has also been behind successful reforms to the energy sector, welfare and pensions and reduced unemployment, as well as becoming the first Albanian PM to visit Serbia, as part of a programme of reconciliation with Kosovo. Yet as well as being criticised for overspending and lacking transparency in the awarding of lucrative public contracts, the two Rama governments have also been accused of presiding over Albania's gradual slide into a narcostate.

Some disagree that Albania deserves the label, which is applied to countries where the economy is fully or partially reliant on the drugs trade and/or where the highest levels of the state and police are in the pockets of the traffickers. Colombia, Peru, Mexico, Honduras and Afghanistan are some of the clearest examples of a narcostate. Nobody is saying that Albania's current levels of violence are on a par with those countries. But dozens of Albania's politicians, from mayors to cabinet ministers, have been implicated in the drugs trade, as well as police officers of all ranks, judges and prosecutors. And while Albania's economy is today stronger than ever, with vibrant energy and agriculture sectors, as well as a booming tourism industry, there is little doubt that vast profits from narcotics are being laundered through the construction industry, which has seen luxury apartments, hotels, cafes, bars and nightclubs being put up at a rate of knots.

The anti-corruption organisation Transparency International ranks Albania 36 out of 100 on a scale where zero is "highly corrupt" and 100 is "very clean". The 2019 Freedom House report on Albania also gave the country low ratings on freedom, political rights and civil liberties. It notes that "corruption is pervasive, and the EU has repeatedly called for rigorous implementation of antigraft measures". It also says that while a Special Prosecutor Service to deal with high-level corruption was created as part of the 2016 reforms, it is "yet to achieve full operational capacity".

The report said there are also problems facing journalists trying to report on crime and corruption, including intimidation and even automatic weapons being fired at reporters' homes.

"While the constitution guarantees freedom of expression, the intermingling of powerful business, political, and media interests inhibits the development of independent news outlets," it said. "Most are seen as biased toward either the PS or the PD. Reporters have little job security and remain subject to lawsuits, intimidation, and occasional physical attacks by those facing media scrutiny." But some of the most scathing criticisms were reserved for the legal system:

"The constitution provides for an independent judiciary, but the underfunded courts are subject to political pressure and influence, and public trust in judicial institutions is low. Corruption in the judiciary remains a serious problem, and convictions of high-ranking judges for corruption and abuse of power are rare. In 2016, parliament approved a variety of reforms designed to boost the independence and capacity of the judiciary, including the evaluation of current and prospective judges and prosecutors based on their professionalism, moral integrity, and independence. Vetting processes are ongoing, and in 2018 again led to the dismissal or resignation of many judges over unexplained assets.... Constitutional guarantees of due process are upheld inconsistently. Trial procedures can be affected by corruption within the judicial system, and are sometimes closed to the public.... Drug-related crime remains a problem, as Albania is a transit country for heroin smugglers and a key site for European cannabis production. Traditional tribal law is practiced in parts of northern Albania, and sometimes involves revenge killings."

This is not to suggest that the Albanian state is a root and branch corrupt body that does nothing to tackle the mafia. For example, in October 2018 a major operation involving more than 1,500 police officers targeted four organised crime groups. The nation-wide raids saw nearly thirty people arrested, including former SP MPs, Arben Ndoka and Arben Cuko. Also held were Flamur, Astrit and Jasim Avdyli, as well as Arben Ndoka's older brother Xhevahir Ndoka, and twenty other people from the Shijak area for involvement in the drug trafficking network allegedly behind that February's huge seizure in Durres.

One of the warrants was reportedly for another trafficker, Lulzim Berisha, who was suspected of helping to courier the drugs to Germany. But he couldn't be found after apparently being tipped off about the raids. His lawyer later denied that a warrant had been issued and said Berisha had done nothing wrong. The prosecutor's office also allegedly had wiretaps featuring conversations between the SP Mayor of Durres, Vangjush Dako, and members of the Avdyli clan discussing securing votes in exchange for public works contracts.

One of the MPs, Arben Ndoka, was arrested over an alleged plot to falsify documents in order to buy up state-owned land in coastal areas of the Lezhe region. He had a controversial history, having been previously convicted of human trafficking in Italy in 2004 and sentenced to seven years in jail.[44] Yet he was able to become a state official after the courts reduced his sentence to just three years. Ndoka became an SP MP in 2013, until he was forced to resign two years later due to pressure being heaped on Edi Rama. Meanwhile the other MP, Arben Cuko, was accused of taking bribes when he served as head of the General Directorate of the Penitentiary Service.

---

[44] His brother, Aleksander, was killed in Lezha, Italy, in December 2017, by an assassin who sprayed his car with Kalashnikov rounds.

The Democratic Party was not impressed by the arrests, claiming they were nothing but an effort to deflect attention away from the ongoing Balili scandal. In fact, the inclusion of Lulzim Berisha in the arrest warrants only helped to remind the public of another recent judicial outrage. Berisha had been arrested in 2006, accused of leading the Gang of Durres, which terrorised the town during the pyramid crisis and beyond, committing at least five murders and dozens of robberies. He was jailed for life in 2012, but in 2014 the High Court cut the sentence to twenty-five years. Then, in December 2016, he was unexpectedly granted early release. The decision was secured by the aforementioned Mayor of Durres, Vangjush Dako, who provided a written letter guaranteeing work for Berisha as a volunteer in a local government-run business. The court ruled that Berisha "suffers from a serious disease and his life is at risk if he stayed in jail".

US Ambassador Donald Lu poured scorn on the ruling, saying, "The liberation of Lulzim Berisha has happened for unknown reasons. I would like to say to the corrupted courts that this decision is unacceptable. We should be scandalized".

Prosecutors from Tirana were called in to investigate the judges. DP leader Lulzim Basha was equally outraged.

"Vangjush Dako has used the power and office entrusted to him by the citizens of Durres to release from prison a criminal who has murdered and terrorized the citizens of Durres," he said.

A further example of the apparently inextricable links between the SP and organised crime came in August 2019, when the mayor-elect of Shkodra was forced to resign before taking up his post. It was revealed that he had a drug dealing conviction in Italy dating back to 2003, for which he received an 18-month suspended sentence. He described it as a "totally banal" event from his past, but it still didn't look good. More serious was the arrest of Vora's SP mayor Agim Kajmaku. He had earlier fled Greece while facing a charge of distributing counterfeit bank notes, a crime which could have seen him locked up for ten years. Meanwhile, another SP mayor was allegedly caught on camera in January 2020 appearing to snort cocaine. He claimed the film was a "montage" and a frame-up aimed at toppling him for doing a "good job".

Overall confidence in the Albanian criminal justice system — at least where serious organised crime is concerned — has not been helped by legal changes made in 2017, when the SP-dominated Parliament approved the government's amendment to Article 491 of the Albanian Criminal Procedure Code making it illegal to extradite an Albanian citizen without a bilateral extradition treaty.

It meant that drug traffickers convicted in absentia in places like Italy would no longer be returned to face justice and, crucially, Klement Balili would not be extradited to Greece. It also meant that Agron Xhafaj — the brother of then-Minister of Interior Fatmir Xhafaj— who had been convicted in Italy of being a member of a drug trafficking organisation, would also not face extradition to complete a seven year sentence handed down in 2002.

Although critics were careful not to try to hold Xhafaj to account for his brother's crimes, DP politicians noted that Fatmir was responsible for the State Police, which should have been tasked with arresting his brother. However, Agron later handed himself in and was indeed extradited to Italy. But the new law also had wide-ranging benefits for a number of other high-profile traffickers.

For example, Edmond Bega, a former member of Aldo Bare's Gang of Lushnje, was facing eleven years in prison in Italy (a sentence reduced from the original twenty-one). He had been arrested in Tirana in 2009, but the High Court reduced the Italian sentence to just four years and four months. In the end, Bega served just one year before he was released on parole for good behaviour.

Another notorious gangster, Safet Bajri, was facing twenty-two years in a Belgian prison for human trafficking and prostitution. He headed up a family-run criminal organization, alongside brothers and cousins Enver Bajri, Ilir Bajri (also known as Rustemi), and Behar Bajri (also known as Brajgovic), whose empire stretched into Holland and Albania. Both Behar Bajri and Ilir Rustemi had previously been arrested in Albania for an attempted murder of a gang rival in 2016, but they were subsequently released. Safet Bajri was arrested in Tirana on September 22, 2018. He cannot be extradited because there is no agreement between Albania and Belgium. At the time of writing, Bajri is in prison awaiting trial on separate charges.

Another beneficiary of the law was former SP MP Mark Frroku. He was sentenced to ten years by the Serious Crimes Court of Nivelles, in Belgium, for the murder of Aleksander Kurti in 1999. Both men belonged to rival gangs controlling prostitution. He was only arrested nearly two decades later in Tirana in 2017, prompting allegations that the arrest warrant and extradition request had been buried by the authorities. Instead of extraditing him to face a new trial, the Court of Serious Crimes tried Frroku itself and found there was insufficient evidence to convict. However, he was found guilty of money laundering and failing to explain his wealth, and subsequently jailed for seven years and six months. He was released three years later for good behaviour.

The extradition law is not the only procedure to benefit drug traffickers. The abbreviated trial rule gives the defendant the right to be judged by an accelerated procedure that means all the facts do not need to be aired in court, similar in some ways to the plea bargains used in the US justice system. It also means the defendant can get a one third reduction in jail term and cannot receive a life sentence.

There are no jury trials in Albania and judges are appointed by the president and waved through by parliament. All of which adds up to a rather unsatisfactory state of affairs where judges are often — rightly or wrongly — accused of showing bias towards defendants with political ties.

***

By far the most serious legal scandal Albania has faced in recent years is the case of former Interior Minister Saimir Tahiri. Drug trafficking allegations first surfaced in 2015, when he was still in post. A former police officer, Dritan Zagani, claimed Tahiri had blocked his investigation into the notorious Habilaj drug trafficking organisation and ordered his arrest. Zagani, a member of the Fier anti-drugs squad, had passed his findings about the network onto other departments, and this was deemed by his superiors to be "leaking" the details of the investigation. He was tracked down and placed under house arrest.

Zagani later claimed publicly that Tahiri was related to the Habilaj men and had given them access to his private Audi car so that they could evade roadblocks as they trafficked drugs into Greece. Zagani fled to Switzerland where he sought political asylum. Some of Albania's most dogged journalists sensed blood.

Tahiri initially responded to the claims by saying he was not related to the Habilaj brothers and that he had sold the car after he joined the government. But reporters easily exposed the ruse and dug out records which showed the Audi used by the Habilaj brothers was still registered to Tahiri. The minister then suggested that he had failed to declare the sale of the car because he owed money to the court after losing a slander case against Sali Berisha. Tahiri didn't want to part with the cash, he said. Some suggested that trying to welch on the court fine alone should have been a sackable offence in itself. Then, an even more damning revelation emerged. Tahiri had used the Audi in Greece twice after supposedly selling it to the Habilaj crew. He explained this latest embarrassment by claiming that he'd borrowed the vehicle back because he didn't want to use a government car for personal trips. Of course, it meant that he had to confess to knowing the gang. He admitted that they were "distant cousins".

An official investigation was opened into the Habilaj brothers and their use of the car, but it came to nothing. Tahiri celebrated the collapse of the case on Facebook.

"Now that the prosecution has checked the lies of the fled policeman, the PD has also lost its stream of lies," he wrote. "This is one of these cases when the lie slaps you back in the face, and the DP members now got a black eye. The police is built on truths (sic), and always has value. The lie is greedy and is never full. This holds also for DP members."

Tahiri's ebullient mood didn't last for long. He was sacked as Interior Minister in 2017 amid the ongoing Klement Balili scandal, and then regained his seat as an MP a few months later. But Italian police later arrested Moisi Habilaj for trafficking 3.5 tons of cannabis in a plot that was said to net the gang twenty million euros a year. This time, Tahiri was directly implicated in wiretap transcripts released to the Italian media.

One of the conversations, which was intercepted in December 2013 between Moisi Habilaj and another drug trafficker, Sabaudin Celajt, suggested both men had spoken with Tahiri.

Moisi Habilaj was recorded saying, "He [Tahiri] has more [money] than us." Celajit replied by saying that Tahiri had power and prestige, but fewer riches. Moisi also claimed that Tahiri had made five million euros in one month, while in another conversation, Habilaj said that 30,000 euros "should be given to Saimir". Both men said Tahiri would use the money to finance the SP's election campaign. Of course, Tahiri vehemently denied any wrongdoing.

"Two criminals, very distant cousins of mine, have mentioned my name and it is not the first time when criminals have used a minister's name," he said.

Edi Rama initially stood by his former minister and called for a thorough investigation.

"We want the truth as soon as possible. What came out of the conversations is disgusting and shocking," Rama said on his Facebook page. "I have known Tahiri for years and I have only words of support and encouragement for him as a person of good intentions, skills and integrity. But, Albania and Albanians today want and deserve to know the truth, only the truth and nothing but the truth."

But when prosecutors sought an arrest warrant, the SP-dominated Parliament blocked the request, calling the move politically motivated. Tahiri resigned from Parliament in May 2018, after being charged with corruption and drug trafficking, paving the way for his arrest. By that point, further damning evidence had emerged of Tahiri's links with the Habilaj family. In August 2014, a year after joining the Rama government, Tahiri had travelled by private boat from Albania to Lefkada, Greece, on holiday with his family and that of another Socialist MP and her family. The boat broke down and had to be anchored off the coast of Greece. Tahiri called for an Albanian police officer to come out to fix the boat. The man he asked to fetch the officer was called Artan Habilaj.

Both men then returned the next day in the infamous Audi, which Tahiri used to drive back to Albania. Habilaj stayed with the boat and later sent it to Brindisi to be fixed. It was then picked up by Moisi Habilaj and two other men, one of them a police officer, who gave a witness statement to that effect. Border records backed the story up. They showed that the men arrived in Bari via ferry from Durres and then used the train to get to Brindisi. Typically, Tahiri denied everything when the allegations were aired in Parliament, but his boating licenses were later uncovered.

"Up to the day when the whole truth is made known, I will not be an MP but a commoner," Tahiri insisted. "As a common citizen, I will face prosecutors, the courts, justice and the law. I will do the same with the clowns of politics that have stolen this country," he added.

Tahiri was placed under temporary house arrest, but after the flurry of allegations, things moved slowly. The investigation led by the government-appointed Temporary General Prosecutor Arta Marku took an unusual twist when she allowed a crucial witness, Nazer Seiti, to be extradited to Italy in contravention of Albania's new criminal code. She also caused uproar by transferring ten prosecutors out of the office and dumping them in regional offices, midway through the investigation. In addition, Tahiri was released from house arrest and handed back his passport.

Ambassador Donald Lu again sounded warning bells, saying, "We have heard several reports from independent sources about serious pressures in this case, also including bribes that have been offered to the judges. We call upon civil society and the media to follow this case attentively."

In June 2019, an Italian court sentenced Moisi Habilaj to fifteen years in prison. Two other gang members, the aforementioned Nazer Seiti and Meridian Sulaj, got eight years each. More members of the gang, including Seiti, were still facing trial in Albania, but it was not clear how things would proceed at time of writing.

Tahiri eventually asked for an abbreviated trial, on charges of "participation in a structured criminal group," "trafficking of narcotics," and "passive corruption by high state officials". Three senior police officers from the Ministry of Interior faced the same charges, but they went on the run and as a result the trial was delayed. Tahiri said the request, which was granted, did not mean that he accepted guilt.

In July 2019, the trial was delayed for a third time. Case prosecutors announced that the translated witness reports given by

197

Moisi Habilaj, Nazer Seiti and Meridian Sulaj in Italy could no longer be found. They asked for more time to obtain new translations.

Tahiri finally had his day in court in September 2019. Much to the dismay of prosecutors, a panel of judges decided to drop the charges and instead convicted him on a single charge of abuse of office. He was handed a five year prison sentence, reduced to three years and four months thanks to the abbreviated trial process, before the sentence was commuted to three years on probation. Tahiri instantly lodged an appeal. Lulzim Basha called the decision "shameful" and said "justice is taken hostage by organised crime".

FUTURE PROSPECTS

As of December 2019, there is little indication that Albania's organised crime and state nexus will be dismantled any time soon. Local elections scheduled for June 2019 were initially boycotted by the DP and LSI, over allegations that the SP would collude with organised crime gangs to swing the vote. It left more than half of the sixty-one municipalities with only SP candidates. There were violent protests across the country and President Meta tried to postpone the elections until October. But the vote went ahead anyway. The Organisation for Economic Co-Operation and Development noted that during the elections, "The opposition decided not to participate, and the government determined to hold the elections without it. In the climate of a political standoff and polarisation, voters did not have a meaningful choice between political options."

There were also claims of voting irregularities, with state employees reportedly coerced into voting for the SP, and electoral commissioners voting on behalf of people they knew. Lulzim Basha, the leader of the Democratic Party, which had boycotted Parliament since February, said, "This is a very dangerous situation. Feeling betrayed by the very institutions whose values Albanians aspire to is a very dangerous development. And it will potentially lead to civil unrest, social unrest ... if there is not a clear condemnation of the farce that has already happened."

Even Edi Rama was forced to concede it was a shambles. "We have to face it, these elections in terms of what they should have been were not the best for the country," he said.

The animosity between the leading figures in both parties will rumble on into 2021, when the next Parliamentary elections are due.

Whatever happens then, it's not at all clear that an overhaul of the government will improve the situation. After all, it is only fair to point out that the Democratic Party has also been accused of having links to organised crime. In 2011, convicted drug dealer Emiljano Shullazi was arrested in Farka, near Tirana, for allegedly disrupting a Socialist Party rally during the election campaign while wearing a bullet-proof vest. Eleven other people, some armed with guns and carrying walkie-talkies, were arrested alongside the gangster. A number of firearms were recovered.

That being said, Shullazi's apparent allegiance to the DP didn't last long. By 2015, he was being accused of running a violent extortion racket in Tirana and Durres, allegedly under the protection of SP politicians.[45] Shullazi was later linked to a string of shootings in Tirana, including one in which one man was killed and four injured, including a police officer. When he was brought to trial in 2018, ten prosecutors had to be disciplined for refusing to take the case. He was eventually found guilty of leading a criminal organisation and acquiring property through threats, along with four co-defendants. Shullazi was ultimately jailed for fourteen years. One of his lawyers had been Ravik Gurra, the Hertfordshire-based dad-of-two whose murder is still unsolved. It was later claimed that Shullazi was being allowed to hold meetings inside Durres Prison with other members of his gang. A senior official was suspended.

---

[45] At one point, Edi Rama sued two opposition MPs for defamation when they said Shullazi had been freed from custody on his orders. They were found guilty by the High Court and fined 1,500 euros each.

In any case, the DP is still the party of Sali Berisha, the man who oversaw Albania's slide into anarchy in 1997, largely thanks to his government's support for corrupt pyramid schemes. While he has been an outspoken critic of the SP and its alleged organised crime links, the current party leader, Lulzim Basha, has also faced money laundering claims, although these are linked to lobbying contracts in the US rather than drugs and the DP says the case is politically motivated. In addition, the LSI has also faced allegations, not least over the Klement Balili affair. Furthermore, in 2011, then-Deputy Prime Minister Ilir Meta was filmed discussing kickbacks for public contracts with Minister of Economy Dritan Prifti. No charges were brought.

The United States has also reportedly refused travel visas for up to 170 Albanian politicians, including the leader of the new Social Democrat Party of Albania, Tom Doshi. A former Socialist Party politician and one of the richest men in Albania, Doshi was expelled from the SP after claiming that Ilir Meta had plotted to have him killed. The US State Department said Doshi is involved in "significant corruption". He denies all wrongdoing.

The fact that Albania is such a relatively tiny country would make most of these shenanigans largely irrelevant to the rest of the world, if not for the fact that Albania's biggest export is by far and away organised crime. In June 2019, the Dutch parliament voted against the EU opening accession talks with Albania, citing widespread corruption and the insidious nature of the Albanian mafia. France and Denmark joined the opposition in October.

Meanwhile, the ties between Albania and Kosovo have strengthened since Kosovo declared independence in 2008. The two countries now share an open border, have joint, or at least complementary foreign policies, and are set to share embassies after a 2019 agreement. Hashim Thaci has also proposed a referendum on unification. While these moves might provide great benefits for the citizens of both countries, it is easy to see how they might also offer potential opportunities for the mafia.

The trials and subsequent re-sentencings of murderous villains such as the cop-killer Dritan Dajti, heroin kingpin Aldo Bare and gang boss Lulzim Berisha, show that even those convicted of the most heinous crimes can receive leniency in Albania. But this is not simply an internal problem. While Albanian mafia chiefs might face a justice of sorts, the high crimes of men such as Klement Balili, one of Europe's biggest drug traffickers, actually take place in countries such as Britain, France, Germany, Belgium and Italy, where their extended networks make millions supplying street dealing gangs.

Even when caught, many of the top bosses only receive the type of sentences that would be handed to low level drug dealers in Britain and the United States. It is not unheard of in British courts for drug dealers to receive two years in jail after being caught with just three grams of cocaine. That is longer than former dictator's grandson Ermal Hoxha served for a plot involving an estimated 120 kilos. In British courts, it is common for people to be given eleven or twelve years for handling just one or two kilos of Class A drugs. Naser Kelmendi, who made millions if not billions from the heroin trade, was serving just six years, until his release pending retrial. And this book, of course, only covers the cases that have come to public attention. There are undoubtedly Albanian narco networks yet to be uncovered.

One possible solution is for EU countries to stop sharing intelligence with Albanian authorities until the corruption problem has been brought under control, or the extradition laws are changed. Instead, they could try to nab the top narcos when they go abroad. For example, Germany and Greece have both led extensive investigations against Albanian crime syndicates, only to see mafia bosses given soft sentences in their home country. Alternatively, some countries could widen the scope of their investigations. For instance, unlike the United States, the authorities in Britain rarely, if ever, bring charges against foreign-based drug traffickers. As the DEA's long involvement in South America has shown, the US is willing to investigate and bring to justice the traffickers behind the drugs trade on their turf even if they live abroad. Britain traditionally deals only with the criminals who are physically present on its own territory. As I've shown, this is largely futile when the ultimate gang bosses never set foot here. Instead, police hail the imprisonment of middle managers like Klodjan Copja and Tristen Asllani as the downfall of kingpins, while the flow of drugs across the Balkan Route and over the Atlantic into Europe, remains undisturbed.

Advocates for drug reform can point to the fact that the power of these criminals would be drastically curtailed if narcotics were decriminalised, as they are in Amsterdam or Portugal, for example. I don't feel strongly about the issue either way. But supporters of such reforms too often look at the issue from the ground up, arguing that the prohibition of drugs leads to the needless criminalisation of millions of people. While that may be true, do we really want to turn gangsters such as Aldo Bare, Klement Balili and Naser Kelmendi into legitimate businessmen? Could we really stomach them obtaining more power and influence than they already have?

Amid all this, it's important to remember that the Albanian mafia does not have an absolute monopoly on the drugs trade in Europe. Indeed, as I've shown, the 'Ndrangheta, Serbian mafia, Spanish, Turkish and British gangsters are all major players, and in some cases these groups have produced crime lords whose power far outweighs that of any Albanian mafia don. Instead, it is the ubiquitous nature of Albanian organised crime, with its ability to operate across extended networks simultaneously, in multiple countries, and with little disruption when parts of the machine are dismantled, that sets it apart.

Bosses come and bosses go. But for the foreseeable future, at least, the Albanian mafia remains one of the most formidable criminal threats facing the continent.

EPILOGUE: LOCKDOWN

On March 9, 2020, Italian prime minister Giuseppe Conte announced a nationwide lockdown, the first in Europe, in response to the wave of serious illness sweeping through the north of the country. By that point, which Conte described as Italy's "darkest hour," there had been 463 deaths nationwide suspected of being caused by Covid-19. By the time his British counterpart Boris Johnson announced similar measures on March 23, there had been 5,476 deaths in Italy, and rising. By the beginning of May, around one third of the world's population was on some form of lockdown, with 146 countries imposing draconian quarantine measures or travel restrictions. By mid-June, it was reported that there had been at least eight million cases worldwide and nearly half a million deaths.[46]

It was obvious that the lockdown would have serious implications for drug traffickers and dealers. This book was first published in January, just two months before the crisis erupted, and

---

[46] As far as the virus is concerned, at time of writing Albania had suffered a thankfully minimal death toll, with fewer than fifty fatalities and under 2,000 cases overall. Britain, sadly, lagged only behind the USA and Brazil, as one of the world's worst-affected countries.

while it is probably tempting for writers of most current affairs books to provide regular updates on the subject of their work, I felt any book about drug trafficking published in 2020 should take account of the coronavirus pandemic. What follows is a brief summary of what has taken place in the first three months of this hugely unsettling and somewhat dystopian new reality we have found ourselves in.

Questions were asked fairly early on about what would happen to criminals in a state of lockdown. In some respects, this was a lighthearted and welcome distraction. Burglars were almost certainly out of business with huge numbers of people barely leaving their homes. There was also some speculation about low level drug dealers. Would they break lockdown rules to continue to deliver drugs? Would customers dare to venture out? There was some early anecdotal evidence that dealers were increasing prices, while some in London continued to drop off to customers by leaving their wares several feet from the front door, to ensure social distancing rules were abided by. At least one enterprising weed dealer produced baggies carrying the British government's slogan, "Stay home. Protect the NHS. Save lives." But much more significant moves were afoot at the top end of the drugs underworld.

For law enforcement, the almost global shutdown presented something of an open goal. Wanted criminals became easier to target, spot and follow. For example, fugitive 'Ndrangheta boss Cesare Antonio Cordi was arrested in March hiding out in an abandoned house in a remote Calabrian village. The house had been put under surveillance after a crony provided the address when he was stopped while shopping for groceries. Officers later caught Cordi after spotting the light from a cigarette glowing inside. Italian police also arrested an 'Ndrangheta member with 537 kilos of cocaine that had been smuggled into the port of Gioia Tauro. Unable to move the shipment into northern Europe, the gangster had buried the stash in a lemon grove. He was spotted breaking lockdown and followed to the grove, where the drugs were recovered.

Similar round-ups took place in Britain. In one case, two Albanian men were allegedly found with a gun, ammunition, three kilos of cocaine and £25,000 in cash in a flat in Hornsey, North London. The

National Crime Agency claimed one of the men had tried to jump from a first floor balcony when officers burst in. Another incident in London involved a high speed car chase and the recovery of a Scorpion submachine gun.

But the most notable successes came at European borders. By the end of May, Britain's NCA was able to boast of making seizures amounting to a staggering twenty five tons of Class A drugs and some £15m in cash, with at least 130 arrests — all since the start of the lockdown. The agency concluded that "Covid-19 restrictions have made criminal groups take additional risks in moving cash around". Additionally, it said, the "closure of many cash-based businesses in recent weeks has robbed OCGs of an opportunity to stash or launder their cash making it harder for criminals to conceal the proceeds of their crimes".

According to the NCA's assessment, production of cocaine in South America and heroin in Asia had been "almost unaffected" by the crisis, meaning that drug lords still needed to bring their products to market. But because of the unprecedented lockdowns, shipments were far easier to track. As the NCA put it, "Travel restrictions have meant fewer opportunities for criminals to move drugs in smaller more discreet amounts, especially through passenger traffic, which in turn means that they are having to take more risks and move drugs in bulk. Criminals may believe that authorities are distracted, particularly at ports, and think there is an opportunity to import larger quantities. We have shown this to be far from the truth."

Across the world, organised crime gangs also began to steal medical supplies, as well as items such as face masks and testing kits, proving that there is no nadir where the search for illicit profit is concerned. But there is evidence that the crisis was also used to facilitate drug trafficking and dealing. In Latin America, this sometimes took the form of 'narco-ambulances' — vans disguised as emergency vehicles to move drugs around a city, while in Britain drug dealers made fake NHS identification documents in case they were asked to justify being on the street. In Britain, one of the NCA's biggest seizures, a quarter of a ton of cocaine found at Dover on May 5, was hidden under a load of medical dry ice, described as "medical supplies" and addressed to a London hospital.

One of the biggest seizures came in Essex, where police recovered 280 kilos of cocaine at Purfleet. Six men were arrested. This mirrored seizures in Antwerp and Vlissingen, were one discovery amounted to four-and-a-half tons. As well as drugs coming into Britain, the NCA helped with other seizures including two tons of cocaine seized off the coast of Panama, four tons off the coast of Spain and Portugal, and hundreds of kilos of heroin seized in Afghanistan and Pakistan. In Spain, authorities seized fourteen tons of cocaine in March and April alone, six times higher than the same period the previous year. Seven of the cases involved shipments of over 100 kilos, with four of them weighing more than a ton.

One of the more unusual cases to take place in Britain during the lockdown involved two Albanian men, Mariglen Bajraktari, aged twenty, and Romario Vukzaj, aged twenty three, who were charged after allegedly breaking in to the container terminal in Tilbury to retrieve around £1m worth of cocaine. According to the NCA, the refrigerated container had arrived from Belize three days previously and contained sixteen kilos. It appeared that the spate of seizures had spooked someone in the underworld and an order was given to get hold of the goods by any means necessary.

The authorities back in Albania also had some success stories. Towards the end of May, customs officers in Durres stopped a truck carrying thirty eight kilos of heroin destined for Italy. The driver, a man from Tirana, was arrested. Another Albanian driver was arrested in Bari in April, with twenty kilos of cocaine and heroin which had transited through Durres. In May, four Albanian men were arrested after trying to smuggle one ton of cannabis into Greece. Elsewhere on the Balkan Route, border officers in Azerbaijan seized a massive 826 kilos of heroin in three days, most of it being smuggled from Iran to Ukraine hidden in a cargo of melons.

In contrast, there were eighty percent fewer drug seizures in Italy, which the police, in something of a non-sequitur, put down to their increased vigilance at ports. In reality, there is evidence that some Italian mafia groups switched to bringing cocaine into Spanish ports after anticipating the effects of the lockdown.

And it wasn't just drugs that were uncovered. In Eindhoven, investigators found nearly thirteen million euros hidden in a flat, alongside two firearms. One man was charged with money laundering.

Life was changing for the narcos just as it had for everyone else. In Latin America, the crisis led to a flurry of pleas from organised crime figures to be freed from potentially dangerous prisons and placed under house arrest. They included the likes of Jessica Oseguera, daughter of the founder of Mexico's Jalisco Cartel New Generation Reuben Oseguera Cervantes (El Mencho). The woman known as El Negra was denied her request, as were most other serious criminals. Meanwhile, those already on the outside were adjusting, sometimes even assuming the role of the state.

For example, in Venezuela armed gangs known as 'colectivos' were the first to order lockdowns in certain neighbourhoods. They enforced the curfew by driving through the streets in flatbed trucks, using a megaphone to order all citizens indoors. In one incident, five men playing dominos after curfew were shot, three fatally. The gang blamed for the attack, Tres Raices, in turn claimed right-wing paramilitaries were responsible.

In Mexico, the aforementioned JCNG was one of a number of groups that distributed food packages and other essential items during the lockdown. Cynical labels on boxes handed out in the state of San Luis Potosi read, "On behalf of your friends from the CJNG, Covid-19 contingency support." The Zetas and the Gulf Cartel carried out similar relief efforts/PR stunts. In Guadalajara, the eldest daughter of former Sinaloa cartel leader El Chapo went one further. Alejandrina Gisselle ensured people received supplies stamped with her father's face and name.

While the cartels saw the crisis as an opportunity to ingratiate themselves with the people, they also needed to keep business ticking over. It was reported that the Sinaloa Cartel ordered its dealers to increase meth prices by five, in order to make up for shortfall in demand. A similar situation developed in Colombia, where dealers started selling basuco, a crude form of unadulterated form of cocaine, for four times its usual price. In New York, the price of cannabis soared by more than fifty percent, while cocaine and heroin prices also increased. Street prices in Europe increased by around thirty percent, while the price of a kilo reportedly increased to around £35,000 in some parts of Europe.

An investigation published by the OCCRP in late May suggested the lockdown had been partially mitigated by the narcos. While public health clampdowns in Peru, where around twenty percent of the world's cocaine is produced, had all but stopped production, the opposite was true in Bolivia, which produces around ten percent of the global supply. There, according to a report by the United Nations Office on Drugs and Crime, the state had found it more difficult than ever to clamp down on illicit farming. In Colombia, the authorities tried to take advantage of the situation by destroying nearly 2,000 hectares of coca plantations in the first three weeks of lockdown. But, as one Gulf Clan member told reporters, the group typically keeps between forty and forty five tons of processed cocaine in reserve, enough to maintain the business for two months. The drugs are hidden in jungle outposts, beaches, and banana plantations. "There has always been a stock, it's a very organized chain," he explained. "It's the way to control everything, especially the price."

As well as the cocaine held in reserve, Colombia had another advantage. Its banana industry was exempt from the lockdown, meaning hidden cocaine shipments to Europe could continue to flow freely. A number of large seizures were made at sea ports, but smuggling routes were also adapted to keep the flow going. For example, while Colombian cartels often employ speedboats and submarines to move drugs north, they switched to using indigenous couriers to move smaller quantities through Panama on foot. It was slower, but less likely to result in a seizure. Drug seizures on the Mexico border did increase by twelve percent during the start of lockdown, but that was put down to the cartels sending larger and less frequent shipments and did little harm to the business. Meanwhile, routes into Europe were also adapted. For example, while routes into Italy were partly shut down, the traffic was redirected to Spain.

A Europol report published in May shed further light on the efforts of drug cartels and street dealers to overcome the coronavirus challenge. The biggest disruption in the supply chain was said to be at distribution level, with little impact on wholesale importation, despite the seizures. However, the report added that the "current instability has led to an increasingly volatile environment for criminal businesses along the supply chain in Europe and appears to have resulted in increased levels of violence among mid-level suppliers and distributors".

Imports had continued because, just like Colombia's banana trade, the transportation of goods had not been hit in the same way as commercial transport. Therefore, drug trafficking by sea and air had not been put on hold. In fact, far from being a coup for law enforcement, the size of the seizures across the EU suggested there had been little or no disruption to supply, due to the assumption that some equally large shipments must be making it through. In addition, according to the report, when it came to heroin seizures nine countries noted no change to the quantity seized during the same period in the previous year, while six reported a decrease. When asked about cocaine, ten countries reported no changes, while another six reported fewer cocaine seizures.

The report made a number of predictions about the future. Firstly, it said narcos are likely to continue to adapt their methods in the wake of the crisis. For example, European-based wholesalers might follow the example of Latin American cartels by keeping larger stockpiles for such emergencies. In terms of retail, the crisis has moved more dealers online, where they use social media and encrypted apps to arrange dead drops, often accepting cryptocurrency in payment. These methods will continue long after the crisis passes. It was noted, however, that if pubs, clubs and bars continue to remain closed, this could have a long-term impact on the demand for recreational drugs.

Investigators will also need to keep an eye on money laundering methods. The Europol report warned that crime groups will escalate efforts to wash money via the offshore system, while the "expected emergence of a post-pandemic recession may lead to a reduction in the prices of goods and a downturn in economic sectors favoured by criminals". This will make the real estate sector even more attractive to criminals wanting to wash their ill-gotten gains.

There is no clear indication of how the coronavirus crisis might impact Albanian narcos specifically. Given the lack of any significant cocaine seizures at Durres during this period, it might well be the case that shipments bound for Albanian gangs on home territory were redirected to Spain, avoiding Italy. This is more than likely, because the Albanians work closely with the 'Ndrangheta clans who reportedly made the decision to switch. It would present some serious logistical issues, particularly if the situation persists, because cocaine is now often processed in Albanian labs and distributed within the country to a variety of criminal networks.

Also, because of the loose-knit nature of Albanian organised crime groups, it is possible that some smaller organisations could have been wiped out if they were indeed the owners of some of the huge seized consignments. However, assuming that demand across Europe, and especially in Britain, quickly rebounds back to previous levels and extended lockdowns do not become the norm, then most will easily recover. The costs of purchasing cocaine at source are minimal and, as we have seen, Albanian networks can turn over millions by combining the wholesale and retail side of the trade, unlike most other crime groups.

There have been some developments inside Albania that are worth mentioning. Concerns were raised about the government's use of new emergency powers granted to deal with the pandemic. The blogging site Medium found itself blocked in late March. Then Ora News, the last Albanian TV station still publicly critical of the government, was shut down by the health ministry, allegedly for breaking social distancing rules.

Long-running disputes about the destruction of public buildings to make way for new luxury developments were solved during the pandemic in an equally authoritarian manner. The National Theatre in Tirana, where protestors had previously fought to stop its demolition, was handed over to the local government which then sent police in to arrest and fine its hardcore supporters. The building was knocked down within a week.

Legal changes were also put forward. A long-mooted plan to legalise cannabis production for medicinal use was placed back on the agenda in May, when Edi Rama announced a draft bill was on its way. Such a move would, of course, allow such places as Lazarat to return to the large-scale cultivation of the crop and it remains to be seen whether a system could be put in place to ensure that all produce is destined for legitimate use. "Illegal cultivation is completely under control," Rama insisted during a virtual press conference. "This is the third or fourth year of consolidation. We plan to pass the bill in this session of parliament." There have already been some doubts expressed about the law. Agron Duka, head of the opposition Agrarian Environmentalist Party and a former agriculture minister, pointed out that "as a state we have not [previously] applied the law correctly, so it can be exploited negatively". And it has prompted villagers in Lazarat to call for a full amnesty and pardons for anyone involved in the illegal trade there.

On that note, an even more contentious legal proposal was announced in early March and pushed through in the summer. The financial amnesty allows individuals and businesses operating in the 'informal economy' (estimated to be worth up to fifty percent of GDP) either at home or abroad, the chance to bank their earnings with no questions asked, on condition of a fee. This gives the government a huge financial boost, not to mention potentially smoothing relations with the EU, which is holding Albania under the money laundering microscope.

The amnesty is set to last for a year, from January 1, 2021, until December 31, 2021. A wide range of individuals will be exempt from taking part, including all serving high officials, such as the president, prime minister, ministers, judges, prosecutors, customs directors, tax office directors, customs officers and their immediate family members. Also exempt will be those suspected of being part of criminal or terrorist organisations, convicted drug traffickers, kidnappers and anyone who has been under investigation, even if the investigation was halted. Former high officials who left their position before 2018 will benefit, as well as any drug traffickers and criminals who have not come to the attention of the state. Nevertheless, it is easy to see how even convicted narcos could quite easily use cronies with clean records to wash their cash. Critics have pointed out that the amnesty could become a de facto money laundering scheme operated by the state itself.

INDEX

Adams Family, 144
Adawi, Naief, 116
Afghanistan, 60, 62, 73, 145, 219
Albanian Football Association, 64
Albanian Troops, 157
Alava, Prada, 193
Albert, Blushaj, 128
Albright, Madeline, 54
Alibej, Endrit 'Tarzan', 190
Alicko, Sajmir, 36
Alicko, Arjan, 36, 67
Alvarez, Carlos, 104
Al Qaeda, 62
Ameen, Renaz, 153, 158
Amsterdam, 116, 146, 214
Antwerp, 2, 115, 187, 219
Arbi Garden, 185-187
Arkan's Tigers, 81, 84
Armagan, Kemal, 150
Arsovska, Jana, 133
Artan, Maskaj, 128
Asllani, Aleks, 165
Asllani, Desar, 165
Asllani, Tristen, 153-156, 158-159, 170
Athens, 86, 94
Australia, 7, 82
Austria, 80
Autodefenses Gaitanistas de Colombia, 186
Avdyli, Flamur, 202
Avdyli, Astrit, 202
Avdyli, Jasim, 202

Avila, Cezar, 182-183
Azemi, Remzi, 106
Azerbaijan, 219
Azzolo, Paolo, 189

Badelli, Eno, 175
Bajraktari, Mariglen, 219
Bajram Curri, 47
Bajri, Behar, 205
Bajri, Enver, 205
Bajri, Ilir, 205
Bajri, Safet, 204-205
Balkan Route, 46, 55, 57-63, 65, 80-81 96, 143, 147, 214, 219
Balkan Insight, 169
Balili, Klement, 193-198, 199, 203, 207, 212-214
Balili, Rigels, 194, 198
Bank of Albania, 28
Bare, Aldo, 15, 22-25, 34-38, 56, 58-69, 71, 79, 88, 101-102, 204, 213-214
Barking, East London, 109- 115, 126, 157-158, 160-162, 170
Barnardos, 20
Basildon crown court, 124
Basha, Lulzim, 203, 209, 210
Batchelor, Mark, 83-85
Baybasin, Abdullah, 132, 144-151
Baybasin, Cagdas, 150
Baybasin (clan), 60, 132-133, 144-151
Baybasin, Huseyin, 144-151, 193

Baybasin, Mehmet, 150
BBC, 136
Beeka, Cyril, 84
Bega, Edmond, 64, 68, 204
Beheluli, Olis, 165
Belgium, 19, 115, 145, 133, 185, 195, 205, 213
Belgrade, 74, 80, 81, 84-86
Belize, 219
Benevento Calcio, 166
Berat, 33
Berberi, Basmir, 166
Berisha, Lulzim, 97, 203-204
Berisha, Sali, 3, 25, 30-32, 51, 196, 212
Beqaj, Arber, 154-156
Beqiri, Gentian, 173-176
Beqiri, Flamur, 115-116
Beqiri, Misse 116
Beqiri, Nezir, 173-174
Beqiri, Sajmir, 174
Beqiri, Valmir, 162
Bici, Mehmet, 93
Biden, Joe, 54
Bilali, Harland, 121
Birmingham, 158, 178
Blair, Tony, 44
Blay, Zoe, 127
Blood feuds, 13, 17-18
Bode, Ridvan, 27
Bojovic, Luka, 81, 87
Bolivia, 59, 84, 100-107, 150, 221
Bombacilar, 132, 147-151
Borici Arben, 67
Borici, Enver, 67
Bosnia and Herzegovina, 61, 70-78
Bournemouth, 158
Bovenkerk, Frank, 145
Boyes, Roger, 42

Brahimi, Edison, 170
Brahimi, Mirsad, 170
Brasco, Donnie, 121
Brazil, 86, 105-106, 225
Brennan, John, 197
Brexit, 109
Broderick, Vincent, 93
Brighton, 169
Budva, 86
Bulgaria, 60-61, 65
Burns, John, 84-85

Caka, Lulzim, 33
Cali Cartel, 102-103
Camorra, 19
Canada, 7, 98, 103
Cape Town, 82, 84-85
Capja (crime family), 5, 189-190
Capja, Agron, 175-176
Capja, Ardian, 176
Capja, Besnik, 176
Capja, Florenc, 175
Capja, Sokol, 174-176
Capone, Al, 80
Caushi, Zani, 32-33
Ceka, Denis, 18
Cekaj, Arber, 186-187
Cela, Lindita, 169
Cela, Rezrt, 175
Cencich, John, 46
Cervantes, Reuben Oseguera, 220
Chapman, Richard, 165
Cici, Erion, 67
Clan del Golfo, 186, 221
CIA, 197
Cohen, Alan, 93
Colchester, 168
Colombia, 2, 59, 100-107, 182-183, 184-186, 187, 193-194, 200, 220-222

Colotti, Nardino, 90-91
Communist Party, 12-13, 23-25, 30, 119, 122
Conte, Giuseppe, 216
Copja, Klodjan, 165, 176-180, 191
Cordi, Cesare Antonio, 217
Corleone, Don, 146
Coronavirus, 217, 221, 223
Corriere della Sera, 47
Corporation, The, 18
Cosa Nostra, 10, 13, 14, 17, 19-20
Costa Del Sol, 102
Covid-19, 216
Croatia, 46, 86, 94
Cuba, 183
Cuka, Gentian, 165
Cuko, Arben, 202
Czech Republic, 46, 80, 83-84

Dacic, Hamdo, 81
Daily Mail, 123
Daja, Artur, 34-38, 58, 65, 67-68
Dajci, Azem, 'Ziro', 159-160
Dajti, Dritan, 1-4, 7, 213
Daka, Grineo, 170
Dako, Vangjush, 203
Dardha, Altin, 33
Darmanovich, George, 84
DEA, 103, 106
Deamer, Andrew, 193
Dedaj, Nikola, 91-92
Dedovic, Igor, 86
De La Vega, 102-103
Delmore, Jack, 93
Demiraj, Arber, 189
Demiri, Xhevat, 35
Denmark, 122, 185, 212
Dervishaj, Plaurent, 96-97
Dervishaj, Redinel, 96-97
Delalic, Ramiz, 70-78

Del Ponte, Carla, 50, 53
Democratic League of Kosovo (LDK), 41-42, 44
Democratic Party, 25, 29-34, 58, 166, 196, 199-209, 210-214
Department of Justice, 7
Dibra, Fatjon 'Stealth', 159-160
Dick, Cressida, 113
Die Weltwoche, 50
Dika, Myfit, 15, 95-96
Dishan, Kamado, 166
Dizdar, Altin, 3
Djordjevic, Ivan, 84
Djuric, Dalibor, 86
Djuricic, Milan, 84
Dobroshi, Princ, 46
Dondollaku, Enver, 64, 67
Dover, 141, 218
Doshi, Tom, 212
Draskovic, Andrija, 81
Drenica, 41-43, 49-50
Driza, Mane, 127-130, 136
Dylgjeri, Arben, 190
Dubai, 25, 85
Dublin, 162
Ducholler, Sajmir, 3
Dudic, Dragan, 85
Durnay, Erdal, 190
Durickovic, Goran, 86
Durres, 1-4, 11, 23, 25, 30, 34, 96, 107, 115, 174, 186-187, 189, 191, 202, 203, 208, 211-212, 219, 223
Dumani, Arben, 164-165
Duzgan, Cem, 150

Ecuador, 105- 106, 186, 193
Elbasan, 5, 33, 173-180, 182, 183, 186, 188, 191
  Football Club, 183
  Elbasan Street, 189

216

El Chapo, 220

Escobar, Pablo, 80, 189, 192-194

Essex, 109, 120, 142, 144, 162, 219

Essex, Joey, 170

Ethemi, Edmond, 136

EULUX, 7, 53-54, 77

European Union, 52, 60, 126, 187, 200, 224

Europol, 19-20, 185, 221

Evening Standard, 153

Facebook, 111

Farley, John, 16, 96

Federal Bureau of Investigation, 14-15, 50

Fici, Skender, 93

Fier, 29, 127 129

First Capital Command, 105

Five Families, 18

Flamuri, Bledar, 36

France, 102, 141, 195

Franz Ferdinand, 70

Freedom House, 201

Freskaj, Kastriot, 3

Frroku, Mark, 205

Fufi, Amarildo, 166

Fufi, Mhill, 166

Galeotti, Mark, 16

Gambino family, 89-90

Gang of Cerrick, 33

Gang of Cole, 32-33

Gang of Durres, 96-97, 203

Gang of Lushnje, 34-38, 131, 174, 204

Gang of Mandela, 33

Gang of Tan Kateshi, 33

Garcia, Jorge, 102-103

Gashi, Agim, 46-47, 64

Gashi, Ekrem, 47

Gashi, Mohamed 'Ali', 71-72

Gavric, Dobrosov, 84

Gelbard, Robert, 44

Genovese crime family, 7

Germany, 12, 19, 20, 25, 46, 54, 60, 94, 124, 134, 146, 182-186, 202, 213

Gheg (ethnic group), 13-14, 25, 51

Gina, Rexhep, 67

Gisselle, Alejanrina, 220

Giuliani, Rudy, 93

Gjallica, 28

Gjoka, Edvin, 177-178

Gjoka, Gazmir, 96

Gjoka, Parid, 98

Gjinushi, Skender, 32

Glasgow, 59, 136, 164

Glenny, Misha, 24

Godfather, The, 2, 146

Going, Shaun, 49

Gotti, John, 91

Greece, 11, 19, 30, 32, 102, 103, 105, 126, 175-176, 178, 182, 193-199, 204, 206, 208, 213, 219

Grezda, Erenick, 99

Group America, 105-106

Gulf Cartel, 220

Gulhaj, Edmund, 131-132

Gurra, Ravik, 5-6, 190, 211-212

Habilaj clan, 206-209

Hackney Bombers, 132, 147-151

Hakim, Karolin, 116-117

Hall, Stephen, 177

Haliti, Xhavit, 50-52

Haradinaj, Ramush, 49-54

Harizaj, Edison, 189-190

Harpenden, 5-6

Hasani, Armando, 175-176
Hawks (law enforcement), 84-85
Haxhiu, Bledar, 37, 67-69
Haxhiu, Laert, 69
Hellbanianz, 6, 151, 153-156, 157-163, 164-165, 170, 190
Hemisi, Anis Fouad, 117
Hidri, Ilir, 106
Hodzic, Elvis, 75
Holland, 75-76, 81, 102-103, 116, 133, 135, 141, 143, 145-146, 205
Holmes, Mark, 138
Homeland Calling, 45
Home Office, 20, 123-124
Honduras, 188
Hoxha, Afrim, 67
Hoxha, Enver, 12-13, 23-25, 92-93, 125, 181
Hoxha, Ermal, 181-183
Hoxha, Ilir, 181
Hoxha, Jurgen, 69
Huey, Sharon, 82
Hughes, Andrew, 77
Hynes, Paul, 178
Hyseni, Ilir, 181-183

Ibrahimi, Ardian, 175-176
Instagram, 111, 158, 160
International Crisis Group, 43
International Monetary Fund, 27, 32
International Narcotics Agency, 15
International Oranisation for Migration, 126
Interpol, 20, 58, 60, 122
Iran, 60, 145, 219
Islami, Ismet, 138
Italy, 11-12, 19, 30, 34-35, 37, 47, 60, 63-69, 80, 94, 102, 116, 126, 128-129, 134, 137, 144, 151, 175, 176, 185, 187, 190, 202, 203-204, 208-209, 213, 216, 219, 222-223
Ivezaj, Prenka, 90

Jagger, Suzy, 42
Jaho, Edison, 189
Jalisco Cartel New Generation, 220
Janissaries, 86
Jashari, Adem, 43-44
Jocic, Sretan (Joca Amsterdam), 106
Johannesburg, 83, 85
Johnson, Boris, 216
Judah, Ben, 135-136

Kacanic, Fadil, 106
Kadriovski, Daut, 15, 94-95, 145
Kadiu, Mustapha, 136
Kajmaku, Agim, 204
Kaksic, Zoran, 105
Kannani, Elmaz, 71
Kannani, Lavdosh, 127
Kanun of Lek Dukagjini, 14-18, 51
Kascelan, Slobodan, 87
Kavac Clan, 85-88
Kelmendi, Becir, 75
Kelmendi, Besnik, 73
Kelmendi, Donata, 73
Kelmendi, Elvis, 73, 75-76
Kelmendi, Liridon, 73, 75
Kelmendi, Naser, 47, 50, 56, 58, 70-78, 79-80, 88, 213- 214
Kelmendi, Rexhep, 75, 75
Kent, 125, 166-171, 177
Kettering, 178
Kingston crown court, 155
Kokedhima, Koco, 194

Korac, Filip, 87
Korce, 33
Kotor, 85
Kozar, Alan, 87
K-SHIK, 54
Krasniqi Organisation (Bruno and Samir), 15, 98-99
Krasniqi, Florin, 45, 55
Krasniqi, Jeton, 170
Kray Twins, 135
Krejcir, Radovan, 83-84
Kuci, Fabion 'Gucci', 159-160
Kingpin Act, 73
Kosmajac, Dragoslav, 80
Kosova Petrol, 49
Kosovo, 8, 11, 15, 19, 38, 39-56, 57-58, 61, 64, 71, 73-78, 80-81, 94, 117-126, 129, 134, 140, 157, 200, 212
Kosovo Liberation Army (KLA), 19, 39-56, 58, 61, 64, 73, 74, 94
Kukes, 43
Kulla, Nehat, 34
Kurti, Aleksander, 205

Lacertosa, Antonio, 97
Lammy, David, 111
Lazarat, 59, 200
Latifi, Zamir, 69
Lajqi, Bajram 'Van Damme', 104
Leka, King, 31-32
Lewis, Delroy, 'The King', 112-113
Lici, Petrit, 67-69
Lika, Kujtim, 15, 95-96
Lika, Xhevdet (Ismail or Joey), 92- 95
Limaj, Fatmir, 51-52, 54
Lingard, Anders, 116
Liverpool, 136, 143
Llakatura, Besnik, 97-98

Lleshaj, Sander, 198
Lockdown, 216-225
London, 3, 12, 18, 20-21, 29, 47, 56, 59, 102, 109-117, 118-130, 131-139, 140-150, 153-163, 163-171, 174-180, 217-218
Los Mellizos, 102-103
Los Urabenos, 186
Lu, Donald, 197-198, 203, 208-209
Lufter, Maskaj, 128
Lushnje, 29-30, 34-38, 58, 66, 69, 93
   Football Club, 64
   Lagoon, 68

Macedonia, 11, 20, 35-36, 40, 54, 58, 61, 65, 67, 81, 94-95, 107, 126, 123, 174, 194,
Mahmutaj, Hektor, 129
Malaj, Arben, 31
Malta, 185
Manahasa, Mikel, 18
Manahasa, Petrit, 18
Manchester, 158
Mandela, Nelson, 53
Manjani, Ylli, 196
Mansaku, Besnik, 165
Marbella, 87
Marku, Arta, 208
Marku, Prel, 121-122
Marty, Dick, 50-56
May, Theresa, 150
Medellin Cartel, 192
Medidani, Rexhep, 32
Mehanovic, Haris, 74
Mejia-Munbera, Miguel and Victor, 102-103
Melbourne-Blake, Tanesha, 111
Mema, Erald, 165

219

Mema, Fadil, 175-176
Memia, Albert, 164-165
Messina Brothers, 135
Meta, Ilir, 194, 200-209, 210-211
Metalla, Florian, 132-133
Metropolitan Police, 7, 110, 117, 121, 125, 149, 155, 176
Mexico, 103, 188, 200, 220-221
Michaels, Chrysoulla, 118-125
Mifsud, Frank, 135
Mihaljevic, George, 83-84
Mihaljevic, Miso, 83
Milano (football club), 81
Milosevic, Slobodan, 41, 43-44, 84
Miraka, Asmirald, 165
Moldova, 137
Mone, Stefan, 127-128
Montana, Tony (fictional), 99, 118
Montana, Tony (alias), 127
Montenegro, 11, 20, 40, 61, 72, 74, 76, 80, 83, 85-88, 90, 126, 133
Montgomery, Michael, 53-54
Moodie, Jaden, 110
Moreno, Valter, 182-183
Murder Inc, 189
Musaj, Ndricim, 154- 156
Mussolini, Benito, 12
Mustafa, Xhevdet, 92-92
Muzaka, Jorgo, 67

Nano, Fatos, 32, 34, 200
Narco-ambulance, 218
National Crime Agency, 20-21, 114, 162, 217-218
National Criminal Intelligence Service, 151
National Post (Toronto), 15
NATO, 44
Ndoka, Arben, 202-203
Ndoka, Xhevahir, 202

'Ndrangheta, 19, 46, 65, 85, 102, 105, 115, 187, 214, 217, 223
Nelson, Kobi, 111
Nesic, Goran, 105-106
Newcastle, 135, 162-163
New Covent Garden, 141
New York, 10, 18, 20, 45, 89-99, 125, 131, 221
Nikolla, Denis, 97-98
Northampton, 158
Northern Ireland, 154
Northumberland Park Killers, 111
North Valley Cartel, 102-103
Norwich, 158
Nottingham, 165, 178

Obama, Barack, 73
Odunuyi, Kelvin, 111
Okic, Ferid, 81
Operation Goldfinger, 185
Operations Jezebel and Journey, 102-103
Operation Tiberius, 141-144
Organ Harvesting, 50-59
Organisation for Economic Co-Operation, 210
Organized Crime and Corruption Reporting Project (OCCRP), 7, 186, 221
Oseguera, Jessica, 220
Ottoman Empire, 11, 59
Ozcan, Hasan, 111
Oxford, 165

Pacino, Al, 121
Pakistan, 60, 219
Palmer, John 'Goldfinger', 142, 144
Panama, 219, 221
Partizan Belgrade, 86

Paul, Marius, 166
Paytack, Ahmet, 150
Pearson, Graham, 20
Peduto, Guy, 90-91
Peterborough, 166
Peru, 59, 100-107, 200, 221
Peqini, Eduart, 33
Pistorius, Oscar, 83
PKK, 145
Plakici, Luan, 136-139
Pleca, Zvonko, 81
Podgorica, 86
Populli, 27-28
Portugal, 214, 219
Prague, 87
Prendi, Leke, 129
Prodi, Romano, 32
Prifti, Dritan, 212
Prifti, Leonard, 22-25, 35, 38, 66-69
Pristina, 41, 43, 47, 49, 71, 73, 80, 131
Proshka, Azem, 165
Prizren, 43
Public Health England, 113
Pyramid crisis, 24-34, 43, 117

Qevjani, Niko, 36

Raatikainen, Matty, 53
Racak massacre, 44
Radoman, Goran, 85-86
Radoncic, Fahrudin, 71-72, 76, 78
Rama, Edi, 194-196, 198, 200-209, 211, 224
Raseta, Strahinja, 72, 77
Raznatovic, Zeljko (Arkan), 84
Rebels (motorcycle gang), 82
Revenge for Justice, 5, 30, 190
Rexha, Ekrem, 49

RICO Act, 91
Ristani, Arben, 196
Rodgers, Jennifer, 92
Romania, 16, 20, 38, 60, 65, 79, 114, 133, 136-137, 159, 177, 190
Rotterdam, 2, 107, 115, 141
Rragami, Ardian, 118-125
Rragami, Gentian, 125
Rrappo, Almir, 99
Rudaj, Alex, 18, 20, 89-99, 103
Rudaj, Robert, 103
Rugova, Ibrahim, 41
Russia, 11, 16

Sadiki, Baki, 80
Saliuka, Liridon, 170
Saljanin, Duja, 93
Sarajevo, 70-72, 76
    Siege, 61
Saranda, 30, 194
Schembri, Dritan, 175-176
Saric, Darko, 82, 85, 106, 193
Saric, Dusko, 85
Scarface (movie), 99, 100, 131
Scotland, 111, 121, 141, 155, 164
Seiti, Nazer, 209
Sejdia, Hajdin, 26-28
Sejdiu, Bajrush, 81
Selhaka, Shpetim, 18
Selita, Ervin 'Vinz', 159-160
Selmani, Bedri, 49
Serbia, 11-12, 39-63, 70, 72-74, 80-87, 104-105, 133, 193, 200, 214
Shamata, Halit, 34
Shehu, Erion, 99
Shehu, Tritan, 25, 29
Shijack, 202-203
Shkoder, 122-123, 169, 185, 203
Shkurta, Rezarta, 181

Shkurti, Alfred (Aldo Bare), 22-25, 34-38, 58

Shkurti, Ramadan, 35, 69

Shkurti, Xhulio, 69

Shullazi, Emiljano, 5, 190, 211

Shqiponija, 25

Sicily, 11, 128-129

Sigurimi, 23-24

Silk Road, 59

Silver, Bernie, 135

Simmons-Turner, Paul, 170

Sinakolli, Ardit, 175

Sinaloa, 220

Sinani, Ermal, 132-133

Slovakia, 80

Slovenia, 185

Smiljkic, Jugoslav, 85

Smith, John, 73

Skaljari Clan, 85-88

Social Democrat Party of Albania, 212

Socialist Movement for Integration (LSI), 194, 210-214

Socialist Party, 25-28, 31-34, 51, 59, 187, 189, 194-198, 199-209, 210-214

Soho, 127, 135-139

South Africa, 61, 82-85

Soviet Union, 59

Spahiu, Kujtim, 121-122

Spain, 46, 81, 102, 107, 142-143, 185, 219-223

Squitieri, Arnold, 89-90

Stalin, Josef, 23

Stanaj, Anton, 80

Stankovic, Aleksander, 86

Steenkamp, Reeva, 83

Stergu, Ilir, 67

Sudan, 80

Sude, 27

Sulaj, Meridian, 209

Sun, newspaper, 123

Sunday Express, 158, 159-160

Sunday Telegraph, 48

Surcin Clan, 81

Sweden, 116-117, 185

Sweet, Matthew, 31

Switzerland, 75

Sydney, 82, 94

Syla, Azem, 51-52

Syria, 117

Tafilaj, Admir, 189

Tahiri, Saimir, 196-198, 206-209

Taliban, 62

Tahullau, Saimri, 69

Taullajt, Baki, 66-68

Telegraph, newspaper, 53-54

Tendy, William, 93

Thaci, Gani, 48-49

Thaci, Hashim, 8, 41-59, 81, 212

Thaci, Idriz, 49

Thailand, 141

Thaqi, Gjavit 'Doc', 103-104

Thaqi (network), 15, 143

Tilbury docks, 109, 115, 219

Tirana, 1-4, 13, 26-28, 30, 33, 36, 47, 51, 53, 97, 107, 127, 160, 166, 174-175, 184, 189-190, 200, 203-204, 211, 219

    National Theatre, 223-224

    University, 13

    Serious Crimes Court, 36

Toci, Skender, 165

Tocu, Abdul, 165

Tosak, Arjan, 33

Tosk (ethnic group), 13-14, 58

Topalli, Besim, 165

Tottenham, 111, 148-150, 170

Tottenham Boys, 150-151

Transparency International, 201
Treanor, Timothy, 91-92
Tres Raices, 220
Tunbridge Wells network, 166-171
Turkey, 5, 11, 16, 37, 46-47, 58, 60-68, 73, 75-76, 80-81, 86, 92-96, 102, 114, 132, 142-151, 184, 190,193, 214

Uddin, Khalad, 165
Ukraine, 86, 219
Union for the Better Future of Bosnia and Herzegovina, 78
United Nations, 18, 221
United States, 12, 44, 51, 57, 60, 73, 92, 94, 96, 104, 126, 197, 212-213, 225
    State Department, 212
University of Zurich, 42
Uruguay, 82, 105-106

Valachi, Joseph, 10-11, 20
Valencia, 185
Venezuela, 220
Veseli, Kadri, 51-52
Vienna, 87, 96
Vlissingen, 219
Vlore, 30-32, 47, 194
Vory, 16
Vucic, Aleksander, 80
Vulaj, Vuksan, 93
Vujotic, Milan, 86
Vukotic, Jovica, 86
Vukzaj, Romario, 219

Wallace, Ben, 113
Walsh, Peter, 102
Warsaw Pact, 61

Watson, Levi, 165
Whiteley, Richard, 165
White Paper on Albanian Terrorism in Kosovo-Metohija, 49-50, 63
Winstanley, Judge Robert, 138
Wolverhampton, 165
Wood Green, 18
World Bank, 27, 32
World War Two, 12, 40, 125
World War One, 11, 70
Wright, Mark, 170

Xanin, Fatos, 3
Xhafa, Edjan, 67-68
Xhafa, Mario, 166
Xhafaj, Agron, 204
Xhafaj, Fatmir, 204
Xhafferi, 27-28
Xhaja, Enea, 189
Xhixka, Genic, 183, 186
Xhuvani, Gjergj, 189
Xhuvani, Konstandin, 189
Xhuvani, Luiza, 189
Xibrake Network, 181-183, 184

Yesilgoz, Yucel, 145
YouTube, 110, 160
Yugoslavia, 19, 24-27, 40, 43-44, 50, 54-55, 60-61, 92, 95

Zagani, Dritan, 206
Zathynkos, 193
Zemun Clan, 74, 81, 87
Zetas, 220
Zog I, King, 12, 93
Zornic, Haris, 81
Zvicer, Rodoje, 86-87

IF YOU HAVE ENJOYED THIS BOOK OR FOUND IT INFORMATIVE, THEN PLEASE CONSIDER LEAVING A SHORT REVIEW ON AMAZON.

JUST THIRTY SECONDS OF YOUR TIME COULD MAKE ALL THE DIFFERENCE TO THE AUTHOR.

ABOUT THE AUTHOR

John Lucas is a journalist who has written for some of Britain's best-selling national newspapers, including *The Sun*, *The Daily Mirror*, the *Mail on Sunday* and *The Times*.

He has also written *Balkan Warriors: The Rise and Fall of Europe's Deadliest Drugs Cartel*, a companion piece to this book telling the story of the Serbian mafia's biggest gangsters.

John's first book, *Britain's Forgotten Serial Killer*, sparked a review of the decision to move notorious inmate Patrick Mackay to an open prison after the matter was raised in Parliament.

In addition, John has penned:

Dope Kings of London: Brilliant Chang, Eddie Manning, and Secrets of the First War on Drugs — The tale of a loose network of original narcos who shipped cocaine, heroin, and other drugs around the world in the wake of the first anti-narcotics laws.

The Baroness: Unmasking Himmler's Most Secret Agent — A true life spy story about a woman who seduced Hitler's chief henchman in a bid to protect her Jewish son.

For news about future books and free true crime stories direct to your inbox, please subscribe on Substack: **johnlucas.substack.com**

Printed in Great Britain
by Amazon

34358896R00135